MANY FACES OF GENDER

MANY FACES OF GENDER
ROLES AND RELATIONSHIPS THROUGH TIME IN INDIGENOUS NORTHERN COMMUNITIES

Edited by

LISA FRINK,
RITA S. SHEPARD,
and GREGORY A. REINHARDT

UNIVERSITY PRESS OF COLORADO
UNIVERSITY OF CALGARY PRESS

© 2002 by the University Press of Colorado

University Press of Colorado
5589 Arapahoe Avenue, Suite 206C
Boulder, Colorado 80303
www.upcolorado.com

University of Calgary Press
2500 University Drive, N.W.
Calgary, Alberta, Canada T2N 1N4
www.uofcpress.com

All rights reserved
Printed in the United States of America

The University Press of Colorado is a proud member of the Association of American University Presses.

The University Press of Colorado is a cooperative publishing enterprise supported, in part, by Adams State College, Colorado State University, Fort Lewis College, Mesa State College, Metropolitan State College of Denver, University of Colorado, University of Northern Colorado, University of Southern Colorado, and Western State College of Colorado.

The paper used in this publication meets the minimum requirements of the American National Standard for Information Sciences—Permanence of Paper for Printed Library Materials. ANSI Z39.48-1992

Library of Congress Cataloging-in-Publication Data

Many faces of gender : roles and relationships through time in indigenous northern communities / edited By Lisa Frink, Rita S. Shepard, and Gregory A. Reinhardt.
      p. cm. — (Northern lights, ISSN 1701-0004 ; v. 2)
Includes bibliographical references and index.
  ISBN 0-87081-677-2 (hardcover : alk. paper) — ISBN 0-87081-687-X (pbk.) (University Press of Colorado)
  ISBN 1-55238-093-9 (pbk. : alk. paper) (University of Calgary Press)
    1. Indians of North America—Psychology. 2. Indians of North America—Sexual behavior. 3. Indian women—North America—Social conditions. 4. Inuit—Psychology. 5. Inuit—Sexual behavior. 6. Inuit women—Social conditions. 7. Gender identity—North America. 8. Sex role—North America. 9. Sex differences—North America. 10. Ethnopsychology—North America. I. Frink, Lisa. II. Shepard, Rita S. III. Reinhardt, Gregory A. IV. Northern lights (Calgary, Alta.) ; v. 2.
  E98.P95 M35 2002
  305.3'089'971—dc21
                                                                              2002007131

Design by Daniel Pratt

11 10 09 08 07 06 05 04 03 02   10 9 8 7 6 5 4 3 2 1

CONTENTS

List of Illustrations   vii
Acknowledgments   ix

1 Many Faces: An Introduction to Gender Research in
   Indigenous Northern North America   1
    Lisa Frink, Rita S. Shepard, and Gregory A. Reinhardt

I CONTEMPORARY RESEARCH

2 *Kipijuituq* in Netsilik Society: Changing Patterns of Gender
   and Patterns of Changing Gender   13
    Henry Stewart

3 Gender Equality in a Contemporary Indian Community   27
    Lillian A. Ackerman

4 Celebration of a Life: Remembering Linda Womkon Badten,
   Yupik Educator   37
    Carol Zane Jolles

II HISTORICAL AND ETHNOARCHAEOLOGICAL APPROACHES

5 Changing Residence Patterns and Intradomestic Role Changes:
   Causes and Effects in Nineteenth-Century Western Alaska   61
    Rita S. Shepard

6 Re-peopling the House: Household Organization Within Deg Hit'an Villages, Southwest Alaska   81
   Jennifer Ann Tobey
7 Fish Tales: Women and Decision Making in Western Alaska   93
   Lisa Frink

III MATERIAL AND SPATIAL ANALYSIS

8 Child and Infant Burials in the Arctic   111
   Barbara A. Crass
9 Puzzling Out Gender-Specific "Sides" to a Prehistoric House in Barrow, Alaska   121
   Gregory A. Reinhardt
10 Broken Eyes and Simple Grooves: Understanding Eastern Aleut Needle Technology Through Experimental Manufacture and Use of Bone Needles   151
   Brian W. Hoffman
11 Gender, Households, and the Material Construction of Social Difference: Metal Consumption at a Classic Thule Whaling Village   165
   Peter Whitridge

IV SYNTHESIS AND PROJECTIONS FOR INDIGENOUS NORTHERN GENDER RESEARCH

12 Gender Dynamics in Native Northwestern North America: Perspectives and Prospects   195
   Hetty Jo Brumbach and Robert Jarvenpa

Notes   211
References   217
Contributors   247
Index   249

ILLUSTRATIONS

FIGURES

1.1	Map of volume localities	2
4.1	Sketch map of St. Lawrence Island	45
4.2	Linda in her late teens or early twenties	53
5.1	Excavated features at the Tagilgayak Site on the Unalakleet River, Alaska	70
5.2	Structural remains found in Features P3 and P9 at the Tagilgayak Site	71
5.3	Stone net sinker and carved bone fish arrow recovered at Tagilgayak	72
7.1	Yukon-Kuskokwim delta landscape in July	95
7.2	Chance Hill setting whitefish net	99
7.3	Ulrich Ulroan brings whitefish to his grandmother, Mrs. Angelina Ulroan	101
7.4	Mrs. Angelina Ulroan processing herring at her camp	102
7.5	Filleted salmon with fish mark ownership	105
7.6	Dried and smoked salmon at the foot of the smokehouse	106
9.1	The "male" artifact packets	138
9.2	Gender-uncertain objects	139
9.3	Gender-female objects	139
9.4	Gender-male objects	140

9.5	Leather (and other) scraps and debitage	144
10.1	Grooved needle and red fox left tibia with needle blank removed via groove and snap technique	152
10.2	False Pass High School class replicating needles	158
10.3	False Pass needle manufacturing experiments	160
11.1	Map of Qariaraqyuk, southeast Somerset Island, Nunavut	167
11.2	Model of Thule social relations	171
11.3	Map of Eastern Arctic showing metal sources and probable routes by which trade goods reached Qariaraqyuk during Classic Thule times	176
11.4	Distribution of blade thicknesses for 42 Thule blades from Qariaraqyuk, Deblicquy, Brooman Point, and Skraeling Island	178
11.5	Distribution of slot widths for all knives from Qariaraqyuk	179
11.6	Distribution of slot widths for all projectiles from Qariaraqyuk	180
11.7	Distribution of slot widths for all heavy-duty manufacturing tools from Qariaraqyuk	180
11.8	Distribution of slot widths for men's end-slotted, composite, and side-slotted knives from Qariaraqyuk	181
11.9	Distribution of slot widths for ulus and men's knives from Qariaraqyuk	188

TABLES

8.1	Sites with infants, children, or both	112
8.2	Individuals	113
8.3	"Other" burial types	113
8.4	Individuals in single and multiple burials	114
8.5	Multiple burial associations	114
8.6	Significant goods	117
9.1	Reproduction of table 1 from Newell's "Artifact inventories of three functional partitions of the [Mound 44 House]"	126
9.2	Additions and corrections to table 1 from Newell's "Artifact inventories of three functional partitions of the [Mound 44 House]"	128–129
9.3	Gender-ascribed and gender-sided inventory of floor-related Mound 44 artifacts	132–136
10.1	Needle production steps, materials, and debris	155
10.2	Comparison of eyed and grooved sewing needle diameters	162
11.1	Distribution of inorganic finds at Qariaraqyuk, by house	183
11.2	Inferred blade/bit material for Qariaraqyuk hafts based on slot width analysis, by house and artifact class	184
11.3	Distribution of metal finds at Qariaraqyuk, by artifact class and gender category	186

ACKNOWLEDGMENTS

WE ARE GRATEFUL TO SEVERAL PEOPLE who helped make this book happen. We wish to thank John W. Schoenfelder for creating the place map and extend our appreciation to three anonymous readers who gave us exceptional suggestions for improving the manuscript (and, of course, all omissions and commissions are ours alone). We recognize and thank the participants in the original "Approaches to Gender in the North" symposium at the 25th Annual Meeting of the Alaska Anthropological Association held in Anchorage, Alaska, March 1998 (organized and moderated by Lisa Frink): Barbara Crass, Lisa Frink, Gregory A. Reinhardt, Petra Rethmann, Rita S. Shepard, Henry Stewart, Steven R. Street, and Barbara Bodenhorn (discussant). And thanks to all of our contributors for their innovation and hard work. We also acknowledge Allen McCartney, who inspired the publication of this book. Furthermore, our gratitude goes out to our editor, Darrin Pratt (director, University Press of Colorado), for his thoughtful support, and to Cheryl Claassen and Gary Dunham who helped us navigate the publishing waters.

This book is dedicated to all of the women who have blazed the trail and continue to keep the path open.

MANY FACES OF GENDER

1

MANY FACES

AN INTRODUCTION TO GENDER RESEARCH IN INDIGENOUS NORTHERN NORTH AMERICA

Lisa Frink, Rita S. Shepard, and Gregory A. Reinhardt

A demure ten-year-old, wearing typical girl's attire, sits quietly playing with a doll as he dreams of killing his first game animal.

A family sleeps surrounded by the objects of their daily lives, unaware they will soon be crushed by intruding sea ice.

A nursing mother dies, and her family kills the infant and buries mother and child together rather than allow the child to starve to death.

On a Bering Sea island, a woman born in a dome-shaped house of driftwood and walrus hide dreams of seeing a real lawn of green grass.

A man brings the fish he just caught to his wife on the shore, where she cleans, cuts, and marks them as her own.

During a time of major social transformation, seamstresses abandon drilled-eye needles and adopt grooved needles in their stead.

These are a few of the moments whose significance this volume explores. By its nature, our focus on gender takes us within houses and families,

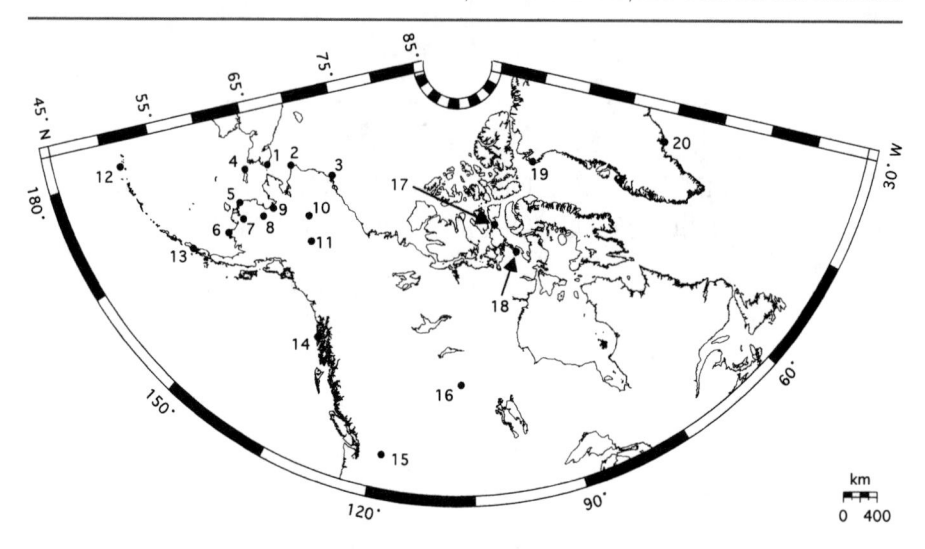

Figure 1.1 Selected localities discussed in this volume: (1) Ekwen; (2) Point Hope; (3) Barrow (North Slope Borough); (4) Gambell; (5) Chevak; (6) Cape Newenham and Goodnews Bay; (7) Bethel; (8) Anvik and Holy Cross; (9) Unalakleet and Tagilgayak; (10) Allakaket (Koyukuk R.); (11) Fairbanks; (12) Amchitka Island; (13) False Pass; (14) Sitka; (15) Colville Reservation; (16) Knee Lake (Chipewyan area); (17) Qariaraqyuk; (18) Pelly Bay; (19) Narssarssuaq; (20) Ammassalik.

putting "the people" back into our studies of broad social, political, and economic trends.

This volume has two basic aims. First, we want to begin to fill a gap concerning descriptions and analyses of women's and men's prehistoric, historical, and contemporary roles in northern Native communities. Second, we wish to present anthropologically comprehensive discussion and analysis of past and present gender roles and relationships.

Our book casts a wide net of current research on gender issues, with a vast geographical and temporal breadth. The research sites range from Greenland to the Canadian north, Alaska, and into the Pacific Northwest. Chapters include investigations of pre-Christian child and infant mortuary behavior, nineteenth-century Deg Hit'an household organization, archaeological material patterning and emergent social difference in a prehistoric Thule whaling village, and a contemporary Alaskan Yupik woman's navigation of her life amid a rapidly changing cultural and economic landscape.

GENDER AND ANTHROPOLOGY

Since the last third of the twentieth century, anthropologists have produced a staggering array of research focused on gender. But relatively little of this outpouring is attributable to scholars' analytically addressing gender dynamics among the indigenous people of northern North America.[1] Furthermore, the comparatively meager number of published northern works does not fully reflect the possibilities for synchronic and diachronic anthropological contributions from such a broad and diverse region.[2]

At the outset, we must discuss what we mean by *gender*. Clearly, gender analysis has entered the mainstream of anthropological thought.[3] As others before us have stressed, we also want to get readers past the idea that *female* equals *gender*, because they are not the same (Moore and Scott 1997). Gender studies are ultimately about people and the social significance, performance, and marking of gender. The cultural meaning of gender can change whether a person is elderly, disabled, a child or an infant, a woman or man, or a member of any other chosen social category. Moreover, the past no doubt contains the same degree of diversity the present holds (and maybe more). Gender is not just about females and males, who peek out from the data in selective studies; it is not just about sex roles but about relationships. Ideally, it is about complex interpersonal interactions rather than two-dimensional dichotomous stick-figure people (who behave like we do because, let's face it, they are often tacitly modeled on our society's standards of how the sexes act). We believe gender studies *should* consider human values and emotions, loyalty and rivalry, triumph and tragedy, love and fear, success and self-expression, desire and competition. That is, gender should examine the limitless ways humans in different cultures choose to create, re-create, and change their personal identities and their interactions within (and between) their societies and environments in meaningful ways. Imagine the possibilities if we invested more into putting faces (Tringham 1991) to the lives that we, as anthropologists, want to understand.

Having said this, a certain danger is inherent in gender research (especially in analogy-founded archaeological interpretations) in foisting today's patterns on the past, a warning initially sounded by Margaret Conkey and Janet Spector (1984). This stasis can create what Susan Kent (1998:18) aptly characterized as a gender that is "timeless," denying recognition of differently constituted gendered categories and changing roles and power relations over time (Lepowsky 1993). In fact, Brumbach and Jarvenpa (Chapter 12, this volume) caution us that "we may be on Arctic 'thin ice' when we employ Euro-American frameworks of gender and gender roles for interpreting other people's lives." For instance, although Arctic ethnographers have analyzed gendered assumptions (Ackerman 1990a; Bodenhorn 1990; Guemple 1995), few researchers have tested the somewhat "petrified" model of northern Native women's and men's complementary but equal roles. This book, however haltingly, endeavors to address the complex diversity that makes up synchronic and diachronic social, economic, political, and material gender relationships in the circumpolar north.

In addition, this volume contributes in large measure to the basic understanding of the position of women in Native northern societies, a relatively neglected topic in northern research. Indeed, Laura Klein and Lillian Ackerman (1995:3) claim that "silence surrounds the lives of Native North American women." Our authors give fresh voice to some of these women past and present, revealing their vital individual, familial, and communal roles; their life stories and modes of generational transmission of knowledge and tradition; and their perspectives and impacts on social, cultural, economic, and technological change. Each author has individual aims in revealing aspects of gender in anthropology. Still, the editors hope to influence readers' thinking on two salient issues concerning anthropological research in the north.

"ANTHROPOLOGY" AND GENDER RESEARCH

The first issue is that anthropology as a four-field approach is coming under increasing scrutiny. In this time of division within anthropology, gender provides a rich conceptual focal point from which cultural, physical, archaeological, and linguistic anthropologists can inform one another's research.[4] Our intent is not to deliberate on this debate but to demonstrate the convergent position gender research continues to offer anthropology's four subfields. This effective interdisciplinary approach has a long tradition in gender studies (di Leonardo 1991; Hager 1997; Reiter 1975; Rosaldo and Lamphere 1974). The data and analyses resulting from sociocultural, biological, and archaeological gender studies will enhance, enlighten, and caution each other, as well as benefit from discipline-wide critical review.

This book's materially focused chapters uncover aspects of diversity and complexity that make up the past and consider dimensions of present behaviors that can be integrated into archaeological interpretations. All of the authors recognize the difficulty of finding gender in the archaeological record at a fine-grained level. For instance, Reinhardt cautions us that, although discovering "female" and "male" house-floor sides may appear methodologically straightforward (based on artifact distribution), it is in fact rife with difficulties in "puzzling" spatial relationships among material remains and the roles that may be ascribed to them.

Hoffman and Whitridge illuminate change, agency, and the utility of gender-focused research in archaeological theory building. They challenge us to understand the social issues embodied in seemingly simple objects, showing that material items can signal countless (if not disparate) relationships and active social and economic shifts through time. As Whitridge emphasizes, gender relations may be the seed from which emergent inequality grows.

Shepard and Tobey steer their examinations to include households as well as families, reiterating that both can be diverse, fluid, and clouded. They point out that lines dividing men's and women's roles, their association with a distinct space, or their daily activities within a household can be very blurry. What is more, children and elders need to be integrated into the study of household organization and production. Adding to the complexity that goes beyond just gendered women and men, Frink introduces readers to the profound resource management and economic contribution of Native elder women. Going further, Crass encourages us to incorporate infants and children into our analyses. These types of multifaceted and diachronic considerations of gender relations and change should be seen as a valuable and useful comparative data set for all anthropologists.

To appreciate the complexity in archaeological communities, we must continue to enrich our models of the past and become more aware of the broad variability of gender patterns among contemporary gendered individuals, families, and communities. The cultural anthropologists in this volume—Ackerman, Jolles, and Stewart—invite us to value the intricate nature and emergent patterns of people's lives today. Stewart questions both the dichotomous representations of gender and the incorporation of a third gender category, for the Netsilik *kipijuituq* does not comfortably fit into this gender paradigm.

Jolles, relying on one indigenous woman's life history, accentuates the tremendous changes that have accompanied the relatively recent contact history in Alaska, emphasizing the ability of individuals to engage and respond actively to sometimes dramatic social and economic shifts. In addition, Ackerman extends gender and equality investigations to the community level. Her work reinforces the idea that indigenous gender relations (and ideology) can endure (as well as mitigate and mediate) tremendous economic and social change. These researchers impel us to accept the profound complexity of experiences in the present day and so provide an additional guide in understanding and questioning the archaeological record.

Finally, this interdisciplinary approach allows us to continue to create models of past and present gendered social behavior and relations and to answer some thorny questions in cultural, biological, and archaeological anthropology. Who or what determines someone's gender, and how do we identify possible markers? Was European contact a detriment or a benefit to indigenous women? Do changes in living space imply changes in social structure? Does ideology prescribe or describe living space? Does women's production within the household indicate their subjugation or their power? *Can* archaeological activity areas and tools accurately identify women's and men's patterned actions? How can we understand human-environment interactions within the framework of variable and shifting roles in modes of production and social and economic relationships? Is gender at the heart of emergent inequality? These are the threads of questions and musings, relevant to many anthropologists, that weave through this volume.

NATIVE PEOPLE AND ANTHROPOLOGICAL RESEARCH

The second issue we underscore relates to continuity. Three things combine to make Native northern North America an optimal location for anthropologists to examine modern, historical, and prehistoric representations of gender in action: (1) the late contact (from mid–eighteenth to late nineteenth century) between indigenous people of the far north and Europeans, (2) the fairly well-preserved archaeological record (as a result of prevalent permafrost and minimal development), and (3) the history of cooperation between Native peoples and anthropologists (Cruikshank 1990; Mather 1995; Morrow and Schneider 1995). Thus the modern anthropological data and historical records generated in this vast region can provide details not readily available in other environs. Moreover, many of these Native communities have adaptively retained some of their economic and social institutions, such as subsistence pursuits and community celebrations.

As Brumbach and Jarvenpa (Chapter 12, this volume) observe, the activities and pursuits of "both women and men in contemporary northwestern communities are highly visible." This visibility allows archaeologists to expect reasonable success in analogical model building. Besides that, it offers an especially useful tool for analyzing cultural resources (such as oral history) and testing archaeological models of social development. We believe studies of contemporary behavior, combined with the relatively recent connection to the past, provide a fairly sturdy translational bridge from which we can try to "see" past societies and in particular to understand and test modes and directions of change.

In addition, archaeology in the far north can offer cultural anthropologists (as well as those in other disciplines) an invaluable diachronic model of gendered behavior, a resource these anthropologists seldom appropriately recognize and employ. For instance, first contact with Europeans led to few social or cultural changes among many Native peoples for several decades, although new material goods appeared in settlements almost immediately. It seems some Native North Americans revised their living spaces by integrating new tools and technologies into their old lifeways while retaining both their physical and social structures (houses and communities). The collection of *new* objects in *traditional* places indicates enduring cultural and social conservatism. Such a model of social action can be used and tested for comparative analytical and theoretical purposes (see Chapter 5, this volume).

AVENUES TO UNDERSTANDING GENDER

Although our strategies vary, we do not seek to reinvent the methodological or theoretical wheel. One of our aims is to present data and analyses that can and must be integrated into mainstream anthropological currents. Doing so will throw light on the complicated nature of social, economic, and material relations in past and present northern Native communities.

This volume begins in the ethnographic present, considering contemporary issues of gender identity and change. In his captivating portrayal of Canada's Netsilik *kipijuituq,* Stewart informs readers about the social production, performance, and perception of self and gender. His research serves as a caveat throughout this book, a warning that there are certain pitfalls to relying on Western dichotomies, given that the *kipijuituq* does not quite fit typical anthropological notions of a third category such as the Native Californian two-spirit (Hollimon 1997).

Furthermore, in her case study of the Northwestern Plateau's Colville Indians, Ackerman investigates an anthropological paradigm first posited by Eleanor Leacock (1978) that sexual inequality necessarily follows participation in an industrial economy. According to Ackerman, this Native Plateau community is steadfast in its ideology that women are valued for their productive contributions and remain the "backbone" of the economy.

Finally, Jolles takes us on a life history journey with an Alaskan Yupik woman, including the familial (and community) shift from use of semisubterranean structures to aboveground houses. She uses oral history and personal testimony to chart this Native woman's extraordinary accomplishments and ordinary daily activities in order to help us understand the challenges facing an individual in the midst of dramatic economic, social, and material changes.

Many social issues broached by the ethnographers (e.g., impacts of missionization on Native domestic life, gender marking and labor, materiality, and culture change) are further addressed in the work of the archaeological anthropologists. Both Shepard and Tobey use ethnohistoric data to assess household and community organization and culture change resulting from missionization. Shepard suggests that the position of women and men in western Alaskan Koyukon Athapaskan households underwent a fundamental transformation when belief systems changed in the mid- to late nineteenth century. The changing organization of household space helps to identify these shifts in social relations. Tobey also investigates the likely effects of missionization on household and community organization among the Deg Hit'an Athapaskans of southwestern Alaska. She suggests that the anthropological conception of a "household" must incorporate the full range of active members during different daily routines. She further believes Native spatial, social, and economic patterns were significantly disrupted (and likely challenged) during the American missionary period.

An issue that winds through several of the chapters concerns women and the meaning of their productive activities. Frink further develops previous anthropological inquiries concerning Native women and modes of labor and production. She integrates interviews of western Alaskan women with participant-observation studies at a subsistence fish camp. Frink demonstrates that women are not just passive processors but are essential both to production and control and as critical resource managers—patterns that ought to impact archaeological model building and interpretation in this region.

Crass, Hoffman, Reinhardt, and Whitridge analyze material culture as a route to understanding gender identity, the production of place, and inequalities between women and men. As Ackerman (Chapter 3, this volume) points out, a community's interest in the well-being of women and children can inform gender equality. Thus the "visibility" of children should also be a basic concern of archaeologists interested in past social systems. Crass reviews and analyzes 305 pre-Christian Inuit and Eskimo infant and child interments, discussing the differential postmortem treatment of infants, children, and adults. She then considers the possibilities for interpreting these burial discrepancies.

By using experimental replication with Unangan (Aleut) schoolchildren and incorporating data from the Agayadan village site located on Unimak Island in the eastern Aleutians, Hoffman investigates the enigmatic shift from eyed to grooved bone needles. He explains how late prehistoric shifts in needle manufacture may signal gendered relationships, particularly women's active involvement in social, economic, and material change. According to Hoffman, Native women likely intentionally altered the design of needles to facilitate producing finely made parkas, considerable status symbols and trade items in the changing Unangan political economy.

Extending the household analysis approached by Shepard and Tobey, Reinhardt reanalyzes one interpretation of a "frozen family," a prehistoric North Alaskan Thule household in which the occupants succumbed to an encapsulating ice flow. The excavated objects were subsequently used to posit female and male "sides" within this prehistoric house. In his thorough reconsideration of the data, however, Reinhardt alerts us to the dilemmas that arise when trying to assess the relevance of spatial data and gender attribution in archaeological interpretations.

Finally, by focusing on household activity areas and material remains, Whitridge challenges readers to think more deeply about "egalitarian" and "simple" household and community organization and social change. His interpretation of archaeological data at the prehistoric Classic Thule site of Qariaraqyuk in the Central Canadian Arctic connects the ways materials are used and activities take place within a particular space and thereby identifies economic and social jockeying between the sexes. Whitridge explores the emergent inequalities in this small-scale hunter-gatherer community and calls for archaeologists to consider an analysis that may "logically" precede more complex, less egalitarian systems.

In the final chapter, Brumbach and Jarvenpa contextualize each of the contributions in this volume. They elucidate the critical nature of gender research in the American region of the circumpolar north and emphasize that this research will encourage fresh approaches and new lines of inquiry. Beyond that, they further develop the cautionary tale woven through this volume, that gender attribution and the interpretation of the "female-male nexus" are filled with biases and traps. They warn that unevaluated gendered associations may confound rather than clarify the many ways individuals and communities live and impact their social, economic, and material lives.

The editors and authors of *Many Faces of Gender* hope our book contributes to fuller understanding of the endless variations of social and cultural life found among indigenous peoples of the far north. We encourage other anthropologists to look more broadly at the diverse roles and relationships in the communities they are studying and implore archaeologists to remember that people—people with faces—once lived at the sites they excavate and once used the artifacts they now scrutinize. We want these chapters to be enlightening and constructive, and we hope they will motivate our readers to delve further into the ideas we have raised.

I
CONTEMPORARY RESEARCH

2

KIPIJUITUQ IN NETSILIK SOCIETY
CHANGING PATTERNS OF GENDER
AND PATTERNS OF CHANGING GENDER

HENRY STEWART

GENDER STUDIES, dating back to the late-nineteenth-century suffragist movement, underwent great change in and after the 1960s. Recent gender studies—variously referred to as the second feminist movement, second wave gender studies, or the radical feminist movement—fostered many cultural anthropological studies of gender, biological sex, and sexuality. At first these studies tended to center on Europe, the United States, and other regions of Judeo-Christian influence. Recent reevaluations of the berdache in North America since 1980, however, and other examples of transvestism, homosexuality, gender change, and gender role change throughout the world, have raised questions concerning the universality of European (Judeo-Christian) concepts of gender, biological sex, and sexuality (Bodenhorn 1990; Callender and Kochems 1983; Davis and Whitten 1987; Fulton and Anderson 1992; Gilmore 1993; Guemple 1986; Jacobs, Thomas, and Lang 1997; Lang 1998; Morris 1995; Murray 1994; Robert-Lamblin 1981; Saladin d'Anglure 1990, 1993, 1994a, 1994b).

In these studies there is general agreement that the dichotomy of man/woman, either as gender or as sex, may not be a universally applicable model. For example, the existence of a third gender among the Inuit (Eskimo)[1] and other non-European societies (Saladin d'Anglure 1994b; see also Murray 1994) is one aspect of an ongoing reinterpretation of a Western folk model of gender in Northern studies.

Here I shall discuss the *kipijuituq* in Netsilik society, a newborn male child raised as a female, and how the *kipijuituq* may reflect on Euro-American concepts of gender and biological sex. Data used in this chapter are primarily those I gathered in the hamlet of Pelly Bay, Nunavut, Canada, from 1989 through 1996, in addition to supplementary data from the literature. Based on my observations, it appears that the *kipijuituq* is unique and differs from other examples of gender change known for the North American Inuit/Yupik. For example, gender change in the case of the *kipijuituq* apparently did not serve a particular communal social function, as did other examples of gender change in the Arctic.

Following a review of Inuit sex and gender in the literature, I propose that in the Netsilik and other Inuit societies ideally there may have been one "sex" and three or possibly more "genders."

THE KIPIJUITUQ

In the Netsilik (Arvilingjuarmiut) society of Pelly Bay in Nunavut Territory of Canada, certain biologically male (in the scientific sense of the term) children are brought up as females until they take a prescribed animal, usually at age fourteen to sixteen.[2] Such children are subject to various taboos (a state referred to as *tiringnaqtaq*), foremost of which is that the child's hair must not be cut before catching a prescribed species of game.[3]

BECOMING *KIPIJUITUQ*

The decision of whether a newborn male child should become *kipijuituq* is in many cases made by the grandparents, mainly in the following ways. First, if the namesake of the infant is (was) *kipijuituq*, the child automatically becomes *kipijuituq*.

Second, the grandmother or grandfather talks to (*hanaurajuk*) the infant, and by observing the child's reaction to those words, the grandparent may know what course of life, or destiny, is in store for the infant. An infant, named either in utero or when it is born, takes on the personality and disposition carried in the name (Rasmussen 1931:219) and thus is believed to be born with a fully developed personality. Knud Rasmussen (1931:259, 505), discussing Netsilik naming practices, wrote that the child becomes the name(s) spoken when it leaves the mother's womb. This latent personality becomes manifest as the infant grows. It is said that by observing the reaction of the infant thus endowed with a full-fledged personality, it is possible to determine whether the infant is destined to become *kipijuituq*. Male infants judged to be *kipijuituq* become socially female: they are dressed in female clothing, expected to act as girls, and are referred to by female kinship terminology. They do not, however, take on all elements of culturally defined feminine gender roles. That is, a *kipijuituq* may play with dolls and otherwise behave in a feminine manner but is not taught sewing, cooking, and other traditionally feminine activities.

In the event that an infant is judged to be *kipijuituq*, that judgment must be obeyed by the child, its parents, and kinspeople. It is (was) believed that if that judgment were ignored, the infant and its kinspeople would be visited by misfortune, such as a hunting accident or a poor catch.

Many restrictions apply to the activities of the *kipijuituq* and to how members of the community treat the *kipijuituq*. The most stringent restriction is an admonition against cutting or trimming the hair. As mentioned earlier, the hair must be allowed to grow naturally until the first catch of the game animal prescribed by the grandparents. If this admonishment were disregarded, misfortune would be visited upon the *kipijuituq* and, in some cases, also upon its kinspeople. Such misfortune might include poor hunting, health problems, or an accident during subsistence activities. Other taboos include prohibitions against eating certain game or portions thereof. Several years ago one *kipijuituq* prematurely cut its hair and was severely chastised by its parents and grandparents.

B of Pelly Bay was a *kipijuituq* until his first catch.[4] I first noticed ten-year-old B in 1989, but it was several seasons later before I realized B was a male. For several seasons I thought B, always demure and unobtrusive, with hair done up in two long braids, was a female. Because persons in a *kipijuituq* condition have become rare in recent years, B said he was at first embarrassed by his situation.[5] By the time he reached age eight, he became used to being *kipijuituq* and ceased being embarrassed. Having to use the girl's toilet at school was the admonition that troubled him most.

B took a seal when he was ten years old, but because his grandparents felt a seal was insufficient in B's case, it was not until he was fifteen and took a polar bear in 1994 that he was released from the *kipijuituq* condition.

TRIMMING THE HAIR

Informants were unable to explain why so much importance is attached to the admonition that a *kipijuituq* must not cut or trim the hair, but an excerpt from an ethnography of another Inuit society suggests a possible explanation. Gustav Holm (1914) noted that among the Angmagsalik (Ammassilik) of eastern Greenland the hair is worn long and has never been cut, it being regarded dangerous to lose any of one's hair (Holm

1914:32). When Holm asked for a lock of hair for research purposes, the Ammassilik usually said their father had told them they were never to cut their hair or they would die. Holm (1914:86–87) surmised that they were afraid that an *ilisitsok* (exorcist or witch) might use the hair in a *tupilek*, an animal effigy of bad omen with power to cause death (Kleivan 1984:619). William Thalbitzer stated that Ammassilik men almost always had long, uncut hair (1912:600). According to informants, the fact that some Netsilik shamans did not cut their hair to retain vitality may indicate a similar belief in the Netsilik society.

RELEASE FROM THE STATE OF BEING *KIPIJUITUQ*

The most common way a person is released from the *kipijuituq* condition is by taking the prescribed game animal. If the person(s) judging that an infant is to be *kipijuituq* states that a caribou or a seal is the suitable game, taking an animal of that species can release the person from the state of being *kipijuituq*. In some cases, if so specified by the grandparents or namesake, a *kipijuituq* may be obliged to take several kinds of game or more than one of the same species. For reasons I discuss later, the polar bear seems the most potent game for release.

There is another situation by which the *kipijuituq* state is terminated in the Pelly Bay society. That occurs when on their deathbed the *kipijuituq*'s grandparents, parents, or namesake leave testament that the *kipijuituq* need no longer be bound by the taboo against cutting his hair. At that time the child becomes male by gender and is no longer considered a *kipijuituq*.

Traditionally, when the *kipijuituq* took the specified game animal or was freed from his *tiringnaqtaq* (tabooed) state by a deathbed injunction, all the people in the camp gathered for a celebration.[6] During the celebration all adult females gathered in one house (tent or snow house), and the men formed a single line in front of the entrance. Women came from the house one at a time and kissed each man in the Inuit fashion (*kunigatuk*), holding the man's face in her hands. A woman did not kiss men of her own kin group (*ilagiimariktut*), however. As each woman came out she grabbed the former *kipijuituq* from the preceding woman and kissed its face. After being kissed by all of the women, the boy was completely released from being *kipijuituq*. Following this ceremony a drum dance was held for the former *kipijuituq*. In recent times the kissing and drum dance ceremonies have not usually been performed, and they were not performed in the case of B.

After taking a polar bear, B cut his hair in the presence of his grandparents and was released from taboo restrictions. He seemed happy to be a normal boy and, at the same time, seemed proud of having undergone the experience.

While a *kipijuituq*, B did not seem to receive special treatment from his cohorts. It is difficult for an anthropologist such as myself who is over fifty to commune with young teenagers, but I was able to observe interaction between B and his best friend Keith (pseudonym), the youngest boy of the family with whom I stayed in Pelly Bay. B visited often, and the two boys joked and played together as other teenagers. I was struck, however, by the fact that B never joined in contests of strength and wrestling or other Inuit male games that took place often in the house and at camp. It appears his female gender restricted participation in such male activities, although he hunted like other young males.

The *kipijuituq* is becoming a rare, possibly discontinued social phenomenon in Pelly Bay. Informants told me this was because of the influence of Christianity. My impression is that television, projecting forceful images of gender roles corresponding to biological sex (in the Western sense), is also a possible factor. I have seen many young people in Pelly Bay model their appearance and actions on images of gender portrayed on television and in videos. Many studies have been conducted on the effect of television on Inuit/Yupik society since concerted broadcasting commenced in 1980 (e.g., Alia 1999; Koebberling 1999; Stenbaek 1999; Watson 1980), especially its influence on language (Graburn 1982). Although Richard Condon discussed in detail the influence of television on the behavior and values of Inuit teenagers in Holman (Condon 1987:125–128), his discussion of gender and sexuality (Condon 1987:132–143) does not refer to the influence of television on Inuit/Yupik views of gender, sex, and sexuality. Laila Sorenson's (2000:174) apt observation on the role of television in conveying, formulating, and transforming beliefs, values, and myths guiding modern perceptions, however, is without doubt applicable to arguments concerning the influence of television on Inuit/Yupik society.

GENDER CHANGE IN THE ARCTIC

Many facets of the *kipijuituq* phenomenon have yet to be recorded and interpreted. For example, there are conflicting statements as to whether a female infant could be *kipijuituq*. Based on my observations at Pelly Bay, it appears that females do not become *kipijuituq*, although for different reasons they may be classed as *tiringnaqtaq* (under a special state of taboo). As I discuss later, many researchers have recorded instances of Inuit/Yupik female children being male gendered until coming of age or, in some cases, throughout their lifetimes (Lang 1998:165–166, 186,

302). Some of these instances may parallel the *kipijuituq,* but no data exist to either support or repudiate such a supposition.

The *kipijuituq* differs from the 148 examples of the berdache[7] recorded for North American indigenous peoples (Callender and Kochems 1983; Fulton and Anderson 1992; Lang 1998:4–5) and also from the catamite reported from the Aleutians. In the Aleutians the catamite (*shupan*) acts as a sexual partner for renowned hunters or powerful leaders (*Musk-Ox* 1994) but remains male in gender. As far as I was able to ascertain, the *kipijuituq* did not participate in sexual acts with adult males but was only treated socially as a girl before menarche.

A review of the literature reveals several instances of gender change among the Inuit and Yupik.[8] Sabine Lang (1998:4–5), in her definitive study of gender change in North America, has gleaned from the literature instances of gender change in Inuit/Yupik society from southwest Alaska to Greenland: southwest Alaska (Chugach, Koniag [Alutiiq]), Kotzebue Sound (Malimiut), St. Lawrence Island, Quebec, Cumberland Sound, and southeast Greenland. Lang (1998:281) stated that male gender change (woman-man) has been reported only for western Alaska, although her own data (Lang 1998:78, tables 2, 4, 5, 6, 7, 8) seem to contradict this statement.

It is not certain whether the notion of gender change applies to the Chugach. According to Kaj Birket-Smith, in Chugach society no known cases exist of boys raised as girls or of women who lived or behaved like men, but a half man/half woman (*aranu'tiq*) appears in historical traditions. The *aranu'tiq* are said to be male on one side and female on the other; they performed the work of both sexes and were considered more skilled than ordinary persons (Birket-Smith 1953:94). Although Birket-Smith refers to the *aranu'tiq* as a transvestite, in the Chugach intellect the *aranu'tiq* more aptly refers to a third gender, not an either-or category.

Women-men (*anasik*) on St. Lawrence Island were considered to be especially powerful shamans, and in fact all *anasik* were shamans, although all shamans were not necessarily *anasiks*. In the case of the *anasik* it appears that gender change was a means of becoming invisible to malevolent spirits, possibly an influence from the Chukchi (Lang 1998:165–166). Lang (1998:261) also mentions men-women in the St. Lawrence society, as well as among the Mahlemut (Malimiut) of the Kotzebue Sound coast.

Because of geographical proximity and a common historical background rooted in the Thule tradition (McGhee 1984b:376, 1996:211), examples of gender change in Greenland and the eastern Canadian Arctic may likely have more relevancy to the *kipijuituq,* so I shall discuss those examples in greater detail.

In her study of exchange in the Ammassilik society of southeast Greenland, Joelle Robert-Lamblin (1981) notes that not only were girls raised as boys (*tikkaalia*), that is, made into boys, but also that boys were brought up as girls (*nuliakkaalia*), that is, made into girls. Several reasons are cited for reversing gender roles, one being that when a newborn was not of the sex the parents desired, newborn children were raised in the gender opposite their biological sex. Thus a boy might be raised to fill a woman's position or a girl to be a hunter (see also Holm 1914:67). Or if a daughter (son) died prematurely, the next-born daughter (son) might be raised in the gender role of the dead child. Concerning this transformation, Robert-Lamblin (1981) does not cite the metaphysical reasons known for the Netsilik *kipijuituq* but theorizes that this practice was intended to remedy sex-ratio disequilibrium within a family. This social device may have functioned as a substitute for infanticide as practiced among the Netsilik (Remie 1985). To the best of my knowledge, however, the *kipijuituq* did not function as a sex-ratio equalizer.

Another instance of gender change in east Greenland is the *piaarqusiaq* (*piaaqqusitat*), a young boy or girl dressed in a ridiculous manner and wearing a specially made cap (Ostermann 1938:191; Thalbitzer 1912:588, 1941:602). The *piaarqusiaq* is a child whose brother or sister died in infancy and for this reason requires special treatment to reach adulthood safely (Ostermann 1938:191; Thalbitzer 1912:588). The special clothing is thought to make the child invisible to hostile spirits (Ostermann 1938:191; Thalbitzer 1941:604). In this way, the *piaarqusiaq* is a practice to ward off evil spirits and as such differs from the *nuliakkaalia* and *tikkaalia,* a practice said to equalize gender balance and assure division of labor according to gender.

An example of gender change to avoid a hostile spirit is cited by Bernard Saladin d'Anglure (1994b:98) for the Quebec Inuit. In this case a person ordered by the group to execute a dangerous camp member became afraid the soul of the executed person would seek revenge and became a transvestite to evade that hostile soul.

An example of sex crossing is found in traditions recorded by William Thalbitzer (1923:511–516) from east Greenland and Franz Boas (1901:248, 323) from Cumberland Sound and Hudson Bay. In these traditions, an old woman took to living like a man and married her daughter-in-law. In the Greenland version the old woman changed into a man and procreated as a man.

Saladin d'Anglure has also recorded instances from the Quebec Inuit society of girls dressed and socialized as boys (1994b:91), a boy dressed alternately as a girl and boy every other day (Saladin d'Anglure 1994b:94), and a boy taught both sewing and hunting and dressed in the coat of a boy and the pants of a girl (Saladin d'Anglure 1994b:92). The reason given for these gender changes was that the sex of the child's namesake differed from the sex of the child; therefore the child was gendered according to its name. In all of these examples, the transvestite girl or boy eventually had to make the transition to his/her biological sex. In the case of a boy, the transition to his biological sex was accomplished when he killed his first game animal (Saladin d'Anglure 1994b:97), at which time he abandoned his feminine clothing.

It is not certain whether this phenomenon corresponds to the Netsilik *kipijuituq,* as there is no mention of taboos associated with the Quebec transvestite. The Quebec example, however, is similar to the Netsilik *kipijuituq* in that a boy's transition to his biological sex was effected by his first catch.

DISCUSSION

As I pointed out earlier, the *kipijuituq* most commonly makes the transition to the male gender by taking a polar bear. The role of the polar bear in gender conversion may be rooted in the Inuit worldview. In Inuit creation myths, according to Saladin d'Anglure, at the beginning of the world humans and other animals were undifferentiated and thus were able to mutually metamorphose. In the mythical world, of all the animals the polar bear was most closely associated with humans. This close association is evidenced in Inuit mythology as follows: (1) at the beginning of the world, a sterile woman came to possess a polar bear cub and brought it up as a human (Saladin d'Anglure 1990:179); (2) polar bears also stand up on two legs; (3) polar bears eat the same things as humans (marine mammals and fish); (4) they hunt in the same manner as humans; (5) like humans, polar bears can travel either on the sea ice or on land; and (6) they live in a winter shelter similar to an iglu (snow house) (Saladin d'Anglure 1990:183).

Another aspect of Inuit creation myths relating to the importance of the polar bear is the allusion to antagonism, or opposition, between human females and polar bears. This allusion suggests that the polar bear symbolizes males as well as sexual desire (Saladin d'Anglure 1990:180, 184) and thus may be the most suitable first game for the *kipijuituq* transition to male status. Also, in mythology the polar bear is portrayed as the original male and as such is considered to occupy a status equal to humans, males in particular, and is seen as a supermale with the power to fertilize sterile women (Saladin d'Anglure:1990, 1994a:208). In some cases, the polar bear is depicted as a kinsperson and a rival of high respect.

Thus by taking a polar bear, which symbolizes reproduction and vitality, the *kipijuituq* would be imbued with vigorous vitality and hunting ability and would be blessed with numerous descendants (Saladin d'Anglure 1990:186, 189). This worldview is one plausible explanation of why, by taking a polar bear, the *kipijuituq* may become a male and how in many cases a young boy becomes recognized as an adult. As mentioned before, B had taken a bearded seal when he was ten, but because his grandparents had directed that the state of being *kipijuituq* would not terminate until he took a polar bear, only then was he able to make the transition to the male gender.

The concept of sex and gender in Inuit societies also needs to be discussed. Pelly Bay informants state that the fetus is male and that the conduct and condition of the mother-to-be at the time of childbirth determine whether the fetus will be born a female or a male. Saladin d'Anglure (1994b:84), based on his research in Quebec, also stated that from the time of birth, neither sex nor gender is fixed. Saladin d'Anglure wrote that the embryo always begins as a male, but during pregnancy or under certain conditions during childbirth it may be born as a female. If the mother breaks a taboo during pregnancy or experiences a difficult delivery, the penis of the male fetus will audibly rupture and change to a vulva. Such a fetus will be born as a female and is called a *sipiniq*[9] (Saladin d'Anglure 1994b:84, 94). Sex change of the fetus is often accompanied by signs such as a cracking sound when the vulvar fissure is formed and the penis retracts, or a clitoral hypertrophy (Saladin d'Anglure 1994b:85). According to one Pelly Bay informant, the male fetus holds on to its penis when coming down the birth canal. In the event of a difficult birth or other extenuating circumstances, however, if the male fetus lets go of its penis, the newborn will be a female.

Such beliefs may be rooted in Inuit legend. In his volume on the intellectual culture of the Iglulik Inuit, Rasmussen (1929:252–253) recorded these stories:

> Women appeared on earth. They came from hummocks of earth: they were born so. They were already fully grown when they emerged from the ground. They lived together as man and wife, and soon one of them was with child. Then the one who had been husband sang a magic song:

A human being here
A penis here.
May its opening be wide
And roomy.
Opening, opening, opening!

When these words were sung, the man's penis split with a loud noise and he became a woman, and gave birth to a child. . . . Also, women grew up from a hummock of earth. They were born and fully grown all at once. And they wished to have children. A magic song changed one of them into a woman, and they had children.

For the Netsilik, Rasmussen (1931:208–209) recorded this story.

That was the time people lived in darkness, in the very first beginning, when there were only men and no Woman was made by man. All the animals died, and there were only two men left. They lived together. They married, as there was nobody else, and at last one of them became with child. They were great shamans, and when the one was going to bear a child they made his penis over again so that he became a woman, and she had a child.

The Ammassilik have a similar belief. Pierre Robbe (1981:74, quoted in Saladin d'Anglure 1994b:86) noted that the Ammassilik believe all fetuses are masculine and that the fetus holds his penis until birth. At that time if he wants to be a girl he does not hold his penis as he moves down the birth canal, and the penis is transformed into a vulva, resulting in the birth of a girl.

Many legends also tell of change of sex by individual volition (cf. Rasmussen 1929:158–159, 302; Thalbitzer 1941:511).

CONCLUSION

In this chapter I have discussed the *kipijuituq*, which to my knowledge has not been heretofore reported in the literature. Other examples of gender change in the Arctic literature are reported to relate to gender/sex equilibrium (Greenland), a tactic to avoid malevolent spirits (St. Lawrence Island, Greenland, Quebec), dual sexuality by birth (southeast Alaska), spiritual powers (St. Lawrence Island, Kotzebue Sound), or a replacement of a child who died prematurely (Greenland). None of these reasons applies to the *kipijuituq*, except that when the namesake of a newborn male is or was *kipijuituq*, the newborn male necessarily becomes *kipijuituq*. The *kipijuituq* differs from gender change in Quebec as a result of one namesake, however, in that (1) in Quebec, gender change arising from one namesake applies to both male and female infants (Saladin d'Anglure 1994b), but only male infants become *kipijuituq*; (2) the *kipijuituq* always changes back to the male gender; and (3) the *kipijuituq* is not recognized as having special powers. Although being *tiringnaqtaq*, or subject to special taboos, leaves the *kipijuituq* vulnerable to misfortune or visitation by evil forces, this condition may apply to any person and is not unique to the *kipijuituq*.

What, then, was the function of the *kipijuituq*? In spite of repeated questioning and observation, I was unable to establish a communal function for the *kipijuituq*. Negative evidence leads me to surmise that birth conditions may deprive a male infant of his male completeness or full male potential. That is, what should have been born a girl came out as a boy, and raising that child as a girl until the age at which it should attain manhood allows the child to be transformed back into a male, imbued with sufficient masculinity to cancel sex/gender ambiguity. A particularly deficient case could be remedied by taking a polar bear, which would imbue the child with supermale power.

Although I repeatedly asked why only certain male infants were destined to become *kipijuituq*, I always received the rejoinder "I don't know." When I suggested the reasoning posited earlier, the response was neither positive nor negative, probably because the Inuit refuse to hypothesize or make presumptions concerning suppositional situations or matters of which they lack intimate knowledge (e.g., Briggs 1969:44, 53).

A newborn male child is determined to be *kipijuituq* through the process of *hanaurajuk* (talking to). Here also, repeated questioning did not reveal what criteria or circumstances obliged a male infant to become *kipijuituq*. The answer to my queries was always that one can know by *hanaurajuk*. Again, I can only surmise that during *hanaurajuk* it becomes apparent that the infant is predestined to be *kipijuituq*. Except when the namesake was a *kipijuituq*, in which case the newborn child automatically becomes *kipijuituq*, I was unable to ascertain what criteria or circumstances played a part in that determination. It appears that through *hanaurajuk* the grandparents perceive signs that the child should become *kipijuituq*.

Data from the literature cited earlier, and information provided by informants at Pelly Bay, suggest that in the cosmologies of many eastern Canadian and Greenland Inuit there was only one sex, the male. In the beginning, a man's penis ruptured and formed into a vulva, or a magic song changed a man into a woman—a transformation making procreation possible. Such a transformation may be the basis for the explanation that the fetus is fundamentally male but may be born a female if he does not hold on to his penis during parturition. From this I conclude that the Netsilik and other eastern Arctic groups posited a single original sex: the female sex deriving from the original male.

There is, however, a problem in this interpretation—namely, that the word *inuk* (and its plural forms) appearing in myths may refer to both male and human being. Where Rasmussen includes the original text with a translation, *inuk* is translated as human being (Rasmussen 1929:252). He does not record the original text for his other stories (Rasmussen 1929:253, 1931:208–209), but if consistency in translation can be assumed, *inuk* in creation myths concerning humankind should mean male (cf. Saladin d'Anglure 1994b:89).

In conclusion, I shall address three questions. Is the *kipijuituq* a phenomenon restricted to the Pelly Bay Netsilik (Arvilingjuarmiut)? The term *kipijuituq* does not appear in the literature and, as discussed earlier, differs from other examples of gender change in the Arctic. For these reasons I propose that the *kipijuituq* is one example of gender change widespread throughout the Arctic but is distinctive in its rationale and manifestation. As such, the *kipijuituq* may be postulated as a unique Netsilik phenomenon.

Did becoming a *kipijuituq* and later acquiring a male gender endow certain males with the symbolic reproductive attributes often associated with females (cf. Bodenhorn 1990)? This question can be answered only with further data.

Finally, in the Inuit intellect are (were) there categories or concepts that correspond to gender, biological sex, and sexuality? There are terms for human males (*anut*) and females (*arnaq*), but I have not found terms in Inuktitut corresponding to gender, biological sex, or sexuality. In this chapter I have used gender not because it correlates to an Inuit concept but because it is essential to describe an Inuit social phenomenon in English. It is important to remember that gender and associated terms are vehicles to translate Inuit social phenomena into English and are not translations of indigenous concepts. As Henrietta Moore (1994b) has pointed out, social scientific research contests the premise that sex difference is natural and that outside of biomedical discourse, sex is not a universal concept rooted in presocial, physiological parameters. Examples presented in this chapter aptly emphasize the fact that gender is a process rather than a category (Moore 1994b:820). Research is needed to establish whether the concept of gender and sex exists (existed) in non-Western societies. Stated otherwise, we need to reexamine our projection of oppositional dualism as a paradigmatic structure (Kehoe 1997:266; see also Chapter 12, this volume).

Research and hypotheses concerning these problems are prerequisites to discussions of the third sex/gender or conjectures concerning the ascendancy of the biological male alluded to earlier in this chapter. All of these a priori suppositions implicitly presuppose the pertinence and universality of a two-sex dichotomy in anthropological research.

ACKNOWLEDGMENTS

I thank Simon Inuksaq (deceased May 1997), Josie Angutinguiniq, Martha Kutjuutiqu (Tunnuq, deceased October 1998), and Guy Kakkiarniun of Pelly Bay for their hours of consultation and patience with my interminable questions. I also express appreciation to Petra Rethman (McMaster University) and Gregory A. Reinhardt (Indiana University), Lisa Frink (University of Wisconsin, Madison), Rita S. Shepard (UCLA), and Masao Kashinaga (Tokyo University) for pertinent comments and advice.

3

GENDER EQUALITY IN A CONTEMPORARY INDIAN COMMUNITY

Lillian A. Ackerman

Gender equality has been described in several hunting-gathering societies (Draper 1975; Schlegel 1977), but no one so far as I know has described gender equality operating in a society that is part of an industrialized nation. Indeed, Eleanor Leacock (1978) wrote that such equality was impossible in a complex society. She believed gender equality and industrialization were incompatible.

On the Colville Indian Reservation in north-central Washington, however, gender equality and industrialization do appear together in the same society. The people of the reservation are descended from Indians who had a fishing-gathering-hunting culture in which the practice of gender equality was not only present but necessary. Women provided at least 50 percent of the society's subsistence, and their other functions were extremely important in keeping the economy and other cultural systems viable.

The modern period of Colville culture is rooted in the Euro-American conquest of the Plateau Culture Area, which is a fairly recent event. Plateau Indians were forced to sign treaties in 1855, consenting to be placed on reservations. When the Colville Reservation was formed in 1872, eleven tribes/bands were eventually located on it, but they shared the same culture; that is, they were all Plateau Indians. Traditional Plateau cultures became very similar as a result of the extensive intermarriage required by their incest regulations, which forbade marriage with any known kin (Ackerman 1994:289; Hunn 1990:217). Consequently, tribes and villages far apart geographically often intermarried, evening out cultural differences. This practice is followed to the present day.

After the reservation was formed, the people farmed as the government expected them to, but they continued their foraging lifestyle as well as they could with the decreased land area available. This situation continued for some years. A crisis point in cultural change took place in the late 1930s. In 1938 the separate bands or tribes were required to surrender their independent political structure of chiefs and assemblies. These institutions were dissolved—not without a furor—and a reservation-wide tribal council was formed that administered the reservation as a whole. Then in 1939 the construction of Grand Coulee Dam began, and by 1941 it flooded much of the reservation land, destroying areas where wild root crops flourished and also destroying the salmon runs that could not get past the dam to spawn. As salmon provided one-third of the food supply and roots and other plants provided about half, the people were forced to give up extensive foraging and turn almost completely to the Euro-American economy to survive.

I will not go into detail here as to how the people adjusted to these changes. Suffice it to say that after great effort and astute management by the tribal council beginning in 1970, the Colville Reservation today is one of the most prosperous in the nation. This may not be saying much, since unemployment is still over 50 percent, but the reservation has been successful in many economic projects and continually plans for more. Today the reservation has organized businesses including lumber mills, logging, grocery stores, gambling casinos, and houseboating for tourists. The tribal bureaucracy provides employment mostly to tribal members to run these establishments and to perform the administrative work on the reservation. In 1986 the reservation injected about $5 million into the economy of north-central Washington as a result of purchasing materials, paying salaries, and paying taxes. The economy of the reservation, then, is similar to the Euro-American economy in that the reservation staffs offices, manages forests and businesses, maintains roads, plans economic development, and administers health, education, and welfare offices. Nevertheless, the economy remains a somewhat separate system from the rest of the country in that the tribal administration does its hiring by its own rules and runs its businesses based on its indigenous traditions and values.

EQUALITY IN THE ECONOMIC SPHERE

Because the Colville people have a legacy of gender equality inherited from their traditional foraging culture (Ackerman 1995:78–98), they have achieved without pain that elusive goal in Euro-American society: equal pay for equal work. Men and women not only earn equal salaries for the same work but have equal access to all jobs including management, logging, ranching, and, at one time, mining. I once asked a council member if she was aware that equal pay for women was not the norm in Euro-American society. She replied that everyone on the reservation was aware of it, but the council took as a given that women had to support their families, and the philosophy was that the welfare of their society was dependent on the welfare of children. Thus ideology is a factor in the preservation of gender equality.

As noted earlier, women in the past were extremely influential, as they provided at least half of the food supply by gathering roots, berries, and other plants and sometimes capturing small animals. Their work was regarded as the backbone of the economy, recognized by both genders. Today women are still considered the backbone of the economy, still recognized by both genders. Women are expected to support their families today, as they did in the past with their gathering activities. In 1979, when the economy was good, almost 90 percent of women were employed in a formal job. The remaining 10 percent, who had no employable skills or no child care resources, took care of other people's children along with their own to earn money. Often Colville women are the sole supporters of their children because of the high divorce rate in Plateau societies, past and present.

As a consequence, girls as well as boys are raised as potential breadwinners and are equally encouraged to obtain higher education or vocational training. Since the work of both genders is recognized by the society at large as of equal value and importance, a ceremony in the form of a feast persists that recognizes that value. Some wild resources are still available, so when a boy captures his first fish or animal or a girl brings back food from her first independent gathering effort, a feast is held in which the child's food is completely consumed. Elders particularly are invited to attend the feast because their presence bestows good fortune on the young person. New permutations of this custom have arisen and are observed as well. A girl's first loaf of bread is given to an elder as a sign of respect. A child's first powwow prize money is shared with elders.

Individuals of both genders commented that women are generally more efficient and reliable workers than men. One male Euro-American consultant admired the speed and skill displayed by a group of Colville women who built a road on the reservation. He noted that women generally are more industrious and more thorough about completing a task, and they keep an eight-hour day more conscientiously than men.

This modern opinion is reminiscent of the phrase "men don't work," which encapsulates the emic or Native perception of the male economic role in the traditional culture. Of course men "worked" in the past by providing fish and animal flesh to the diet, and their defense of the community was risky "work" that was highly valued. Apparently, however, these activities were not regarded as "work." Male economic activities in the past occupied long hours during a few weeks each season and occurred in strenuous spurts, with leisurely periods in between, whereas women more often were continually occupied with tasks on a daily basis. In my opinion, the traditional economic role of Colville women better prepared them for the eight-hour day and five- to six-day work week required of workers in an industrial society. The traditional pattern, on the other hand, did not prepare men for this schedule. Accentuating this difference is the cultural lack of a "moral imperative" for Colville Reservation men to earn money for its own sake, which equals power and prestige in Euro-American society.

The traditional Indian male pattern of intermittent work may account for the observation that women in many North American tribes acculturate more readily than men to modern society (Maynard 1979; McElroy 1979). It is argued that this differential acculturation among the Oglala Sioux occurs because women are able to continue their homemaker roles in contemporary times and thus experience less cultural disruption than men. In contrast, men are completely deprived of their former roles as warriors and hunters (Maynard 1979:12–13).

This explanation cannot apply to the Plateau tribes of the Colville Reservation because little continuity has occurred in women's roles either. Although childbearing and rearing continue, all else is changed. Office employment is as different from gathering and preserving wild foods as lumbering is from hunting. What remains from the past is the ethic that women do what they must to support the family and even provide the major share of support if needed, as they did in the traditional culture. Women's better adjustment in contemporary times may result from their being accustomed to sustained rather than strenuous intermittent work. It would be interesting to see if other North American tribes have conceptions on the nature of male and female work similar to those in the Plateau and to correlate those conceptions with the differential adjustment of the sexes to the Euro-American economy.

EQUALITY IN THE DOMESTIC SPHERE

Consultants say that in the past, men were seldom home, since they were away getting food. Indeed, since the annual round often separated a married couple involved in disparate tasks in different areas, they must have been together consistently only in the winter, when the subsistence round was completed, and perhaps in the fall, when parties consisting of both sexes participated in the hunt. Women butchered the game the men brought in and dried the meat. Whether men were home or not, it was considered the domain, or at least the realm, of women. They were considered the owners of all the food in the household; they processed it, distributed it, and used the surplus for trade.

Within the home today, often an extended family, Colville women still control the economic resources of the family, as they did formerly. The oldest woman runs the household and makes most of the decisions. Women are considered more economically astute than men and still handle their husband's income as well as their own. The idea that women control all resources within the household still lingers, even though men are present year-round (see Chapter 7, this volume). The separation of men and women continues to some extent. I observed that men socialized in groups, whereas women socialized in their groups at large social gatherings. When I mentioned this pattern to consultants, they agreed that this is common.

Women today usually keep young children after a divorce, although some inequality is beginning to creep in. In the past, no one expected a man to provide for his children after divorce because it was impossible for him to do so. One spouse or the other usually left the community. This caused no economic hardship for the woman and her children, for her work was extremely productive, and it was easy to acquire a surplus for trade. Women could trade their vegetal foods for meat or fish, and they always received meat and fish in communal distributions. Today I have seen elders deride the few women who defy custom and seek support after a divorce. Unfortunately, although most women work, divorced or not, it is harder to support children on only one income in modern conditions. Consequently, single mothers are finding it harder to sustain their families than in the past.

A married couple continues to own property separately. A husband and wife will each have their own car. Consequently, if a divorce occurs, the woman, who sought a loan for her car and paid for it out of her income, will automatically own it. Neither a husband nor a wife, even in a long-term stable marriage, will borrow the other's vehicle without permission.

Each marital partner pays for different things to run the household. He might pay the taxes and make the mortgage payments, whereas she will pay for the children's dental work and food. Each partner keeps a separate savings account. The division of financial responsibility is different for each household, but an attempt is made to make it equal.

EQUALITY IN THE POLITICAL SPHERE

In the political arena, men and women both speak publicly with equal frequency, and they vote independent of each other. I was told that a husband or wife never learns how the other votes in national or reservation elections. In a spirit of experimentation I once informed a young Colville man that married couples in Euro-American society discuss candidates before an election and influence each other on which candidates to vote for. He was incredulous, even scandalized. His reaction indicates how seriously married people view their political independence from their spouses.

A problem of women's access is developing in the political sector. When the tribal council started in 1938, fairly equal numbers of men and women were elected to the council. Around 1970, after the tribal council successfully fought termination of the reservation, the workload for the council increased tremendously, and all members were required to travel extensively. Young women felt the travel particularly was incompatible with their parental duties to their young children. Older women who have older or grown children, however, do seek and win office without trouble. This leads to a situation in which young men sit on the council along with mostly older men, but young women are not present alongside older women. Despite the age imbalance, the gender balance is about equal. The chairperson is currently female (2002).

Many consultants say they generally prefer to have women represent them on the council, as women are more aware of problems and will aggressively fight Euro-American demands more readily than men. Women, they say, "have a stronger spirit" and will fight for what they believe, whereas men are trained to be reticent and dignified.

DISCUSSION

In all aspects of contemporary Colville Reservation culture, gender equality has survived industrialization and modernization, with only the two exceptions noted earlier: the currently threatened welfare of children after divorce, and young women's limited access to leadership in the political sphere. Overall, however, I would judge that gender equality continues to be a necessary element in the contemporary culture. A significant difference occurs in the nature of gender equality from the past, however. During the foraging period, men and women exercised mostly balanced, complementary rights. In the present they exercise mostly identical rights in every aspect of culture, suggesting that access to identical rights is the only way to have equal rights in an industrial society.

Why has female status been reduced in other parts of the country and the world by colonialism and capitalism and yet escaped that fate on the Colville Reservation and, in fact, in the entire Plateau Culture Area? Missionaries were successful in destroying several female leadership positions in the culture, but they were not successful in ranking men and women by, for instance, giving superior value to men's work. Perhaps women's work was too important. This may not sufficiently explain the persistence of gender equality, but a few other speculations may provide some clues.

Gender equality may have persisted on the Colville Reservation because Euro-American settlers did not appear in the Plateau in large numbers until the 1890s, reducing the time for negative impact on the culture. Further, the eleven tribes on the Colville Reservation were not confined there until 1872. The missionaries may have failed in the area because they had too little time to solidify the culture changes they engineered before the influx of settlers reduced their influence. Moreover, the Plateau people have a strong oral tradition and trace their genealogies five to seven generations back, along with the life histories of most of their ancestors (Ackerman 1994:302). Consequently, they also have a strong cultural tradition, which has not been easily suppressed.

Finally, gender equality may have survived because it is not something that a casual observer can see. It is largely invisible to outsiders. With part of Euro-American society trying to win equal rights for women, the existence of gender equality on the Colville Reservation might even be applauded rather than condemned.

I have stressed the importance of the economy in this chapter, since so much theory points to it as the source of gender equality (e.g., Sanday 1974). I believe that ideology (Schlegel 1977) also supports the gender equality found among the Colville people; thus equal pay for equal work is a principle among them, as explained earlier. Their ideology extends further. Despite the theoretical universal inferiority ascribed to women by some researchers (Chodorow 1974; Ortner 1974) because of their childbearing, child-rearing, and lactating functions, Colville women are honored by men for those functions. Consultants of both genders say men honor not only their own mothers and grandmothers—important figures in a boy's development—but all women. Men readily confide in women and expect their mothers, grandmothers, and wives to be strong. They expect their daughters to be strong and train them appropriately. The Colville women's enculturating functions earn them a position of authority within the extended family in their old age, and they are able to exert influence within the community as well. At any age, women are not considered inferior within Plateau culture because of their natural functions but are honored and receive economic and domestic rewards for exercising those functions.

The Colville Reservation data reveal that gender equality exists not only among foragers but also among participants in an industrial society. The facts suggest that equality may flourish at any level of socioeconomic integration and may be present in other unlikely or unexpected places, since modern economic conditions do not appear to be incompatible with gender equality after all. Where the Colville Reservation people have the authority and power to direct their society, they have adapted modern economic conditions to fit their ideology of gender equality.

IDENTICAL AND CONTEMPORARY RIGHTS

In contrast to contemporary Colville culture, where gender roles tend to be identical, gender roles in traditional Colville culture were different from each other. Men hunted and fished and women gathered, for instance. Both genders, however, had equal access to power, authority, and autonomy in the various spheres of the culture. This access was not identical as in modern Colville Reservation culture but was balanced or complementary. One example is that only men were chiefs in most groups, but women chose them. Interdependence of husband and wife occurred in the Plateau as it does among the Inupiaq and Yup'ik (Eskimo) cultures. The descriptions of this interdependence leads many ethnographers, myself included, to view the status of Yup'ik and Inuit men and women as at least approximately equal, although it is an equality of the complementary kind.

A fine example of complementary access to the social spheres of a culture is described by Barbara Bodenhorn (1990) for the traditional Inupiaq of the Alaska North Slope. She points out that Euro-American culture often uses the Eskimo in general as an example of inequality between men and women. Because men hunt, the reasoning goes, they dominate. Further, men control the public sphere because they "work"— that is, they hunt—while the women stay home. In contrast, the Inuit view of reality is that hunting is not simply a matter of men capturing animals. The wife of the hunter attracts the animals to the husband so he can catch them. Since hunting is a sacred act, the wife who is generous and skillful at womanly tasks leads animals to give themselves to the hunter. As Bodenhorn (1990:61) says, "It is the woman to whom the animal comes."

Ideology enters the picture here, as it does in the Colville gender system. A man of the North Slope whose wife has died can realistically seek help from female relatives to raise his children and butcher his catch, but he does not have a wife to whom an animal can give itself. Thus his view is that his hunting is handicapped. Consequently, women's activities—such as sewing, butchering, and sharing with others—are viewed as hunting skills by the Inupiaq (Bodenhorn 1990:62). This situation is comparable to the concept that the whale comes to the whale captain's wife at Point Barrow. There the wife has an important role during the launch of the whaleboat, and her behavior and generosity at home while the men are hunting affect the outcome of the hunt (Bodenhorn 1990:61).

I argued in a recent article that Yup'ik women must have had even greater autonomy than many women in hunting-gathering societies, since their men lived in so-called men's houses (see also Chapters 5, 6, 7, and 11, this volume). Men's houses had the effect of isolating men as individuals (Ackerman 1990a:214). They were excluded from the company of their male kin, since they were scattered over a wide territory into patrilineal dispersed clans, whereas residence was and is matrilocal, at least in Goodnews Bay, Alaska, and some other Yup'ik villages (Ackerman 1990b). Thus women lived with their mothers, sisters, children, aunts, and cousins, which formed a support network, whereas men were isolated from their kin of both genders. The men of King Island in their men's houses were reported to be often hostile, competitive, and suspicious of each other (Bogojavlensky and Fuller 1973:73, 76). Thus the existence of men's houses within a community is not an index of male dominance within the society (for a different view see Chapter 11, this volume). It seems unlikely that the separation of men and women in different dwellings has anything to do with gender status, and in fact such an arrangement may be socially disadvantageous for men because of their social isolation, referred to earlier (see also Chapter 9). Bodenhorn (1990:67) pointed out that one translation of the word *kashim,* generally translated as "men's house," refers to a ceremonial, communal, dancing, or festival house. This definition seems to fit the situation more accurately than "men's house."

I attempted to evaluate gender status among the Yup'ik (Ackerman 1990a) using my research at Goodnews Bay, Alaska, plus the literature, and concluded that the genders were approximately equal. I leaned heavily on Margaret Lantis's study of the Nunivak Islanders, using such data that men secured half the food and 90 percent of the raw materials necessary to sustain life (Lantis 1946:245), whereas women provided the rest of the food. This share of food production compares favorably with the gathering prowess of traditional Colville Indian women, who collected 50 to 70 percent of the food supply in a milder climate. Yup'ik women also produced clothing, boots, and pottery and prepared and stored all the food. Finally, as Lisa Frink (Chapter 7, this volume) reports for women in Chevak, the women distributed the food and were regarded as its owners, like their counterparts on the Plateau.

Lantis (1946:246) judged that the status of Yup'ik men and women on Nelson Island was little different. Bodenhorn (1990:61) wrote that Alaska Native women today are moving into power positions, thus extending gender equality from the traditional past into contemporary Inupiaq and Yup'ik cultures. Men and women in all three cultures—the Yup'ik, Inupiaq, and Plateau—were equally valued for the economic and other contributions each could make, leading to an evaluation of equal status in all three societies.

ACKNOWLEDGMENTS

The early part of this research was supported by fellowships from the Woodrow Wilson National Fellowship Foundation and the American Association of University Women Educational Foundation and by grants from the Phillips Fund of the American Philosophical Society and Sigma Xi. I thank them for their support.

4

CELEBRATION OF A LIFE
REMEMBERING LINDA WOMKON BADTEN, YUPIK EDUCATOR

Carol Zane Jolles

LIFE HISTORY NARRATIVES HAVE BEEN RECORDED in conjunction with North American ethnographic research since the 1920s. Until the 1970s, however, these locally generated texts were often regarded as complementary, colorful data that could buttress and enliven formal research. It is not my purpose to detail the emergence of the life history narrative as an ethnographic endeavor in its own right. Rather, in this chapter I describe one among many of the remarkably skilled and knowledgeable women who have contributed in major ways to northern Native research and the enduring friendships that so often develop from collaboration with them. Thus my intent is less theoretical than descriptive. As an aside, it is worthwhile to note that the movement of life history narratives from the wings to the stage of ethnographic research can be used to illustrate the relatively greater importance assigned to men's roles and men's lives in the ethnographic record.

By the late 1970s, narrative life histories coauthored by indigenous women and female ethnographers became more commonplace, the result of a more general attention given to women in anthropological research. Such attention, spurred in part by the dynamics of the feminist movement and the development of feminist anthropology, paralleled a revitalized interest in matters of gender. Marjorie Shostak was especially critical in popularizing indigenous women's narratives.

Shostak, who died in 1997, recorded the story of "Nisa" (*Nisa: The Life and Words of a !Kung Woman,* 1981), a !Kung-San woman from the Kalahari Desert region of northeastern South Africa. Nisa's story, compiled after dozens of interviews with a cross section of !Kung women, included a carefully edited and restructured life history narrative plus ethnographic background and interpretation.

For researchers focused on Native American societies, indigenous biographies and autobiographies are familiar resources. Many will recognize the coauthored narratives of Albert Yava (*Big Falling Snow: A Tewa Indian's Life and Times and the History and Traditions of His People,* 1978), Don Talayesva (*Sun Chief: The Autobiography of a Hopi Indian,* 1942), Left Handed (*Son of Old Man Hat,* 1938), the stories of Lame Deer and Black Elk, and numerous other narratives featuring Native American men. At the time they were written, these too were regarded as complementary to "real" research, although they often captured the public imagination. Coauthored life history narratives of Native American women from the "States" were few. Stories revealing the lives and contributions of northern Native American women (Alaskan and Canadian women of the Arctic and Subarctic regions) were practically nonexistent.

THEORY

Postmodernism, in conjunction with feminist thought of the 1970s and 1980s (see, for example, Behar and Gordon 1995; Clifford and Marcus 1986; di Leonardo 1991; Finn 1995; Marcus and Fischer 1986; Mukopudhyay and Higgins 1988; Ong 1995; Pratt 1986), changed our understanding of the gendered landscape even as other efforts were made more generally to open up our view of history, to give voice to the silent, and to balance the cultural and historical record (Wolf 1982). One corollary was greater attention to first-person narratives collected over the last century. Regardless of our new willingness to acknowledge the lives and contributions of women, however, Native American women are still less likely than others to be featured in life histories. Many Native women's narratives remain in archives along with other basic data. I would speculate that this lack of attention comes in part because Native women's lives even now are often perceived as extensions of men's lives. In the North, for example, because of a persistent subsistence-systems bias in local research, more attention is paid to male hunters than to women food harvesters, processors, and seamstresses; and neither men nor women are given much consideration as members of the modern global community.

For many of us who began research in the late 1980s and early 1990s, the exceptional work of two women anthropologists, Margaret Blackman and Julie Cruikshank, critically influenced our own investigations. The portrayals of Florence Edenshaw Davidson, a Haida woman from the village of Masset in the Queen Charlotte Islands, Canada (Blackman 1982); Sadie Brower Neakok, an Inupiaq woman from Barrow, Alaska (Blackman 1989); and three Yukon women elders of Athapaskan and Tlingit descent from interior British Columbia, Canada (Cruikshank 1990), grew out of longitudinal studies in the women's home communities (see, for example, Blackman 1991). Each anthropologist worked closely with her indigenous collaborator-consultants, spending several years tape-recording them. In dialectic fashion, each author also attempted to shape and edit the stories of these northern Native women in ways that could be appreciated by the women themselves, by their own families and communities, and by a readership that included the broader Native and non-Native public.

Unlike Shostak's text, the works of Cruikshank and Blackman amply illustrate the contributions these women made to their societies, stressing their talents and accomplishments. The women were not chosen as "Everywoman." Rather, they were selected for their individual and unique qualities. Nevertheless, Blackman's two volumes, *During My Time* (1982) and *Sadie Brower Neakok: An Inupiaq Woman* (1989), and Cruikshank's *Life Lived Like a Story* (1990) are exemplary not simply because they highlight the very interesting lives of their consultants. Both authors present their consultants in ways that adhere to local traditions of tact and propriety without either unnecessary sensationalism or abrogation of traditional values that preclude drawing attention to the individual at the expense of family or clan. Blackman's descriptions of Florence Davidson, for example, emphasize Davidson's accomplishments within the framework of her marriage and the demands of Haida tradition. Blackman's collaboration with Sadie Neakok is executed in a similar fashion.

Cruikshank's groundbreaking work in *Life Lived Like a Story* not only records the lives of its three Yukon elder protagonists, Mrs. Smith, Mrs. Sidney, and Mrs. Ned, but also takes into account postmodernist concerns with voice and perspective. Cruikshank relinquishes Western tradition with its reflection, attention to explication, and reliance on a linear chronology of events in favor of the categories and perspectives preferred by her collaborators, creating as she does so cultural relevance deriving from the protagonists' cultures rather than her own.

PURPOSE

It is with the work of these two anthropologists, especially with the women whose stories are the subjects of their cooperative enterprises, in mind that I turn to this chapter. My task is both to pay tribute in some small way to my friend, adviser, and consultant, Linda Womkon Badten, a St. Lawrence Island Yupik[1] woman of extraordinary character and talents who passed away in the spring of 1997, and to draw attention to the critical and various roles northern indigenous women play in documenting their cultures.

DISCUSSION

A life is many things. At the very least it is constituted of a multifaceted self. Obviously, that self is composed of the singular characteristics of personality and personhood that distinguish self from other. These include a congeries of qualities that result from cultural background, on the one hand, and from interactions with others both within and without one's own culture on the other. Self is shaped by tradition and historical moment, by belief—the monumental elements of spiritual congress that form the self—and by discourse, the language with its cognitive and substantive qualities through which that self, that life, is expressed and made familiar. These forces are at work as self emerges, "becomes aware," gains in confidence, and achieves adulthood (for a discussion of Yup'ik personhood, see Fienup-Riordan 1986a). Postmodernist theory suggests that anthropology too is bound up with such processes. If this is so, then any rendition of a life story should be marked by its acceptance of the multiple voices and embodiments of experience of which it is constituted. Minimally, it must acknowledge interactions between consultant and interviewer (Clifford and Marcus 1986; Marcus and Fischer 1986; Pratt 1986).

In the present context I attempt to acknowledge the relationship between myself as friend-anthropologist-interviewer and Linda as friend-consultant-adviser. Eventually, it must do much more. Cruikshank noted that a life history narrative "simultaneously reflects continuity with the past and passes on experiences, stories, and guiding principles in the present" (Cruikshank 1990:x). Here I combine Linda's collaborator-protagonist's story and her (protagonist's) past and present, my own story and my past and present, and the common experience of the two of us.

TRIBUTE: A COLLECTION OF THEMES

In tribute to Linda I present a brief outline of her extraordinary life along with recollections of the moments where our lives came together, and I try to place her life within the frame of her own (Yupik) and our own (her Yupik and my *laluramka,* or "white person") cultures. I begin with an account of our friendship and our work together; I follow with background information about Linda's culture, that of the St. Lawrence Island Yupik, and a much abbreviated account of Linda's life. I conclude by comparing aspects of my friend's life to those heroines of Yupik traditional stories whose adventurous mythic journeys encompass so much of Yupik values. By drawing on traditional stories, I hope to place Linda's life within the larger context of Yupik experience while adding a second implicit Yupik voice to the discussion. I look to these stories for possible explanations of her achievements, her cheerful multicultural perspective, and her successful management of a complex multicultural existence.

An Extraordinary Woman

Linda Badten was a close friend. The circumstances of our friendship and my personal sense of loss at her passing therefore color what I say here and my understanding of her life. That said, let me begin. I met Linda in 1989. I had completed ten months' residence and research in her birthplace, the village of Gambell, St. Lawrence Island, Alaska. We had not met previously because she had lived for many years in Fairbanks, Alaska, several hundred air miles away. Although we had not met, I had been told about her by younger women in her large extended family, the members of her *ramket,* or clan, who still live in the village of her birth. For these women Linda was a role model, a living example of what faith, intelligence, perseverance, and hard work could accomplish. I knew little about her personally except for her publicly acknowledged achievements. When her family members learned I would be traveling to Fairbanks to work in the Polar Archives at the University of Alaska, they suggested I call her. I did so, and Linda immediately invited me to stay with her, not just that one time but whenever I was in Fairbanks. Thus began our friendship, based originally on her hospitality, our shared interest in her culture, and her knowledge that I had spent almost a year living among her relatives and caring for her father's brother's elderly widow. I stayed with her thereafter whenever I traveled to Fairbanks.

As Linda and I came to know each other, I found she had the gift of humor. Each time I visited her we stayed awake until two, three, and four in the morning. We talked, we laughed (sometimes without much of an excuse beyond the pleasure of laughing together), and we sang songs—Linda was an ardent and enthusiastic piano player with a large repertory of Broadway show tunes, old-time favorites, and an endless supply of hymns. She played with such gusto and forte that we used to joke about her having to have a house that wasn't too close to anyone else. And we played *Scrabble.* Night after night Linda beat me at *Scrabble.*

I can't remember winning a single game. At her memorial service I learned I was not the only person Linda had beaten at *Scrabble,* leading the minister to ask for a show of hands among those in attendance who had once "played a board game with Linda." Many hands in the church were raised. Sometimes Linda cooked for the two of us, sometimes we cooked together, and sometimes we went out to eat. Often we visited her daughter and her family.

Only after several years of friendship did we begin to work together formally. Almost from the beginning, though, Linda served as my critical reader and adviser, going over an article I was writing or had just finished. The two of us discussed the points I was trying to make and mulled over my supporting evidence and examples from my personal experience within the community. Often the writing became a starting point for a philosophical discussion on the nature of marine mammal hunting communities and culture change to which we would return several times in the course of a visit. She expressed her approval of the work I was carrying out in the community, saying she felt both the past and the present history of the community needed to be documented. She was particularly interested in the combined political, economic, and cultural changes taking place in Gambell and saw those processes as history in the making. And she was curious about my experiences as a non-Native person living in her home community.

As we talked about the community and her perceptions of it, I became aware of the great psychological distance Linda had traveled from her homeland. Often she seemed surprised at the conservatism of the Gambell community. Once, after she had returned to Fairbanks from a visit to Gambell, she said with some amazement that she had encountered what she called "clan politics." She said she had not realized anyone in Gambell still attached much importance to the *ramka,* or clan system. She wondered after her visit whether she had actually experienced culture shock in her own birthplace. And we pondered together over the differences between rural tribal village life and life lived in the city, regardless of identity and origins.

In 1991 we worked together formally for the first time on a project to document the ethnographic content in the paintings and drawings of a well-known St. Lawrence Island artist. We recorded a number of audiotapes that described that content, employing an interviewer-consultant format. In 1992–1993 Linda and I continued our work on St. Lawrence artists and received, along with several others, a planning grant to explore possibilities of an exhibit at the Otto Geist Museum. Toward the end of 1994 she and I began to discuss recording her own story. With what seems in retrospect a sense of premonition, Linda was preoccupied with two concerns. The first was to leave a meaningful narrative for her children and grandchildren. The second was her desire to find a publisher who would allow the greatest percentage of profit to return to her family. She wanted to leave behind not only her story but also some small measure of financial support for her family. She thought a book about her life might do both.

In this, Linda's reasoning was similar to other women from St. Lawrence Island with whom I have worked. The conventions of the life history format, combined with the cultural constraints at work in northern communities, make drawing attention to individual accomplishment a complex task. Certainly, Linda's modesty about her experiences and achievements was a product of the Yupik values she cherished, which suggest that one should not broadcast one's achievements. Nevertheless, she wished to go ahead with a book about her life. I have no doubt that she would have agreed with another of my St. Lawrence Island consultant-collaborators who told me, "I'm not doing this for myself; I'm doing it for the grandchildren."

In 1995 I obtained a small grant from the University of Washington (Seattle) that would allow us to begin our project together. Thus in the fall of 1995 Linda and I recorded what would become the only tapes of her life story narrative. Because Linda was troubled by family concerns and the first signs of physical discomfort eventually diagnosed as cancer, we spent far more time talking, going for walks, and eating than we did recording. Nevertheless, those tapes substantiate Linda's capacity for objective cultural analysis, her drive, her enduring and scholarly interest in and curiosity about her own culture, and her energy. During that visit we began to discuss traveling to the Smithsonian National Anthropological Archives together. We hoped to persuade one of her close childhood friends from Gambell to go with us. We envisioned this trip as an exciting opportunity to explore life histories together. We planned to stay in my mother's house where I had grown up, a house filled with my familiar ancestral memorabilia, and we anticipated working each day at the Smithsonian surrounded by the ancestral memorabilia of Linda and her friend. Our plan was distinctly postmodernist in concept, involving three women plus the unpredictable but interesting possible contributions of my mother, but, sadly, it never took place. By the fall of 1996 Linda was too unwell to undertake such a journey.

When I last spoke to Linda, at the end of April 1997, she had just learned that the cancer which had plagued her for more than two years was terminal. She was clearly shaken by this news and was trying to sort out the collapse of her physical strength from the enduring religious strength that sustained her. Neither she nor anyone else realized that she had only a few weeks to live, not the six to eight months she imagined. When she died she left a heartfelt void: in her family, among her friends, and in the small community of northern scholars who focus on the history and culture of Alaskan and Siberian Yupik peoples.

The memorial service for Linda brought together many people: her children, grandchildren, and in-laws; her Yupik relatives, among them highly respected bowhead whale hunters; college professors, researchers, and former students from the University of Alaska; students and friends from her Bible study group and Sunday school classes; a well-known Alaskan author; the nurse who attended her in the hospital; parishioners from her church; former colleagues and students from the elementary school where she had taught so many children to read and to love language as she did; and a collection of people from all walks of life who had met her and wished to pay their respects on her passing.

GROWING UP YUPIK [LINDA WOMKON BADTEN, 1923-1997]

> In many cultures the lives of natives span periods of critical and rapid culture change. (Blackman 1982:5)

> You learn everyday. It seems like, even as old as I am today, I learn new things. You don't cease to be a student (Sadie Brower Neakok, in Blackman 1989:221).

Linda Badten was a gentle, determined, intelligent woman. On her death, many people recalled her personal qualities and described events that illustrated her generosity, her devotion to friends and family, her willingness to share her cultural knowledge, and the deep religious faith that supported her in all things. Beyond this Linda was a person whose achievements were celebrated in two cultures.

Linda's birthplace was the Yupik (Eskimo) community of Gambell, St. Lawrence Island, Alaska, in the north Bering Sea. In the 1920s, the time of her youth, Gambell was effectively isolated from contact with mainstream American life for nine months a year. Radio contact was limited in those days, and the first plane landed on the frozen lake that borders the south side of the present community in 1916. Gambell had no regular, dependable scheduled air travel until the late 1970s, no television until 1980, and no running water until 1994. During the brief summer months, ships frequented the shores with deliveries of staple goods and the few luxury items that came to the community: oranges

GAMBELL

SAVOONGA

BERING SEA

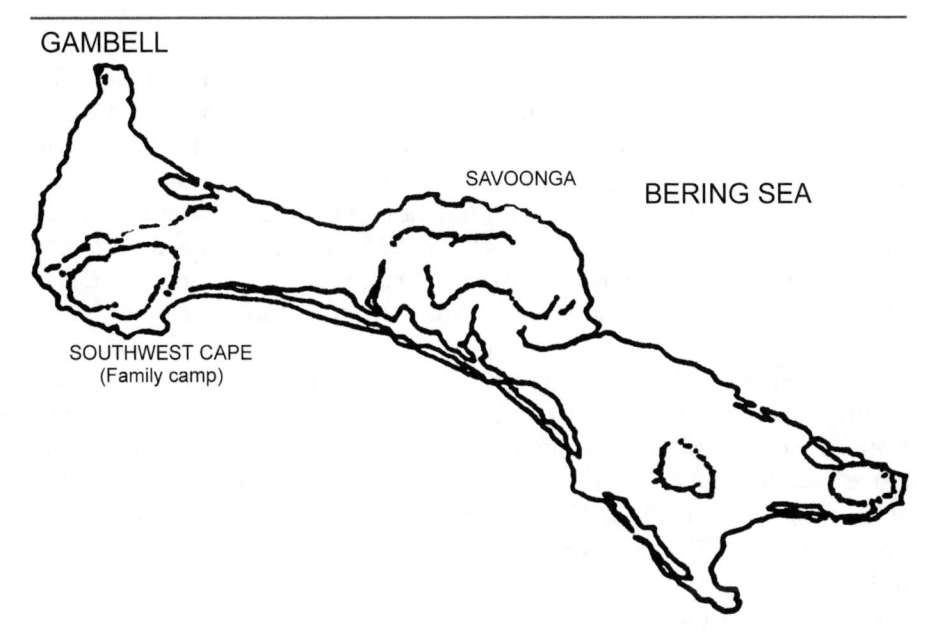

SOUTHWEST CAPE
(Family camp)

Figure 4.1 Sketch map of St. Lawrence Island

and apples, dried fruit, hard candies, pilot bread and cookies in large wooden containers, flour, tea, and bolts of colorfully patterned cloth. When the supply ship arrived, the whole village turned out to help unload. These were some of the outward signs of the commercial world, which might have impressed a young girl growing up in the 1920s. Boat travel between the island and the Siberian shore only thirty-eight miles to the west was still common, although that would slow down and then come to an abrupt halt in 1948 when the border between Russia and the United States closed.

For Linda and others of her generation, life centered on family and kin. In winter there was school and the local Presbyterian church. Some families spent the winter in fox trap–line camps and returned to Gambell each spring to participate in bowhead whale hunting and the walrus hunting that followed. Others stayed in the village during the school year while able-bodied men from the family left to hunt and trap. In summertime there was camping, and most families traveled to their traditional family lands. Linda's family camped on the south side of the island.

Girls of Linda's generation could expect to follow a predictable life pattern. Girls were carefully guarded and supervised in childhood by their parents, grandparents, and other close adult relatives whose ties were reckoned especially through the father's side of the family. (St. Lawrence Islanders are distinguished from other Eskimo peoples by their patriclan kinship system.) Formal education in the local two-room schoolhouse operated by the Bureau of Indian Affairs generally ended in the fifth or sixth grade. The teachers were recruited from the "States." Alaska was still a territory—remote both politically and culturally from the U.S. "mainland."

If parents needed a young girl's help at home, her schooling ended before she finished the elementary years. Many girls of Linda's generation did not complete the educational sequence available in the village, since formal education for girls was often thought unnecessary. High school was unavailable in the village. Those who desired further education traveled to Sitka or even to boarding schools in the States. If a girl did desire to attend high school, her parents were unlikely to give permission for her to travel to the mainland to do so.

By the time a girl finished sixth grade, she could expect to be kept busy at home helping her mother, aunts, and grandmother with women's chores. These included minding her younger brothers and sisters; fetching and carrying water or other items; assisting in routine gathering of greens, berries, mosses, and grasses (used for a variety of household chores) in summer and ice to be melted into water in winter; assisting in food processing tasks; learning to sew; and generally familiarizing herself with the different meats and other foods her female relatives prepared (for more on women and productive responsibilities see Chapter 7, this volume). Her homely chores anticipated a time when she would be responsible for such duties in her husband's family. She stayed closer to home than her brothers and had more household responsibilities at an earlier age than they. Young men, after all, were destined to become hunters, and travel away from home was a routine aspect of the hunting experience.

In her teens a girl undoubtedly became aware that the elders of her family had long since arranged for her marriage partner. The ideal was for her to marry someone in a cross-cousin relationship to her. Eventually, she went through lengthy traditional marriage ceremonies that included a series of gift presentations and a formal bride service (known in the community as "groom's work"), and finally she would move to her new husband's family home to begin a family. All of this constituted the expected and predictable pattern for a woman who would have reached her seventeenth year in 1940, as Linda had (see, for example, Jolles 2002; Jolles and Kaningok 1991. But it was not Linda's life.

Linda, looking back, said she was "always curious," that she "always wanted to know about the world" beyond the borders of her own community. She felt she was always preparing to leave home. Although her friends seemed to satisfy their curiosity about the world beyond them with pictures from magazines and occasional forays into the pages of books, Linda imagined traveling to that world to see for herself. She exclaimed once that she used to dream of seeing a "real lawn of green grass." And she speculated that this was the reason she so loved to take care of the lawn around her small blue clapboard home in Fairbanks. She didn't consider herself a gardener, but her lawn was something special. It symbolized for her the curiosity that was a signpost of her intellect and the drive that had led her away from her birthplace while others remained at home.

Linda was born in 1923. Her full name was Adelinde Aghanaghaughpik Womkon. Her English given name came from Otto Geist, a German self-educated archaeologist and associate of Charles Bunnell, president of the newly founded Alaska College of Mines that later became the University of Alaska, Fairbanks. The university's museum is named after him, and its original collections donated by Geist came from his stay on St. Lawrence Island. Geist had befriended Linda's father and apparently had asked that Linda be named for his sister, hence the German spelling of her name. She was not particularly fond of the name, although she felt comfortable with the Americanized short version, Linda. Her Yupik given name came from her family and drew on their historical attachment to St. Lawrence Island and the Chukotka Peninsula. Her heritage was a mix of St. Lawrence Island Yupik and Siberian Yupik. Her father was Wamkun. Either when the early missionaries were present in the community (1894–1911) or during the first remembered census on St. Lawrence Island (1937), his name became the formal surname of his family of marriage; he acquired the English given of Patrick. Thus Womkon, as it was spelled by those who gave it surname status, became Linda's last name until her marriage.

Linda, like many others of her generation, was born in a dome-shaped two-room house, a type that came into general use in the community following the abandonment of semiunderground dwellings, or *nenglus,* in the late 1800s (see also Chapters 5, 6, 7, this volume). Its building materials consisted of driftwood and walrus hide. Linda's earliest memory was of watching her mother scrub down the interior walls of this house. By the time she began to "be aware," to use the Yupik phrase, the walrus-hide walls had been replaced by lumber walls. Still, the house in which she spent her youth had one main room and an outer room (unheated) used for storing family belongings. There was also a frame summerhouse, difficult to keep warm in those days because it lacked insulation, and its shape was less amenable to heating with a seal oil lamp or the kerosene lamps that replaced them than the more traditional home with its domed roof and focused living quarters. The family also had a traditional camp on the south side of the island, in an area the family considers its traditional homeland and the source of its *ramket* name. Still later, after the trade in Arctic fox skins proved profitable for her father's family, the family built a very large two-story wood frame dwelling that still stands, a monument to that productive and profitable time.

Linda grew up with her parents, her grandparents, and her father's brothers and their families. She regarded her cousins as brothers and sisters. All lived together in the two-room house. It was a life that brought a smile of fond remembrance to her face when she spoke of it. From that period she drew a strong sense of self, of embeddedness in her culture, and a rootedness in the family values that supported her throughout her life.

My conversations with Linda generally focused on select realms of experience. An underlying theme was her religious faith. It was personal, it was deep, and it supported her through a range of encounters it is hard for me to imagine. Let me backtrack. I first met Linda in the written notes and comments recorded in manuscripts now housed in the Presbyterian Historical Society archives in Philadelphia. She came to my attention originally because so many who had met her as a young girl in the 1940s considered her highly intelligent, remarkable, and strong. There was only one photograph that I recall, though, and it hardly did justice to her beauty. Much later, her daughter showed me a picture of Linda from the time she married. It showed an elegant young woman with great personal poise and presence. It suggests that whatever else one might know of Linda's personality and character, she was at one time a woman who must have attracted attention because of her loveliness.

To return to the narrative, Linda's early life was lived within the safety and security and love of a strong family. She spoke easily and happily of her admiration for the elders who were the centerpiece of her young life. She especially admired her father. And she spoke with nostalgia of the times when, as a young child, she was invited to listen to the stories of her grandparents, to move from her own nuclear family to her grandparents' section. Each segment of the family group had its assigned place in the room. Her oldest sister, who was approaching adulthood, also had a special place. No one, according to Linda, entered another person's space without implicit permission. This gave each space its own sanctity while reinforcing respect among all those who shared the home. She also spoke of mealtimes. Women of each family shared the resources brought in by their menfolk among the rest, and a general feeling of goodwill prevailed. If it sounds romantic, with the hard edges of life in a one-room space smoothed away, it probably is, but that is the nature of memory. It is the image of early life Linda carried with her.

In a separate compartment, away from the delight Linda retained of her home and camp life, she carried her memories of the pain of that life before Western medicine stopped the ravages of tuberculosis, influenza, polio, and other once incurable disorders. Linda lost many in her family, including all of her siblings to tuberculosis (see also Chapter 7, this volume). In her own words (excerpted from the tape recordings of her descriptions of her life):

> Oh it was horrible! It got so that I used to look around the big family to see—I wonder who, you know, who's going to be next? How terrible it was! That death. And they all looked dear, oh, which one of those dear people is going to be next? I had a torturous life because of that.

And in yet another compartment Linda kept both her own curiosity and her impatience and downright boredom with a life in which very little went on and she could envision her future by watching her female relatives. It was offset by her curiosity toward the world around her.

One of the great excitements was school. Very early she was caught by the power of language, of words, of description. They transported her to other worlds, and unlike her girlhood friends, she was driven not simply to hear about them but to see them and experience them firsthand. She brought what she learned in school home with her. She says she was so anxious to do well in school that homework was always the first thing she did, not the last. Of her early life she said:

> Oh, I'm telling you! I didn't prepare for anything over there [for a life on the island]. Yes, I did finish a couple of pairs of boots. But it was an ordeal! It took so much time away from doing homework for school. So because the school was becoming very important . . . fitting into the school was becoming important and doing your homework was stronger . . . you did a little bit of this for your mom, and then you'd get back to your own schoolwork. So I never

did get into the full swing of becoming a member [of her society] that way, as the girl child did. . . . I don't know what [the other girls] did about their school homework, but I was worried about mine. . . . I tried to keep ahead of everybody.

Her friends in school were older, but she held her own—in schoolwork but not always in the social environment of her friends. She remembered that she was often teased as a girl. Both her older brother and some of her classmates taunted her about being "plain." She recalled that her brother was the favorite at home and at school. She didn't like being teased, and she didn't like the favoritism shown him, but he was her brother and she loved him. Before he was seventeen he was gone, swept away by tuberculosis. Her siblings disappeared, one by one, as the TB epidemic took its toll. Through it all, Linda studied hard. At home she did chores. She remembered that even when she wanted to be outside playing, the chores came first. She couldn't believe how much water her family needed, for example. Her task was to go with her brother and bring home the sled with a block of ice on it, which would then be melted for drinking and cooking water. She remarked that they always seemed to need more water for something.

One night when we were talking about the daily chores, Linda yawned uncontrollably. I joked that I was putting her to sleep. She replied that no, it was her early life that was putting her to sleep! She could not find any liveliness in the monotony of her childhood chores. Nevertheless, from the boredom of everyday life, she and her brothers and sisters were inspired to create games to while away the time spent indoors. She related how she and her cousins had invented games inside when it was impossible to go out.

> When I was bigger, they had converted the skin walls [of the house] into wooden walls, and that gave us an opportunity to tear the most colorful pages out of magazines to plaster the walls! To make them pleasant!
>
> And not only that, not only was that pleasant, [but] when we children did not have anything to do we learned to spell, [to do] our letters. [With] magazine pages. And we would continue to learn the hardest words we could find. I remember "hexol resorcinol" solution. There was a pharmacy page that had "hexol resorcinol" solution, and to compete with my cousins, I learned to spell that. There were times when we didn't have anything to do; I guess we were bored, and we learned our ABCs backward and learned how to count as far as we could. In that way we began to learn the

patterning of number systems. . . . I think that was a benefit of being in this type of a home where we were restricted from roaming around, because we had to stay, stay put much of the time in our own areas. So being there, not wanting to disturb the older people, we had to invent something . . . like learning to spell, competing with one another.

Linda liked math and proposed that we find someone who could help us write about the Yupik counting system. It seemed to her to have much in common with the "new" math concept she had taught to her students as an elementary school teacher. At her funeral, a friend related that Linda had once tried to explain the idea of atoms and molecules to her family but found that the Yupik language lacked the right words to convey her thoughts clearly.

She also loved to tell stories. She once described how she had decided to tell some stories by Edgar Rice Burroughs and Rudyard Kipling to the younger children when she was home from school. Linda said, with a twinkle in her eye, that she had silently challenged herself to capture the attention of the adults in the room with her tale without seeming to do so. Carefully, she built up her story with dramatic voice and gesture. She said she was very aware of her uncles sitting in the room talking among themselves about "adult" matters—men she thought of as her second fathers. Studiously, she kept her eyes on the children but raised her voice and her dramatic tone, glancing out of the corner of her eye from time to time to see if the men were listening. Gradually, she said, the men stopped talking to each other and listened, spellbound, to her story. Later she heard one of her uncles repeat the story to some friends. Linda chuckled as she told me, "I had them in the palm of my hand."

Linda was drawn into the world through her fascination with language and ideas. She was a good student. When Linda approached the end of elementary school in the village, her teachers encouraged her to continue her education. It was what she wanted to do. I never knew which of the teachers was most important to her later schooling. Very early she had been taught by Paul Silook, a man from the village. She also remembered a Mr. Thompson whose nose was quite large and whose false teeth, which he pulled out of his mouth to surprise the children, absolutely terrified them. They wondered among themselves whether Mr. Thompson might not be a shaman. As Linda recalled those years, she said, "I was so busy with schoolwork that I never really learned the tasks that a girl was supposed to learn. I never finished those things."

Linda's desire to go to school away from the village was unusual. Imagine her delight when her parents reluctantly gave permission for her to attend Sheldon Jackson High School in Sitka, Alaska, many hundreds of miles away. In Sitka Linda was among strangers, but all of the students had in common the newness of their experience. There were few opportunities to travel back and forth. Letters were the only way to communicate, and that was hardly reliable in Alaska in the 1940s and 1950s.

It is not exactly clear how old Linda was when she attended Sheldon Jackson, but it seems likely she entered around 1948–1950. She apparently did well in her classes and again impressed her teachers with her work and her faith. She was offered support so she could continue her studies at the College of Emporia in Emporia, Kansas. In the early 1950s Linda A. Womkon became the first person from her tribe, from the St. Lawrence Island Yupik community, to earn a bachelor's degree. During her years in college, she stayed with fellow students over vacations and holidays. She went on trips, traveling as far as New York City, and met students from all over the world. Each visit to someone's home or to a new city had its own story, its own appeal for her.

With degree in hand, Linda returned to Alaska to teach elementary school. Her first teaching assignment was in the Athapaskan village of Fort Yukon. She went on to teach in Kotzebue, where she met and married her husband. The couple moved to Fairbanks, where in 1958, waiting for the birth of her second child, she lost her husband, a pilot, in a tragic plane crash. She never remarried. She raised her two children and became known as a highly respected teacher.

Linda was at home in the non-Yupik world in which she had chosen to raise her children. At the same time, she retained an abiding interest in and devotion to her own heritage. She expressed that interest by sharing what she knew with others and by making a substantial contribution to the study of St. Lawrence Island culture. In 1960 Linda was approached by linguist Michael Krauss, a young professor at the University of Alaska, Fairbanks. He was interested in Native languages and was searching for someone who could help him with a Yupik text he had recently acquired by the Russian scholar Rubtsova, written in the Cyrillic alphabet. Linda listened to Krauss's description of how the Cyrillic alphabet worked and set out to learn to use it to read some of the very first materials she had ever encountered written in her native Yupik. At that time Yupik was not a written language in the United States, and Linda became instrumental in transforming Yupik from a spoken-only language to a written language.

Figure 4.2 Linda in her late teens or early twenties

Krauss and Linda became close professional and personal friends, a relationship that ceased only with her death. From their professional association came the first St. Lawrence Island/Siberian Yupik dictionary (Badten, Kaneshiro, and Oovi 1983; Jacobson 1987), numerous transcribed texts, and cooperative endeavors of all sorts. Linda became as at-home in the offices of the Alaska Native Language Center on the University of Alaska campus as she was in her own classroom at Nordale Elementary School. Scholars with international reputations called on her to speak to their students about her language and her culture. Linda inspired others from her community to engage in scholarly pursuits as well, and the dictionary project was a product of her work with two of her cousins, women she considered sisters.

In all of this, what is striking is Linda's uncompromising optimism, her willingness to go forward. Unlike her peers, life away from home was not desolate for her, although at times it must have been lonely. She said later that her ability to survive must have developed from a very young age, from her very early desire to see the world:

> It's a mysterious thing, when I think back, that I would have thought of these things as small as I was. Little dreams. I guess magazines did have a lot of influence to arouse my curiosity about other places, because I loved looking at pictures of outside, outside of St. Lawrence Island. Unbelievable lawns and things like that . . . trees, lawns, what it would feel like to be among trees.

When I reconsider Linda's life, with its myriad accomplishments, it seems appropriate to compare her life with those of the Yupik heroines from the tales I have heard over the last decade. One in particular comes to mind, which I will outline here, drawing attention to the qualities associated with Yupik heroines. Perhaps heroine is not the right term; admirable and virtuous womanhood is probably more appropriate.

This is the story of two young girls. The protagonist of the story must leave home on a journey. She travels a great distance in unknown lands. Everywhere she goes she is presented with challenges. Some come in the form of huge tasks that must be finished. For example, she is confronted with a great pile of fish, not yet cleaned, that sits in the middle of her path. Although no one is in sight, the girl feels obliged to clean all of the fish and leave everything in good order before continuing on her way. On another occasion she finds a stack of partially sewn boots, which she finishes. She also cleans meat that has been left on her trail.

Her honesty is tested. At one point she is asked by an old woman she has met to sort through a tray of beautiful beads but to take none for herself. This she does. She obeys the instructions from the elderly woman without question. As she travels along her road, doing exactly as she has been told, it becomes evident that the journey that has led her from home is also the journey that will return her safely to her home. Even in moments of greatest stress, she withstands the temptation to disobey. She is told on one occasion that if she looks behind her she will die. She does as she has been told, even though she can hear the deep growls of polar bears directly behind her on the path. The reward at the end, once she has faithfully met each challenge, is a strong, handsome young hunter who weds her and cares for her and her family.

The second part of the story tells of a lazy girl who also wants a handsome husband. She copies her virtuous sister and sets out on a journey of her own, but she fails to complete any of the tasks set before her or to respond obediently when instructed by the old woman. She is rewarded in the end with a weak, miserable old man for a husband. She accepts her fate, and because of her willing resignation to circumstance, albeit of her own making, her less attractive husband becomes materially successful, and she too lives, as they say, a long and prosperous life.

A number of Yupik tales exist in which the protagonist, often the youngest daughter, must undertake a difficult journey. The heart of the tale is not how she outwits the enemy or escapes danger so much as it is a test of her virtues: her ability to demonstrate through action her adherence to strong Yupik values. Linda believed these stories were designed to affirm the social order and said with a sigh that she was glad she didn't have to live in those olden times, that she would never have survived. I think there are parallels between Linda's life and the lives of traditional Yupik female protagonists, parallels she was too modest to notice.

First, there is the journey. It seems obvious that Linda envisioned herself traveling toward the unknown from a very early age, caught by the excitement of what lay beyond her own small island. Unlike her peers, she was not frightened by the world outside. When she finally did travel to Anchorage, to Sitka, to Emporia, Kansas, and beyond, she met each challenge in two ways: she worked hard, and she set high standards for herself. She also found pleasure in the challenges of the work, in learning something new, and especially in meeting new people. Unlike her friends who became desperately homesick when they left the island and returned home as quickly as possible, Linda continued the journey. When she did return home periodically, she brought her new knowledge and experience with her and shared it as much as possible with her family.

Most stories about Eskimo women are told quietly, within families. Many of the stories come as legends or as instructive tales that have mythic or metaphoric qualities. Only occasionally are stories told of women one knows or might have known. Only a few are about the recent past or the present. Of these few very real and quite remarkable women, most have engendered the respect of others within their own homes, their own homelands. Their admirable qualities were appreciated within the context of a local community, often the community into which they had been born. Linda Badten was not one of these women who gained prominence because of her homegrown achievements in her birthplace. She was an exception. In an era in which few Native women succeeded away from their traditional homes, she stands out as an uncommon woman, one who managed successfully not only to exist in two cultures but also to contribute in amazing ways to each. As her memorial service so eloquently affirmed, her positive example touched dozens and dozens of people.

In spite of her accomplishments, Linda remained modest and unassuming. Her personal goals had to do with her children, her faith, and her sustained interest in her heritage. Because of this and because she was generous in fact and in spirit, she never became estranged from her family, although she lived most of her life away from her homeland. She became for many a model of the possible, and in this her life, like that of a traditional Yupik heroine, has come to partake of the ideal. As anthropologist Aihwa Ong noted, "Life stories have been defined as testimonials . . . that both reinterpret and remake the world" (Ong 1995:355). I have no doubt that Linda Womkon Badten's life will be held up as an example for young girls to follow and will become instrumental in reinterpreting and remaking the future for new generations of Yupik young women.

ACKNOWLEDGMENTS

This chapter is the result of my friendship with Linda. It is only natural, then, that I offer my thanks to Linda's daughter, Jayne Badten Harvey. I am truly indebted to her for her friendship over the years, for her support, and for her help. I am also grateful to Edna Apatiki Anungazuk, Linda's niece, who followed in Linda's footsteps and became a teacher. It was Edna who impressed upon me the important role Linda had played in her life and in the lives of other women of her generation as a role model. And it was Edna who first encouraged me to seek out Linda when I traveled to Fairbanks. I am indebted, too, to the institutions that made work in Gambell and later with Linda possible. That work was supported by the National Science Foundation (Grants NSF-8721726 and DPP-922032), by the Royalty Research Fund of the University of Washington, and by a grant from the Alaska Humanities Forum. Although each of these grants provided opportunities to work with Linda, only the Royalty Research Fund grant funded the recording of Linda's life history. All, however, made it possible for me to spend time with Linda, to work with her, and to deepen our friendship. For that I am most grateful.

II

HISTORICAL AND ETHNOARCHAEOLOGICAL APPROACHES

5

CHANGING RESIDENCE PATTERNS AND INTRADOMESTIC ROLE CHANGES
CAUSES AND EFFECTS
IN NINETEENTH-CENTURY WESTERN ALASKA

Rita S. Shepard

Significant markers of social transformation may be hard to find in the archaeological record, but historical archaeology allows greater insight into such processes because researchers are able to employ many archaeological and nonarchaeological tools in sketching a group's past lifeway. We have the good fortune to be able to use written records, oral history, photographs, and personal interviews. Yet even these tangible and personally interactive strategies do not make it easy to distinguish a point or cause of social change. Symbols that identify socioideological structure do exist, however. When they are replaced and accepted by the community, the new symbols "crystallize" social change.

I have argued previously that although Native Alaskans readily adopted the technological advances introduced by Europeans in the eighteenth century, they did not change the features of their social organization and their intertwined ideologies until the economic and social values propagated by the nineteenth-century Protestant and Roman Catholic missionaries had been widely accepted (Shepard 1997). In this chapter I suggest further that the *roles* of women and men within a household also underwent a radical transformation when belief systems changed, leading Natives to move into Western-style houses and out of their traditional domestic systems (for more on ideological systems and change see Chapter 3, this volume). The question for the archaeologist is, can these role changes be identified in the archaeological remains we recover and analyze?

First, it is necessary to understand both a "domestic system" and a "household" as I define them. The domestic system includes dwellings and their associated storage facilities, ceremonial structures (i.e., *qasgis*) or other special buildings, and the surrounding plazas, courtyards, or outside use areas (Shepard 1997:12). In the mid- to late nineteenth century, Native winter settlements might contain all or only some of these attributes. Indeed, in their journals explorers often noted nothing more than a single semisubterranean house as a stopover locale.

Jennifer Tobey (Chapter 6, this volume) also calls for expanding the analysis of a household. She maintains that archaeologists must consider the surrounding locale of a house and the associated artifacts to understand the dynamics of the people inhabiting a house. She and I agree that the people who occupy a particular house, although making use of the entire domestic system and drawing on the surrounding locale, must be considered a "household."

QUESTIONS

The move into a Western-style dwelling, in which a nineteenth-century Western-concept nuclear family lived, occurred for the most part from the 1890s through the early twentieth century, after the U.S. missionaries were firmly established. I have suggested previously that much of the sociocultural change seen during this period was based on Native acceptance of Christianity with its new moral standards (Shepard 1997). Consider what a residence change for the household might mean:

1. Did a change of dwelling style discernibly affect household social organization and division of labor?
2. Did a change in living space create observable changes in personal communication and allocation of individual space?
3. If so, how can archaeologists uncover these social changes in the archaeological record?
4. Most important, can archaeologists discover something useful to add to our understanding of household relationships?

Since people of both sexes comprise a domestic unit, we can look for evidence of change in social relations at a microscale, at the level of the household. Obviously, analyzing changes in the cultural remains to understand changes in interfamilial relationships could be a very slippery exercise. Nevertheless, I think it is worth a try.

The remainder of this chapter will address these questions, beginning with a consideration of the problem from a broader perspective. Descriptions of western Native Alaskan households during the Russian and early American periods (i.e., mid- to late nineteenth century), followed by brief discussions of the Moravian mission at Bethel in the Kuskokwim River Valley and the Swedish Covenant missionaries in Unalakleet on Norton Sound, will provide a backdrop for understanding late-nineteenth-century changes in familial responsibilities and gender interactions. Next, strategies and methods of three previous archaeological studies of gender underscore the difficulties of the pursuit; attempts to identify gender at my own research site are included in this section. The chapter concludes with discussion and recommendations for future work.

CONSIDERATION OF THE PROBLEM

Archaeologists often disagree when it comes to identification and interpretation of ideology in the archaeological record. Fewer debates over how to identify ideology might occur if better accord existed over its meaning. It is important to remember that ideology is not just about religion, although it does include it. In the present discussion I define ideology as an explicit body of concepts about human life, accepted by and characteristic of a specific individual or group.

As archaeologists, we should be able to find and identify concrete physical manifestations of ideology, or a *materialization* of ideology (DeMarrais, Castillo, and Earle 1996). If, moreover, we consider ideology to be both a source of social power and a part of the framework that shapes social organization and economic activity, then we can contend that people within groups will be wont to create tangible forms in which to ground and focus their power (DeMarrais, Castillo, and Earle 1996:16).

Ideology can be manifested in various ways. Shared rituals and ceremonies, storytelling, symbolic objects or icons, architecture, and written texts are tangible markers of belief; they reflect political and economic patterns as well as ideological systems (DeMarrais, Castillo, and Earle 1996:16). In highly structured societies like chiefdoms and states, manipulation of one or more of these tangible symbols allows leaders to exploit beliefs and gain and maintain social power.

Materialization plays a different but equally significant role in smaller hunter-gatherer-fisher societies. Elizabeth DeMarrais and her colleagues (1996) examined monuments and ordered landscapes within complex societies (i.e., Inca, Moche, and the Danish Neolithic) to understand how people "materialized" their ideological system. I suggest that domestic structures and interior household design organize social relationships and establish boundaries in less complex social groups. Domestic houses and ceremonial buildings, symbolic images, and artistic motifs are the materialized representations of ideology in nonstratified societies. When a new lifeway supplants an earlier one, the material culture changes; so also do the tangible components of an original ideology change when a new belief system replaces an old one.

It stands to reason that male and female interactions and activities are altered as well. The challenge for archaeologists is to recover and describe these modified characteristics. Specifically, I suggest that archaeologists investigate historical transition-era sites known to be occupied through the period of missionization (see Chapter 6, this volume).

HOUSEHOLDS WITH FACES

Ruth Tringham (1991) has proposed that we think about "the faces" in ancient households. In other words, she wants archaeologists to visualize living people in the archaeological assemblages they discover. Many archaeologists, however, believe such descriptions of archaeological "faces" are fancies of the imagination. Most often they have not been taken seriously by those who approach the field "scientifically" and prefer testable models.

And other problems exist. Archaeologists must guard against interpretations that are limited to analysis of sherds, flakes, bones, and botanicals. It is too easy to simplistically stereotype gender activities or activity loci. Households are diverse and complicated. Lines dividing men's and women's roles or space or activities within a household can be very blurry (see Chapter 9, this volume); moreover, the faces of children and elders need to be incorporated into the study of household organization and production. As Henry Stewart has discovered (Chapter 2, this volume), even personal gender identification can be called into question. If we want to see the full variety of roles present in archaeological communities, we must enrich our models and become more aware of the broad variability in gender relations and household groups (Tringham 1991:118).

What does all this mean in the study of late-nineteenth-century Native Alaskans? The ethnographic record has rendered intensely clear pictures of traditional life in Native settlements (Dall 1870; Fienup-Riordan 1988; Nelson 1983 [1899]; Oswalt 1963a, 1963b; VanStone 1955, 1959, 1968; Whymper 1868). Today's researchers have the rare opportunity to compare household organization before and after contact and the abandonment of *qasgis* (men's residential houses, frequently also used as community ceremonial buildings). This fundamental change in familial structure must have necessitated change in individual activities, whether men's, women's, or children's. Thus when the social order was changed, domestic groups began to relate to each other very differently.

It will not be easy to "see" shifts in male and female domestic roles archaeologically; however, thinking about the process at the household level will lead eventually to a clearer understanding of more general culture change. Our own daily personal interactions and behavior are varied and complex, dependent on those with whom we are associating and in what context. The interactions of people who lived "long ago" were not necessarily simpler. Therefore we must consider the probability of myriad interconnections when we are conducting archaeological investigations.

NATIVE ALASKAN SETTLEMENTS

During the early historic period the predominant characteristic of domestic life for the Kuskokwim Eskimos was that female and male activity spheres were centered on clearly defined separate dwellings (Oswalt 1963a:136).[1] The men's house, or *qasgi*[2], was the center of the community (both physically and figuratively) in Eskimo villages. This structure was a man's world that women visited on errands and for some ceremonial functions but in which they never lingered long (Oswalt 1963a:51).

Several journal entries provide vivid word pictures of some historic-era residential arrangements in western Alaska. In 1841 Lavrentiy Zagoskin described an Eskimo *qasqi* in the area of Norton Sound:

> It is in the kazhim that the men do all their work. Here they tan hides, weave fishnets, rig sled. Here all councils are held and decisions made on communal matters. The kazhim serves as a guesthouse for receiving visitors, a dining room for entertaining them, a hall for communal plays, a general dormitory for all the male population except infants, and finally as a bathhouse, for baths are one of the chief delights of all the Kang-yulit peoples. (Michael 1967:115)[3]

Although his account of the activities in and around small winter houses is not nearly as descriptive as those of the *qasgi*, he clearly specifies separate winter dwellings for the women and children (Michael 1967: 114, 121–122, 152, 193).

Nearly twenty-five years later, George Adams, a member of the Western Union Telegraph Expedition, gave us a peek into the inside of a winter house at Ulukuk, an Indian settlement on the banks of the Unalakleet River: "We entered these underground houses thru a small covered log passage, dropped down by ladder a hole for six feet and then crawled on hands and knees along an underground passage for ten feet into the main house of one room, which was twenty feet square with six feet walls on the four sides" (Adams 1982:46). He goes on to describe a fire that burned on the ground in the center of the room, with straw on which to sit or lie covering the earthen floor along the walls. When Adams entered the smoke-filled room, approximately twenty people already occupied half of it, and the odors were "complicated and awful. Besides the smoke there was an aroma of damp rotting decayed wood and rancid oil" (Adams 1982:46).

In 1877 Edward W. Nelson manned a weather station in St. Michael, Alaska, for the U.S. Army Signal Corp; while he was there the Smithsonian Institution also engaged him to collect ethnographic material from the Native Alaskans (Nelson 1983:11). Thus he traveled widely in southwestern Alaska, collecting artifacts, myths, and stories, as well as documenting subsistence techniques, ceremonial practices, and building construction and use details. He described "family" dwellings as women's houses that one to three families shared, each family independent of the other families living in the house (Nelson 1983:288–289).

> Each woman who is the head of a family has an oil lamp beside her sleeping bench where she sews or carries on her household work. Her own cooking utensils and wooden dishes for food, together with the stock of seal oil, dried salmon, and other articles of domestic economy, are kept at one side of the platform. . . . When the time approaches for the preparation of a meal, a fire is built in the middle of the room and the food made ready, after which each woman places a quantity in one or more wooden dishes, takes it to the *kashim*, and sets it beside her husband, father, or whoever she has provided for. (Nelson 1983:288–289)

By the turn of the twentieth century people who made their homes in Unalakleet and along the banks of the Unalakleet River had begun to live in aboveground log and plank cabins. The oldest resident with whom I visited in 1993 was born in Unalakleet in 1908. Until she was nearly ten years old, her family, along with about ten other Eskimo families, lived in log cabins approximately 25 km upriver from the village of Unalakleet near the place still called Sauyaq (personal communication). She had never seen people living in semisubterranean houses.

NINETEENTH-CENTURY MISSIONIZATION IN SOUTHWEST ALASKA

In searching for information about how missionaries affected day-to-day household life in Alaska, I came across three excellent studies. Wendell Oswalt's (1963a) ethnohistoric study of the missionization process in the Kuskokwim delta stands out and proved an invaluable resource. Thomas Correll's (1972) linguistic research and Joseph Jorgensen's (1990) examination of present-day Native people in three "bush" villages also provided useful data.

THE MORAVIANS

In an early historic-era Eskimo village, the domestic house was *not* the home of a Western-style familial household; men's and women's activities were dichotomized (Oswalt 1963a:147–148). In winter settlements, during a typical day men could be found sitting naked on the floor of the *qasgi*, carving or flaking wooden, bone, ivory, or stone into tools and ceremonial articles. The debris from their work would be scattered on the floor around them. After the day's work the men took daily sweat baths in the *qasgi*, during which the older men often recounted old myths or tales of travel to distant and faraway places (Oswalt 1963a:55–56). At mealtimes the women and young girls would bring food to their men in the *qasgi* (see also Dall 1870:406). Children accepted the fact that they were surrounded by women most of the time, with the men visiting only occasionally and for short times. In tundra camps (for summer fishing or fall hunting), where there was no *qasgi*, the men did live with their spouses, children, and other blood relatives; but even then frequent and extended hunting and trapping trips left little time for household interaction (see also Chapters 3, 7, this volume).

Yet in a relatively short time after the arrival of the Moravians, the mission church had supplanted ancestral ceremonial uses of the *qasgi* in the winter village. Soon it became little more than an inn for travelers and a meeting place for the older men. Even the traditional Eskimo hot bath was replaced by the Russian equivalent conducted in an aboveground structure that eliminated smoke and in which women also frequently participated (Oswalt 1963a:148–149).

The *qasgi* lost its fundamental meaning within the settlement. The men and boys began living in houses with the women and children, following the example set by the Moravian missionaries and their wives.

By the late nineteenth and early twentieth centuries, aboveground sod houses and log cabins had succeeded the semisubterranean dwellings. At first, the people living in one of these houses may have been an extended kindred group living as a single residential unit, but the nuclear family residence was the eventual result (Oswalt 1963a:149).

In addition, with a firmly established Christian ideology, marriage became more formalized and immutable. Men, discouraged from living in the *qasgi*, began living with women under a much more formal contract of marriage, one that considered premarital sex and adultery sinful acts. It soon was commonplace for the bride to move into her in-law's house while she and her husband built a separate dwelling. New social relationships had to be forged to accommodate the new interactions between husbands and wives, couples and in-laws, parents and children, and siblings of opposite sex (Oswalt 1963a:149–150). Children attending mission schools had taken on the new role of translator between their parents and the new American settlers (Oswalt 1963a:158).

Change from traditional lifeways was relatively rapid. The first Moravian missionaries founded their station in Bethel in 1885, and by 1894 they had suppressed Eskimo traditional life to the degree that the major traditional annual ceremony for the dead was not held at any of the largest villages on the lower Kuskokwim River (Oswalt 1963a:157). Nevertheless, it was sixty years from the time the Moravians arrived until the last *qasgi* was abandoned along the central Kuskokwim River (Oswalt 1963a: 148–149). "When the last *kashgee* [men's house] in any community was neglected, then abandoned and finally torn apart for firewood, the old way of life lingered only in the memories of the people" (Oswalt 1963a:51).

SWEDISH COVENANT MISSION CHURCH

In 1887 Axel Karlsen arrived in Unalakleet and established the Swedish Covenant Mission Church; by 1889 the school had been started as well. He provided medical services and encouraged residents to cultivate gardens, teaching them to plant potatoes, onions, and other cool-season vegetables. In his capacity as the healer of the soul and deliverer of the Christian message, Reverend Karlsen also suppressed and finally eliminated traditional plays, feasts, dancing, and songs (Jorgensen 1990:63). Karlsen and his church brought the people a new value system (Correll 1972:82).

The *qasgi* in Unalakleet was also the hub of the village; it was the point where all information chains intersected. In early-twentieth-century Unalakleet, even though Karlsen had declared himself opposed to both the concept and the structures, two *qasgis* were still used for non-traditional social activities, such as playing cards, as well as for the more traditional purposes of tool making and information exchange (Correll 1972:199–200). Eventually, however, the Unalakleet *qasgis* were abandoned, and the community allowed them to deteriorate and crumble away. No sign of either of them remains in the village today, although some elders can point out where they once were located (for more discussion of *qasgis,* see Chapters 3, 6, 7, 9, 11, this volume). The residents of present-day Unalakleet live in single-family houses, the children attend a large public school, medical and dental clinics provide health care, two general stores vie for business, and the Covenant Church remains as one of the largest buildings and most influential organizations in the village. Neighbors now meet each other at church, in the schools, or at the stores.

ARCHAEOLOGICAL CONSIDERATION OF GENDER IN ALASKA

The ideological shifts that resulted from the acceptance of Christianity seem to have led to community reorganization and the transformation of the physical structure of houses. These changes must have also brought about changes in roles and relationships within the household. This section begins with my own research that uncovered gender-specific loci in the archaeological context of a traditional domestic system. Then I examine two other archaeological investigations that also considered changes in roles and relationships as cultural mores changed (Ackerman 1970; Clark 1996).

UNALAKLEET RIVER ARCHAEOLOGICAL PROJECT

My research examined traditional Native settlements situated on the banks of the Unalakleet River. My field project included extensive excavations at one site (Tagilgayak) out of the four I surveyed (see Figure 5.1). I have interpreted the site as having one *qasgi* (P3) and two winter houses (P4 and P10); we also excavated storage structures (P1 and P5) associated with the winter house and a small enigmatic houselike structure—possibly a temporary residence (P9). Historical trade items greatly outnumbered the locally made artifacts, and ceramic chronology of English transferware placed occupation in the mid- to late 1800s.

I identified a *qasgi* based on the size of the structure and tools normally attributed to men (see Figure 5.2). The building was significantly larger than the other two houses at Tagilgayak, and it contained the only fishing-related equipment found at the site: two bone fish arrows and a net sinker (see Figure 5.3). Additionally, although berry remains were

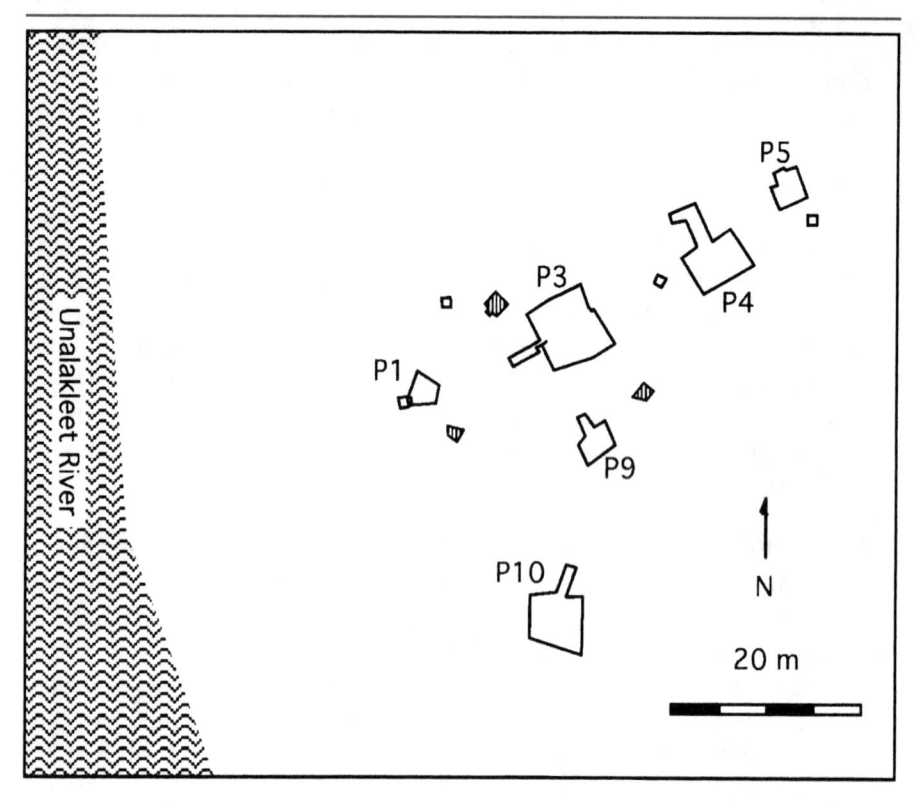

Figure 5.1 Excavated features at the Tagilgayak Site (UKT-022) on the Unalakleet River, Alaska; hatch lines indicate unexcavated features

found in the smaller structures, the higher density and wider variety of berry remains recovered from the building suggested that ceremonies took place there (see also Dall 1870:153; Osgood 1958:73–146).

We must remember, however, that archaeology is not an exact science; artifact context and provenance can be equivocal. Like artifacts from the houses in A. McFadyen Clark's study (1996), those found in the buildings at Tagilgayak can be interpreted in several ways. An antler handle for an *ulu* blade (i.e., a woman's knife) was recovered from the (probable) *qasgi*. If it was used there by a woman, it could mean the structure was *not* a *qasgi* but rather just a larger winter house. On the other hand, a man could have *made* or *repaired* the knife in the *qasgi*, supporting the argument that it was a men's house. Moreover, as Tobey (Chapter 6, this volume) points out, the house and the *qasgi* (or *kashim* in the dialect of

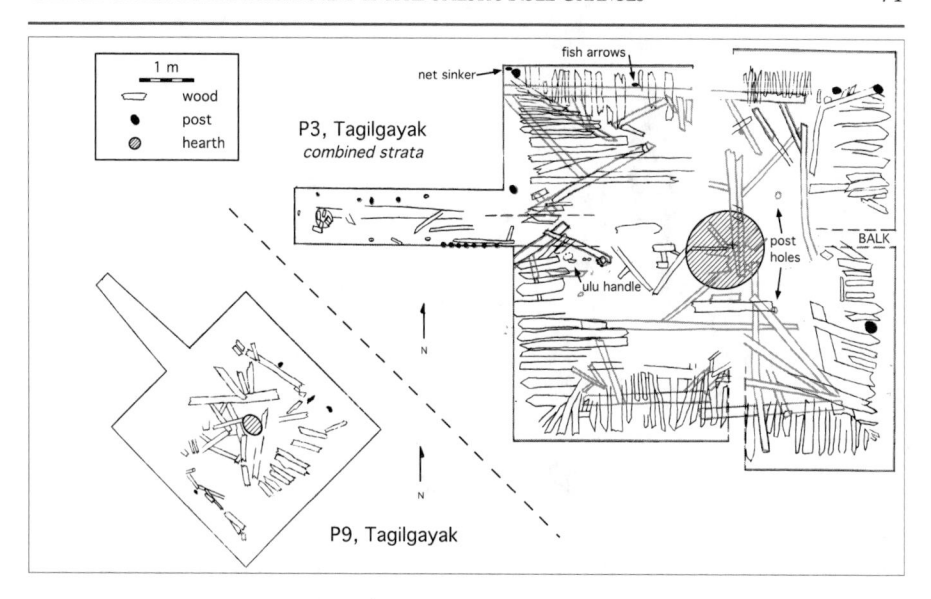

Figure 5.2 Structural remains found in Features P3 and P9 at the Tagilgayak Site; gray outlines in P3 show features uncovered in the lower Level 2 excavations. Drawing by Corinna M. Schoenfelder.

the Deg Hit'an) are not discrete entities but part of a dynamic sphere of activity and interaction across the settlement. To understand the *qasgi* data better, archaeologists need more comparative material from ceremonial structures, but very few *qasgis* have been excavated.

The main living area of the house structures at Tagilgayak ranged in size from 32.5 m² to 7.0 m² (Shepard 1997:37) (see Figure 5.2). The smallest building (P9) presented the biggest challenge to interpretation, and gender played a role in the analysis (see Shepard 1997, appendixes B, C, F, G for data). There was no indication of a delineated sleeping area or bench, but an ephemeral hearth was detected in the center of the floor. Botanical analysis found that this small house had a very high density of grass seed, over ten times that recovered from the large structure thought to be a *qasgi* (Shepard 1997:262). Botanists also identified several types of berry seeds from its float sample; faunal analysis revealed caribou and bird bone in this small dwelling. Glass trade beads dominated the artifact collection from this unit, complemented by fragments of European ceramics and a metal knife.

This combination of cultural material suggests that the building may have been used by women as a seclusion space, either for birthing or at

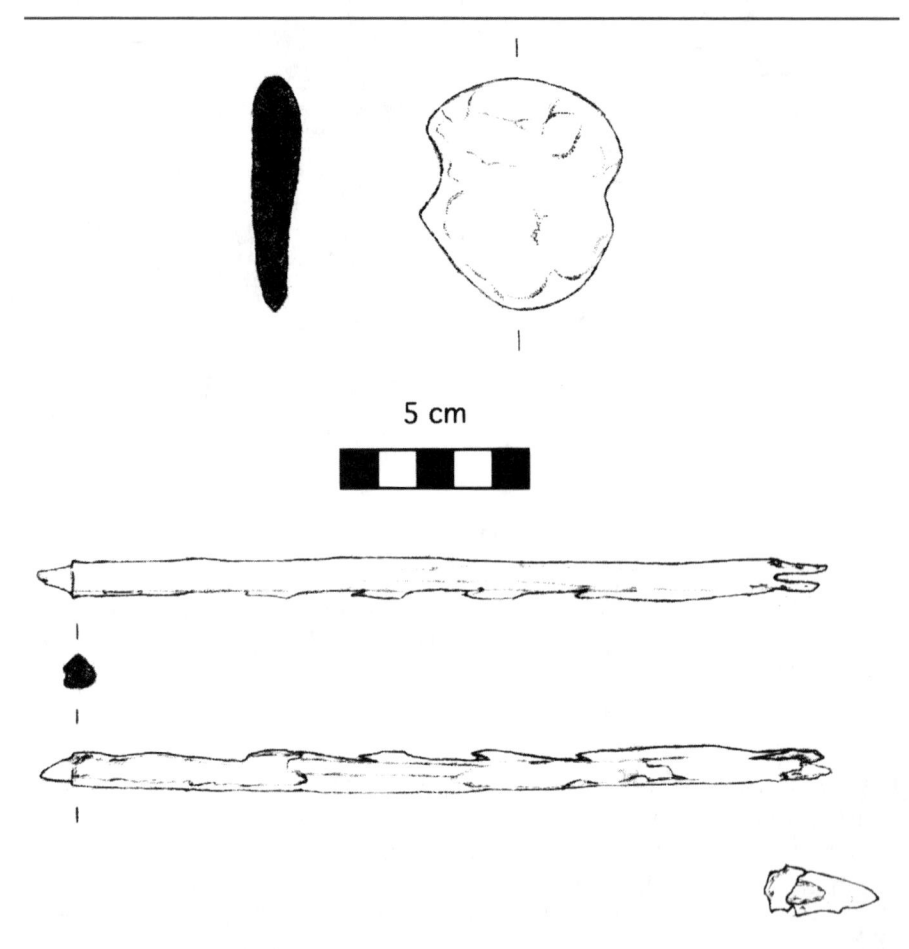

Figure 5.3 Upper: *Stone net sinker, UA-92-129-28, recovered from just outside the walls of the NW corner of P3 at Tagilgayak;* lower: *Carved bone fish arrow, UA-92-129-43, with metal point (*lower right*) found under a plank on north wall of P3 at Tagilgayak. Drawing by Corinna M. Schoenfelder.*

the onset of menstruation (Clark 1981:591; Giddings 1961:153; Nelson 1983:289; Reinhardt 1986:152–156). This scenario entails the accumulation of food remains and a high density of grass to be used either as bedding or for making grass mats or baskets, since young women at their menarche began to learn domestic skills (Clark 1981:591; Giddings 1961:154). Decorative glass beads fit well with this hypothesis and would be expected, too. Other interpretations can be constructed, but this one best unites the archaeological data and the ethnographic record (Clark 1996; Dall 1870; Fienup-Riordan 1988; Nelson 1983; Osgood 1958; Michael 1967).

CAPE NEWENHAM

In 1966 Robert Ackerman questioned the revision and retention of physical characteristics of Native residences in the face of cultural change. He considered the households and household goods found during three periods of occupation: (1) archaeological context at sites on Chagvan Beach, (2) the late-nineteenth-century historic village of Tzahavagamute on Cape Newenham (from data collected in government, missionary, and ethnographic reports), and (3) living people in the modern Native community of Goodnews Bay. He redirected his research from object recovery to feature analysis within these specific cultural frameworks (Ackerman 1970:15–17). Ackerman hoped his methods of comparison would help archaeologists to establish activity spheres and study the stability of cultural patterns from one time period to the next (1970:42).

Over the years, the village residential pattern in Goodnews Bay has shifted gradually toward the store, American school, post office, and church (Ackerman 1970:36). The professed reason many households moved closer to the new "center" was "to be nearer the water" to make washing clothes and personal bathing easier. Ackerman does not question this motive. It seems more likely to me, however, that these institutions, taken as a whole, had replaced the village *qasgi*. Together they had become the new community center. And as along the Kuskokwim and Unalakleet Rivers, people met to exchange information, make group decisions, and worship within the new ceremonial structure.

Next, Ackerman wondered whether distribution of household items could identify gender-linked use of space within a modern house (an aboveground single-room building) that was home to a family of five. He planned to compare archaeological distributions to modern use and work patterns. To do this he compiled a plan view of one present-day home indicating the storage area of tools specific to women's and men's activities, finding fairly direct correlations between gender-specific tools (that suggest particular behavior) and associated activity or storage areas (Ackerman 1970:37–39).

Gender *mixing*, however, appeared in work zones and in tool use (Ackerman 1970:40). Frequent forays by either parent outside of the house meant both men and women often had to be completely self-sufficient and able to use tools or take over tasks more commonly performed by the opposite sex (e.g., cooking, fishing, sewing). Therefore if people living in the past engaged in similar behavior, an archaeologist might have a hard time trying to prove female or male activity at prehistoric sites (see Chapter 9, this volume). In spite of these nonconformities, Ackerman believed the study of modern behavior patterns enabled his group to better discern gender-specific activity areas in a sixteenth-century house pit at the nearby prehistoric site on Chagvan Bay (Ackerman 1970:40–41).

THE KOYUKON: ALASKAN ATHAPASKANS

In her recent book *Who Lived in This House?* Clark (1996) documented three nineteenth-century traditional houses in three different winter occupation sites along the Koyukuk River. In addition to providing a comprehensive analysis of each building's architectural elements and construction, she considered the spatial distribution of the artifacts found in each house. Originally, Clark planned to compare the distribution of objects and faunal remains to information she had collected from informants about use of space and household organization.

Clark's idealized representation of a semisubterranean house, based on her excavations and personal interviews, had a central hearth and hosted two domestic groups. Each group occupied half of the dwelling; the female children were situated closest to the entry tunnel, followed by the wives and babies, and the husbands resided in the center on either side of the hearth. Elders and unmarried adults lived in the back of the house (Clark 1996:145). She tried to compare her artifact collections to the theoretical spatial arrangement within the house. Unlike Gregory Reinhardt (Chapter 9, this volume), however, her artifact assemblage was small, making comparisons inconclusive—both among the three houses and between houses and oral traditions.

Clark created a composite floor plan from two of the excavated houses. She plotted the distribution of two selected groups of artifacts that comprised the majority of items recovered, hoping they might reflect gender-specific use (Clark 1996:142–144). She included scraping stones, metal scrapers, baskets, and a snowshoe needle as probably female associated; ammunition, powder cans, a strike-a-lite, and other iron objects were attributed to men (Clark 1996:153–154). The resulting distribution pattern fit reasonably well with the use of space described by the local elders.

Patterns could *not* be seen, however, in the faunal material, which seemed randomly dispersed around the living area (Clark 1996:158–159). In fact, particularly telling was the fact that excavators found bear bones randomly distributed around the house floors, including areas traditionally allocated to women and children. Additionally, a single lynx scapula was recovered from the woman's area in one of the dwellings. Clark makes special note of this find because neither bear nor lynx bones would be expected in a traditional Athapaskan household with women in residence. Bear meat, bones, and hide are strictly forbidden to pre-menopausal Koyukon women, as is lynx, and would never be taken into a house where women were present (Clark 1996:5–6, 159, 203).

The appearance of animal bones normally prohibited in the presence of women suggested several social scenarios—all dependent on knowledge of present-day gender roles within the group. The simplest explanation is that the people living in these houses were not Athapaskans; they may have been Inupiat who did not hold gender prohibitions against the bear and lynx. Koyukon oral tradition indicates, however, that both male and female shamans were exempt from taboos and restrictions; thus the houses may have been occupied by shamans. Alternatively, elders (including women past menopause) were exempt from food taboos, implying that perhaps only old people lived in the houses. Then again, severe food stress would allow personal survival to take precedence over cultural rules and mores; people would eat anything available rather than starve. Finally, the houses may have been inhabited after long-term exposure to Russians or other Europeans, and the inhabitants may have already begun to accept new beliefs and ideologies, abandoning tradition (Clark 1996:204–206).

ANOTHER NORTHERN EXAMPLE OF THE EFFECT OF CULTURE CHANGE ON GENDER ROLES

Nearly two decades later and worlds away, in an insightful investigation of household change (or what she calls changes in "the internal domestic arena"), Ellen Pader (1988) looked at how objects, organization of objects, and a man's or woman's relationship with objects within a household reflect social action and cultural mores. She studied two very different cultural groups: the nomadic, pastoral Mongolians, and British "Traveler-Gypsies," arguing that the spatial appropriation within a specific locale brought together society and its structures (Pader 1988:251). The Mongolian research specifically addressed issues of gender that can illustrate identifiable changes in material culture in the wake of socioideological change.

Travelers' journals dating back to the thirteenth century detailed the placement of furnishings within a Mongolian domestic tent, or *ger,* and described the ideological values assigned to objects and spaces inside the living area. The western part of the tent and its contents were associated with men and held higher status than objects located in the eastern and female portion of the dwelling. A north-south (or upper-lower) division also indicated status; thus the upper western quadrant held the highest honor (Pader 1988:255).

After the Russian Revolution, the socialist government mandated a change in the lifestyles of the nomadic peoples of the high desert. Studies found that, although the people had obtained many new goods and tools (e.g., sewing machines), they placed them traditionally within the *ger,* retaining the preestablished symbolic order. Status assigned to women and children underwent observable transition, however (Pader 1988:256–257). The children who used to sleep on the floor at the head of the parents' bed moved into their own bed on the male side of the tent, apparently indicating the high importance the Soviet state placed on future generations. Moreover, seating arrangements of male and female children were no longer distinguishable from each other, reflecting a change not only in social relationships but in future power. Perhaps most significant, books became a sign of social change. Prior to the revolution they were the purview of senior men and religious leaders, and women were forbidden to read them. When the Soviets made literacy a priority, women not only began to read, but books began to be kept on a shelf at the head of the bed on the woman's side (Pader 1988:259).

Looking "inside" domestic spatial relations leads to a clearer understanding of the larger process of learning, using, interpreting, and reinterpreting the values and codes of a society (Pader 1988:265–266). Pader argued that members of a domestic group are also part of a spatial interaction encoded by the social group, and the organization of space within a home is part of the social structure. Therefore when a society adopts new socioideological practices, its social roles and structure change and are reproduced by and through the individuals within it. The resulting "recursive relationship between ideology, action, and spatial relations is intensified" as each reflects the others (Pader 1988:266). The Mongolian study should spur archaeologists to search for material evidence that will substantively demonstrate these kinds of sociospatial interactions (see Chapters 9, 10, 11, this volume).

ARGUMENT

Originally I asked whether archaeologists perceive macroscale social change at the microscale level of the household. Eric Wolf (1982:19) has suggested that cultural forms are the "determinate orderings of things, behavior, and ideas" and as such play a major part in guiding human association and interaction. Thus cultural forms influence, and maybe even mold, social relationships.

Therefore I suggest the following sequence of events: (1) New *things* appeared in the community ("community" includes several settlements, linked by their interactions, within a specific geographic area). They were either completely new introductions or traditional items produced by "new" technologies or made of new materials. (2) New people arrived with the new goods (and controlled the access to them), and eventually their different ideas and lifeways permeated the aboriginal domestic systems, affecting the people living in their traditional modes. (3) Native people modified their dwellings to facilitate their changed lifestyle and newly adopted materials.

After ideas changed, *behavior* changed. In due time Alaskans expected their community to include a store, a school, health care, and a church. The ethnographic literature has shown that as the Native population began to accept Christian doctrine and mores and live by U.S. law, they also began to abandon their semisubterranean domestic system and gradually moved into Western-style log or plank cabins (Correll 1972; Jorgensen 1990; Lenz and Barker 1985; Oswalt 1963a, 1963b, 1990; Porter 1893).

Thus in western Alaska, as new people (Russians, Americans, Scandinavians) were integrated into the community, their *ideas* about education and religion also began to be accepted. Fundamental concepts of what made up a community or a settlement or even a proper house and household changed, too. Eventually, wood stoves that radiated better heat replaced open hearths, reducing the physical need for the insulation of semisubterranean houses. Ready-made tools precluded the need to spend time making them in the *qasgi;* wool and cotton fabrics for clothes released women from much of the time spent preparing skins. Moreover, to have easy access to the new goods, some groups moved their entire settlement closer to the trading posts.

Studies to determine gender activity areas are becoming more common. Traditional Native Alaskan wintertime activities took place within the entire domestic system—inside the *qasgi* and the small winter house and outside, in work areas adjacent to buildings and between structures. Therefore changes in the amount and place of work should be visible in the archaeological record. Archaeologists need to consider *social changes* that might have accompanied such movement.

Archaeologists might learn a great deal about transitional social organization and household interactions if we would examine transitional dwellings built in settlements occupied around the turn of the twentieth century (see Chapter 7, this volume). Alaskan archaeologists need to relate material recovered from semisubterranean structures during the late-nineteenth- and early-twentieth-century period to artifact and feature loci in the earliest aboveground cabins. These data would help to identify changes in work places and habits. Thus more homes need to be examined and compared with the ethnographic literature (see also Chapter 6, this volume).

RECOMMENDATION FOR FUTURE STUDIES

All of this raises the question, now what? As always, we must start with standard archaeological method. Without data we cannot interpret anything. But we must try to remember that actual people lived at our sites; they ate and slept, laughed and cried, argued and agreed, made and broke tools, talked about ways to get food, and made love. They participated in all of the day-to-day trivia that we do.

We must consider these activities and relationships when formulating our research models. To do this, archaeologists must think about how people might be likely to behave in certain situations, then use all the research tools available to them—especially ethnographic material and historical records—to find pattern changes that may indicate social change (Tringham 1991:121–124). Clark may have raised more questions than she provided answers to regarding who lived in the Koyukuk River houses, but she *did* propose "faces" for those houses. She may not have known exactly which faces belonged in her houses, but she could paint pictures of real people—working, celebrating, eating, sleeping, and perhaps changing within the parameters of a household.

Could it be that Native Alaskan households moved into aboveground cabins not so much because the Americans brought with them the cast iron, pot-bellied stove that provided much more heat much more efficiently than a small open fire, but rather because, in the Christian faith, married couples were expected to live together in one house with their immediate family? And what were the spatial implications when women then had to share their work space with men? Did less space cause activity areas (e.g., for flaking and grinding stone tools, preparing and cooking meat, sewing skins) to become smaller and more clearly defined, more diffuse, or overlapping? Did tools once kept in separate buildings now commingle in one, or were they stored in very separate places in the new house? Was work once done in the *qasgi* or house now done outside? What happens to ordered space as seasons change? Did outside work areas take the place of the *qasgi* floor? Were more outbuildings constructed for storage or to act as special work spaces? The list can go on and on, but what is important to remember is that, with any of these changes, personal communication and spousal interactions change, too.

Imagine the woman saying to the man, "Take that ivory outside to work—the chips and dust are getting in the food."

Traditionalists (and cynics) may say we are playing at storytelling and that, as archaeologists in the new century, we can never know how the people felt who were living and working at our sites 100 or 1,000 years ago. Indeed I have said so in the past. My recent work at sites where people have modified social organization, switched trade partners, added Western foods to their diet, and adopted new ideology, however, has led me to believe that archaeologists *can* discover and know a more intimate level of change—if only they will look.

ACKNOWLEDGMENTS

The United States Bureau of Land Management in Anchorage provided excavation permits and partial financial support for my research. Further financial support was contributed by the National Science Foundation, Arctic Social Sciences Program: Division of Polar Programs (DPP 9216347). The Cotsen Institute of Archaeology at UCLA provided me with the time and space to write and edit this chapter. Special thanks to Jeanne Arnold for her many insightful comments. Thanks also to the anonymous reviewers for valuable suggestions on earlier drafts of this chapter. Much appreciation goes to Corinna Schoenfelder, who produced the artifact and house excavation drawings. I am especially grateful to Lisa Frink for the invitation to be a part of the original symposium that inspired this book and for encouraging me to look at my research with an eye to gender. I thank Greg Reinhardt for years of friendship and guidance, as well as for his valuable comments on this work. Finally, my sincerest thanks to John Schoenfelder, my colleague, friend, and partner, for his computer mapping skills, his thoughtful critiques, and his unconditional support.

6

RE-PEOPLING THE HOUSE
HOUSEHOLD ORGANIZATION WITHIN DEG HIT'AN VILLAGES, SOUTHWEST ALASKA

Jennifer Ann Tobey

The household is a fundamental social form within human society; it embodies many dimensions of a society's social activities. Examinations of the household can provide insights into economic practices, symbolic meanings, class relations, status differentiation, kin relations, and gender relations. Using a household approach to highlight gender organization in Deg Hit'an society can prove useful to understanding the process of missionization in Alaska and in creating an interpretation that depicts people as dynamic and interactive.

The process of missionization among the Deg Hit'an of southwest Alaska has not been explored in detail at the household level. This chapter offers an approach that focuses on the spatial and temporal organization of the household. Using this approach, I illuminate the importance of research at the household level and provide a brief analysis of the premissionary household. I then discuss important aspects of the missionary period that would have influenced life at the household level and address the need to explore these different aspects in order to understand the routine life of the Deg Hit'an during this period.

A considerable lack of accessible information exists concerning Deg Hit'an social dynamics at the household level during the American missionary period.[1] In general, studies have focused primarily on broadscale approaches (see Mitchell 1997; Simeone 1982; VanStone 1974, 1979a,

1979b). Cornelius Osgood's work in the Anvik-Shageluk area (Osgood 1940, 1958, 1959) is an example of a study conducted at the village level, although his research focused on premissionary rather than missionary life.[2] All of these studies are informative, providing useful comparative and background data to incorporate into household studies. When we apply a household approach, however, the formerly obscure mundane and integral aspects of Deg Hit'an culture are illustrated.

This chapter emphasizes the need to examine these integral aspects and broaden our understanding of the American missionary period in Alaska. I suggest that the way to do so is to use a household approach that permits us to examine the changes and consistencies of daily practices, kin relations, and gender relations and roles. Furthermore, the house is a social space represented as a fluid entity whose composition, meaning, and function are transformed during the day. To understand the effects of the missionary period, one must first examine the premissionary-period household and use this as a baseline of information.

In what follows I describe many facets of the household and discuss the importance of a household study. Using Osgood's data, I offer a brief household analysis, exploring the spatial and temporal organization of the household and the house using a sociospatial lens. By describing a household that was dotted across the village landscape,[3] its members active throughout the day and the year, I show that the house itself transformed, taking different meanings and different roles at various times of the day. In addition, I show that three household-type groups were found in Deg Hit'an society. These groups overlapped, as individuals were members of more than one group. With a dynamic view of premissionary village life as seen at the household level, I set the stage for future examinations of the missionary period, highlight some of the forces that may have affected the household and gender roles, and suggest possible avenues of research.

HOUSES AND HOUSEHOLDS

The house is an important structural element in human societies. Archaeological remains of houses often appear as synchronic signatures; however, through the course of its use life, the house is a diachronic entity. One way to access this diachronic nature is to examine the social group associated with the house and house locale—the household. To envision the household of the past as a dynamic entity, we must first recognize the complexities of that entity and work with them accordingly. Archaeologists utilize a multitude of evidence to reconstruct the household of the past. As Carol Kramer (1982:673) described it, archaeologists use "architecturally bounded spaces, patterns of circulation within and among them, and structural and perhaps artifactual redundancies within them to construct the number and possible relations among the inhabitants of those spaces, which they may term households." Although "bounded spaces" and "structural and artifactual redundancies" may be synchronic, "patterns of circulation" implies movement of household members—a dynamic characteristic.

The numerous forms of evidence we study indeed suggest that the household is a complex entity. All too often, however, the household is reduced to a simple unit of analysis, such as a production unit or domestic unit (for example, see Sahlins 1972; Kramer 1982, respectively). Focusing on a particular aspect or function of the household leads to a manageable analysis, but it often excludes important elements. Although researchers are aware of the multiple aspects, representations often continue to reflect households as simple units, and this can lead to a static view of the household. The difficulty of presenting the household as complex and dynamic is compounded for archaeologists, who must rely on material remains as a data source.

Examining households in terms of activity patterns has been useful to archaeologists who cannot *see* the people they study (e.g., Flannery and Winter 1976; see also Chapters 9, 10, 11, 12, this volume). When we study the house, associated artifacts, and surrounding locale, we are indeed looking at an assemblage of static remains. It is our job through interpretation to put the dynamic life back into these remains.

The first step is to recognize that the house and the household have multiple meanings and functions (Bailey 1990). Because the house assemblage is intimately related to the household, we must acknowledge that the assemblage that represents a dynamic social unit is itself dynamic. For example, when we look at a house and its associated artifacts and features, we must look at the entire assemblage as a single categorical unit. We must acknowledge that just as the house/house locale serves many functions, the household served many functions and filled many roles. Furthermore, examining the spatial and temporal organization of household activities can reveal the complexities of the house and household—for instance, that activities overlap or vary through time, both in a cyclical or seasonal sense and in a progressive sense.

GENDER

At the most basic level of interpretation, gender is a social category that is based on biological sex, age, and sexuality and is specific to a particular culture. It is not analogous to biological sex but rather is distinct from it. Sex is a fixed quality unrelated to culture, whereas gender is "a thoroughly socio-cultural creation" (Pollock 1999:24; see also Nelson 1997:15). Gender roles and classifications may indeed be accepted as natural, predetermined, and unchanging within the society to which they belong. Thus examining gender highlights how culture is organized. Although it may relate to sexuality, roles, activities, behaviors, and responsibilities to others, gender is more than a mere classificatory device; it is "a process that is constructed as a relationship or set of relationships, necessarily embedded within other cultural and historical social institutions and ideologies such as status, class, ethnicity, and race" (Conkey and Gero 1991:9). Moreover, gender varies from culture to culture, both by specific gender designations and by the number of different genders present in society (Nelson 1997). Gender categories may—and often do—consist of more than men and women. The roles and behaviors of unmarried young women or girls may be significantly different from those of married women, and thus unmarried young women may be considered a different gender from married women in certain cultures.

Gender, like the household, is an important organizational principle that transcends multiple aspects of society (Conkey and Gero 1991; Tringham 1991; Yanagisko 1979). Both gender and the household are embedded in, as well as imbued with, multiple characteristics of society. Therefore an approach that explores both gender relations and the household will reveal many aspects of society, and will produce a dynamic integrated view of culture at the village level. I suggest focusing on the organization of household members by exploring the overlap as well as the separation of activity patterns. It is necessary to keep in mind that these activities are not segmenting but rather are transforming the village landscape. For instance, the overlapping activity signatures may give us insights into how activities changed through time—daily and seasonally—and thus into how the house space transformed through time. Furthermore, since we are interested in the social unit, we must follow the members as they came to and went from the house. This means studying activity patterns throughout the village, as well as those in and around the house. With the use of ethnographic and ethnohistoric records during missionization, this avenue of study is feasible (see also Chapter 5, this volume).

A sociospatial approach integrates the physical environment with spatialized experience within the term *space*. Thus space becomes both medium and outcome of social practices (Giddens 1984; Saunders 1990). We must view the house as an entity/artifact in itself. An individual's experience of space occurs through the dialectical relationships among the physical locale, social practices and meanings, and the phenomenological (Tilley 1994). Moreover, different individuals experience space differently based on differences in social practices and relations that correspond to age, status, and gender (Soja 1989; Tilley 1994). We must consider how the house incorporates all of these different functions and meanings.

THE DEG HIT'AN

The Deg Hit'an are an Athapaskan-speaking people from the southwest interior of Alaska. Around the time of contact, Deg Hit'an villages were established along the Kuskokwim and Yukon Rivers and their tributaries (de Laguna 1947; Osgood 1940, 1958, 1959; VanStone 1979b). These rivers were an important resource, supplying a variety of fish and waterfowl and serving as transportation and communication links between villages (Osgood 1940, 1958, 1959; Snow 1981). Because the resources of the Kuskokwim were less rich than those along the Yukon, the Deg Hit'an along the Kuskokwim depended more on hunting and less on the rivers than the Yukon Deg Hit'an did (Snow 1981:602).

Native peoples in Alaska had a well-established trade network with people in Siberia, and indirect contact with the Russians began with the introduction of Russian material items around 1789 (Griffin 1996; Michael 1967:100; Simeone 1982; Staley 1992:16). Trade and contact increased when Russian fur traders reached the Aleutian Islands and later extended into the Alaskan mainland. Members of the Russian Orthodox Church also traveled through Alaska. The Deg Hit'an may have been less preoccupied with trade than other Alaska Natives (see Michael 1967; Snow 1981), but they were not untouched. Even the smallest element of contact would have had an influence.

After the United States purchased Alaska in 1867, the lives and practices of the Deg Hit'an, and of Alaska Natives in general, were affected by U.S. fur traders and missionaries. Unlike the Russian American Company and the Russian Orthodox Church, the American Commercial Company and U.S. churches established trading posts and missions within Deg Hit'an territory. As a result, Americans had a bigger impact than the Russians on Deg Hit'an daily life. The Deg Hit'an began to depend less on traditional means of subsistence and began to rely on U.S. commodities (VanStone 1974, 1979b).

PREMISSIONARY LIFE

The Deg Hit'an occupied three types of villages during the year: the winter village, the canoe village, and the summer village. These different villages were located relatively near each other, with the winter village being the base camp (Snow 1981). Canoe villages consisted of ephemeral shelters, and summer villages were closer to the winter village and were smaller than the canoe villages (Snow 1981:604). Summer villages were characterized by aboveground plank or bark houses, smokehouses, and caches (Osgood 1940). Deg Hit'an winter villages were characterized by semisubterranean houses, caches, and a *kashim*—commonly defined as a men's house (de Laguna 1947; Osgood 1940; VanStone 1979a, 1979b; see also Chapters 3, 5, 7, 11, this volume). I will focus on the winter village. Women told stories in the house, and men told stories in the *kashim*. Numerous games and ceremonies were held, including the Animal Ceremony and the Mask Dance (Osgood 1958). Men, women, and children of the village, and sometimes those of other villages, gathered for ceremonies; during such time the *kashim* was the center of activity for the entire village.

Osgood claimed the house belonged to married women (Osgood 1940, 1958); however, it is not clear if this ownership was shared among all married women or was limited to a specific woman within the household. Even so, it served many members of the community. Two to three families were associated with one house, which stored material items for the many household members. At the start of the day it housed a large group of people, as families gathered to eat their morning meal, after which men and boys left for the *kashim* (or for hunting, trapping, and similar activities). Women and girls remained—sewing, cooking, making pottery, talking, and telling stories. At night, women, their husbands, daughters, and young sons slept in the house; and occasionally the house functioned as a council place for women of the village (Osgood 1940, 1958).

While women worked and socialized in the house during the day, men worked in the *kashim*. This space was the focus of men's lives in the winter (Osgood 1958:33), where they socialized during the day and evening. Here they manufactured and repaired items such as traps, wood bowls, and arrow shafts (Osgood 1958). In the late afternoon they built a large fire and took a sweat bath. Later, women brought the evening meal to their husbands and unmarried sons. After the meal, men and women listened to men tell stories. Like women in the house, old men occasionally held council in the *kashim* (Osgood 1958).

ORGANIZATION OF SPACE

From ethnographic research and archaeological discussions, we can recognize a division of labor and social relations based on gender (see Osgood

1940, 1958; Snow 1981). Within married couples, men provided the majority of food, whereas women cared for children, prepared food, and obtained food from areas near the village (Snow 1981:611). According to Osgood, women and men manufactured different items. Women manufactured twisted lines, tanned skins, nets, grass baskets and mats, birch bark baskets, skin containers, pottery, dry fish, and clothing. Men made awls, chisels, gouges, thimbles, scrapers, knives, axes, adzes, wedges, mauls, grinding stones, weapons, hunting implements, fishing implements, wood dishes and bowls, ceremonial items, and skin lines (Osgood 1940:440–441). These different social roles and activities were then transcribed onto the landscape. For example, as mentioned, women spent their days in the house, and the men were in the *kashim*. It would be easy to create a dichotomy and categorize the house as women's space and the *kashim* primarily as men's space. Following this spatial distinction, archaeologists would expect to find women's artifacts in the women's space and men's artifacts in men's space. The organization of space within Deg Hit'an communities, however, was more complex than this simple distinction (for further discussion of gender and spatial analysis, see Chapters 9, 11, 12, this volume).

Physical places took on different meanings because they housed many different activities during the day. Examination of the house further supports this view of complexity. As mentioned previously, the house was considered to be owned by women; yet both men and women built the house (Osgood 1940:432–448). It housed men, women, and children, its composition changing throughout the day. Also, men and women kept their belongings in it. The roles and functions of the house changed as the household members moved throughout the village landscape.

For purposes of this chapter I define the household as the group of people regularly associated with a particular house-type structure. With this definition, three different household-type groups can be distinguished. The first is the multigender household with married men, married women, unmarried men, unmarried women, and children. This consisted of all members of the two to three families associated with a particular house (see also Chapter 7, this volume). Although the married women owned the house, men took part in deciding who would make up the social unit that lived together. Osgood noted that men who were hunting and/or fishing partners often shared the same house (Osgood 1958). This household group met for the morning meal but did not remain spatially bound together throughout the day. These individuals had particular relationships, roles, and responsibilities with respect to each other; and the house was a social and physical setting in which these activities and interactions took place.

After the morning meal, the house was transformed from a space for a multigendered group to a place occupied by married women, unmarried women, and sometimes children. This second household group consisted of the women and girls of the original two to three families. Although part of a larger household group, they formed another unique group that was based on their association with the house. As they conducted their daily activities within this structure, they formed relationships specific to their social group.

The third social group of interest here is that associated with the *kashim*. The *kashim*-hold included the married and unmarried men of the village (members of this group were also members of household groups) who spent their days manufacturing and repairing tools. Again we see a group in spatial flux. In the morning its members were dispersed at their wives' and mothers' houses, and most men reassembled in the *kashim* during the day. Then, in the evening many left for the night. As we see, group membership overlapped with respect to the landscape.

The three social groups were not only dynamic across the landscape and through time but were also closely linked. Examining the landscape with a social lens, we see that places—such as the house and the *kashim*—are not discrete, isolated entities but are tightly woven into society.

REORGANIZATION IN THE MISSIONARY PERIOD

American missionaries introduced new practices and deliberately tried to persuade the Deg Hit'an to change some of their traditional practices, such as discontinuing their feasts (Simeone 1982). A shift in village residence took place as people converged on the larger communities of Anvik, Holy Cross, and Shageluk[4] (VanStone 1979a). Boarding schools were established at all three villages and enrolled children from neighboring villages (Mitchell 1997; Simeone 1982; VanStone 1979b). Because they removed members from the household groups for significant lengths of time, the schools impacted the groups' labor and activity forces. Church missions were established at Anvik and Holy Cross, and the missionaries worked to convert people and educate them in the ways of American life (Simeone 1982). The missionaries played a significant role in attracting people to these villages. As a result, the household group may have reorganized tasks, which in turn impacted the spatial as well as social organization of gender-differentiated activities.

Missions at Anvik and Holy Cross affected spatial organization in the Deg Hit'an landscape by creating physical distinctions between mission and nonmission land. In Anvik, Natives who became Episcopalian moved across the river from the village (Chapman 1896:523, cited in VanStone 1979a:77). The mission charged residents living on mission land a dollar a year and emphasized that undesirable people were to be kept off that land (Simeone 1982). This created the idea that the mission land was a privileged place, and by 1900 all Anvik residents lived on that land (Simeone 1982). At Holy Cross tension existed between the Roman Catholic Church and a number of Deg Hit'an residents. The latter, led by an influential shaman, moved across the river from the mission; the others moved onto mission land with Father Lucchessi (VanStone 1979b; Simeone 1982).

House form also changed as a result of the American mission period. In Anvik, for example, all inhabitants lived in traditional semisubterranean houses as late as 1892 (VanStone 1979a:77; see also Chapter 4, this volume). Five years later two-thirds of the people lived in aboveground log houses on the mission land (VanStone 1979a:77). Although this change may have taken place only in the structure itself, the household composition may also have changed (see Chapter 5, this volume). The missionaries influenced many aspects of Deg Hit'an life, and it is likely that the role of the house was affected, too. What other changes occurred with respect to spatial organization and role of the house have yet to be examined; however, by appraising how the missionary period is reflected in the house, we can gain an understanding of how society was affected at the household level.

With the increased presence of the church, the importance of the *kashim* declined (Osgood 1940, 1958). The disappearance of the *kashim* may have had significant impacts on ceremonial life, social organization, and gender-differentiated activities. James VanStone summarized the demise of the *kashim*:

> The decline of the Ingalik ceremonial cycle obviously affected the importance and function of the *kashims* in the various settlements. As workshops and lounging and sleeping places for men, they would continue to be important for some time to come, but once the ceremonial aspects of *kashim* activities were diminished, the structure as an institution in Ingalik life would never be the same again. The *kashims* at Old Shageluk and Holikachuk continued as meeting houses until the villages moved in 1966 and 1963, respectively. The structure at Anvik was destroyed by fire in the 1940s and not rebuilt. (VanStone 1979a:76)

The continued use of the *kashim* by men suggests that a division of labor based on gender continued. That division would have changed, however, and, at the least, spatial organization, which was based on gender, continued. Moreover, the activities in the *kashim* may have changed, but, unfortunately, the daily role of the *kashim* during the American missionary period has yet to be fully examined.

MOVING FORWARD

To understand the effects American missions had on mundane life, a household approach as outlined in this chapter should be applied. Following the provided interpretation of the premissionary household, research ought to focus on the organization of household members through time. In particular, an activity pattern analysis should be conducted that investigates artifact distributions and the distribution of household members with respect to the landscape and to the time of day and year.

An appropriate research approach is ethnohistoric in nature, such as described by Oswalt in *Bashful No Longer* (1990). This approach combines multiple lines of evidence such as archaeological data, oral traditions, and historical documents—missionary diaries, journal articles, other articles, and texts. Incorporating multiple lines of evidence is neither a new approach to historical archaeology in Alaska (for example, see Crowell 1997; Kan 1996; Oswalt 1980; Oswalt and VanStone 1967) nor foreign to studies of the Deg Hit'an (see VanStone 1979a, 1979b). Ethnohistory is more than a "fitting" of different lines of evidence. The different forms of evidence tend to have different biases and agendas. As a result, variabilities and discrepancies in historical portrayal may arise, which in turn can contribute to a complex view of household life.

CONCLUSION

The examination of premissionary households presented here investigated several aspects of Deg Hit'an life, such as composition of the household groups and the spatial and temporal organization of daily activities. Unlike activity-area studies that have focused on activities directly associated with the house structure and the house locale, this brief examination focused on activities of the *members* of the social group *associated with* the house. By doing so, a dynamic view of both the household and the house was created. People moved across the village landscape, and the house's meaning and functions were transformed throughout the day. Besides providing a dynamic view of the past, this interpretation highlights different variables that may have been influenced by the American missionary period. Because the household and activities were integrated within society, we are made aware that one change or effect can influence many other aspects. Thus, for example, the removal of children from the household unit to attend boarding schools likely affected the household as a production unit. With fewer individuals within the household, fewer people were present to obtain and procure food (yet there were also fewer to feed). Furthermore, young children in school were unlikely to learn traditional practices of subsistence, ceremony, and daily activities.

Research examining missionary pressures at the household level would increase our understanding of Deg Hit'an life during this time period. Once data from these multiple lines of evidence are gathered, they should be analyzed within a framework that explores the spatial and temporal organization of the household. This type of approach, one that is multifaceted, will illuminate various aspects of Deg Hit'an society—such as issues of gender relations, family relations, and identity—creating a dynamic view of the missionary village. Further, when this interpretation is compared with one of premissionary life, we can then explore the impacts of the missionaries; and issues such as cultural change, ethnic continuation, and acceptance and resistance can be examined. This type of research will not only increase our understanding of Deg Hit'an past, it will also provide information beneficial to understanding the American missionary period in Alaska.

ACKNOWLEDGMENTS

First, I would like to thank Lisa Frink, Rita Shepard, and Greg Reinhardt for inviting me to participate in this volume. Their comments have been both inspiring and informative. Donna MacAlpine of the Anvik Historical Society has not only been a good friend but also educated me about the Innoko Lowlands and the people who have lived there. Thank you. Because this chapter was based on my master's research, I wish to thank the faculty of Binghamton University for their support and guidance. I especially thank Drs. Albert Dekin, Charles Cobb, William Isbell, and Susan Pollock.

7

FISH TALES
WOMEN AND DECISION MAKING IN WESTERN ALASKA

Lisa Frink

ALTHOUGH ANTHROPOLOGISTS HAVE LONG RECOGNIZED the role of women as subsistence processors, insufficient attention has been paid to the entire spectrum of processing activities, including both the details of the skills operating through the full array of the processing stages and the sophistication of postprocessing management and distribution responsibilities. This chapter seeks to begin to fill the gap by examining more closely the mechanics of the production process at a Native Alaskan fish camp, highlighting the scope of women's productive activities.

Clearly, women's productive roles have proven more complex and influential in understanding present and past human behavior (e.g., Brumbach and Jarvenpa 1997a, 1997b; Gifford-Gonzalez 1993; Moss 1993). For several years Arctic anthropologists have increasingly paid attention to the significant role of women and subsistence fish processing. Archaeologists, however, have yet to take full advantage of this bank of knowledge and the new questions these data stimulate (for exceptions, see Chang 1988, 1991; Frink, Hoffman, and Shaw n.d.; Knudson et al. n.d.; Romanoff 1992; Schalk 1977; see also Chapter 12, this volume). Food processing and production is an anthropologically valuable research focus for at least three reasons. First, it leaves the "day-to-day" material remains that are relevant to archaeological investigation (Lightfoot, Martinez, and Schiff 1998:199); second, processing is critical to understanding the full spectrum of women's labor and the social and economic dynamics of prehistoric, historic, and modern people; third, viewing women's processing as "productive" informs our models of women's economic, social, ideological, and material contributions and impacts in hunter-fisher-gatherer communities (see also Ellanna and Sherrod 1995:18).

The data set used for this chapter is the result of ongoing archaeological, ethnoarchaeological, ethnohistoric, and oral historic research with the Cup'ik-speaking Eskimo (a subdialect of Central Yup'ik; Woodbury 1992:12) community of Chevak in the Yukon-Kuskokwim delta of western Alaska. This chapter explores the role of women in fish production, and the research results demonstrate that processing fish is a highly skilled occupation (a concept not often applied to women's activities), that women's roles are highly managerial (e.g., Ellanna and Sherrod 1995; Jolles and Kaningok 1990), and that fish production is complex and warrants continued research.

ENVIRONMENT AND CULTURAL BACKGROUND

The western Alaskan Yukon-Kuskokwim delta appears to be an endless, windy, wet, and cold space; however, for at least part of the year this swampy flat is brimming with life (Selkregg 1976). The approximately 75,000 km^2 triangular-shaped delta is edged on the north by the Yukon River, the fifth largest in the United States and the most extensive in Alaska, and to the south by the Kuskokwim River, Alaska's second largest watercourse. The outwash from these rivers makes up the delta—a flat, treeless, highly active, wet tundra environment. The most prominent features are the Nulato Hills in the north and the Kilbuck Mountains to the south. The low and poorly drained soils of the lower Yukon region are home to the largest seasonal waterbird breeding grounds in Alaska and contribute to providing residents with an amazing quantity and variety of foods including fish, sea mammals, and floral edibles (Ager 1982; Selkregg 1976).

The climate in the delta is variable, with extremes from 44 to 80 degrees F (Selkregg 1976:15–16). The region has 20" of mean annual precipitation, including the water equivalent from snow (Selkregg 1976:12–13), and discontinuous permafrost remains underneath the low ground vegetation of grasses and sedges rooted in mosses and lichens (Selkregg 1976). Around May, ice on the many rivers, lakes, and sloughs starts its rapid retreat to the Bering Sea, and the slowly melting snow heralds the "season of plenty" for the delta residents, in which highly seasonal resources abound (Testart 1982:524, 1988b, 1998c; Ager 1982; Barker 1993;

Figure 7.1 Yukon-Kuskokwim delta landscape in July

Fienup-Riordan 1986b; Fitzhugh and Kaplan 1982; Oswalt 1963b, 1990). (Of course, this abundance can vary according to year, season, and individual circumstances.) For instance, particularly during the early spring and late fall, men hunt several species of seal including the bearded (*Erignathus barbatus*), ringed (*Phoca hispida*), and harbor (*Phoca vitulina*) seals.

The Yukon-Kuskokwim delta is famous for its diversity and quantity of migrating waterfowl. Plentiful streams, small thaw lakes, and marshy sedges create an extremely productive habitat for birds (Selkregg 1976:197). April is *Tengmirvik,* or "where geese arrive" or "geese come" (Andrews 1989:259). Millions of seasonally migrating fowl are a copious resource[1]; they include several species of geese like the Canada (*Branta canadensis*) and black brandt (*Branta nigricans*). Also available throughout the summer are various greens collected by women, such as sourdock (*Rumex articus*), and during August several species of berries are eagerly gathered, such as salmonberry (*Rubus chamaemorus*) and blueberry (*Vaccinium uliginosum*).

The most abundant and paramount delta food, however, is fish. Today men spend many hours using nets to procure the fish, and women work to process this intensively harvested resource (Menager 1962:157–162; Nelson 1983 [1899]; Pete 1991; Wolfe 1989b). The first fish to offer itself to delta residents is the herring (*Culpe harengus*), which begins to run in mid- to late June. Not long after that the most important fish, salmon, continues to run through August. Five species of these anadromous fish—the king (*Oncorhynchus tshawytscha*), the red (*O. nerka*) the silver (*O. kisutch*), the pink (*O. gorbuscha*), and the chum (*O. keta*)—are available in the surrounding rivers and sloughs. Also included in the catch are flounder (*Platchthys stellatus*) and halibut *(Hippoglossus stenolepis*), as well as freshwater fish like the sheefish (*Stenoduc levichthys*) and blackfish (*Dallia pectoralis*).

The "season of scarcity" begins in the fall (Testart 1982:524, 1988b, 1988c; Barker 1993; Fienup-Riordan 1983, 1986b; Oswalt 1990). Migratory birds begin to head south for the winter, and the rivers begin to freeze in November. Although some hunting, trapping, and fishing occur, most people rely on properly stored and managed provisions to make it through the sometimes long and severe winter months. For these storage-based economies, planning, production, and storage of the seasonally abundant harvests continue to be imperative.[2]

Procurement of fish can be an enormous investment of time and energy, since winter prosperity depends on this short-term summer activity (Pete 1991; Wolfe 1989a, 1989b). For instance, Victor Shnirelman (1994:175) estimated for the Cherchez le Chien of the Kamchatka Peninsula that eight fisherman using nets can catch thousands of fish per day.[3] He also documented that the production process was highly intensive, keeping most women busy for twelve hours of continuous labor (Shnirelman 1994:179). During this heightened labor load, Beth O'Leary (1992:vii) observed that Southern Tutchone women cut, on average, 100 fish per woman per day.

CULTURE HISTORY

Very few excavations have been conducted in the delta, making it in many ways archaeologically little known (VanStone 1984a). Evidence suggests that people inhabited the western coast of this region 3,000 years ago (Okada et al. 1982) and lived in the inland territory since A.D. 800 (Shaw 1998). The first recognized culture in the delta is late Norton (Giddings 1964; Oswalt 1952; Shaw 1983, 1998), followed by western Thule culture, the ancestors of modern Eskimo groups (Dumond 1977; Shaw 1998).

As recounted by Linda Womkon Badten (in Chapter 4, this volume), many Native Alaskan people lived in rectangular semisubterranean houses made of wood, hides, and sod into the early/mid–twentieth century (Barker 1979; Shaw 1982; see also Chapter 6, this volume). Typically, particularly in winter villages, the cultural sexual division of space was structurally reinforced by the use of the *qaygiq,* or men's house (for a discussion of the use of the men's house, see also Larson 1991; Lutz 1973; Chapters 3, 5, 6, 11, this volume), and the *ena,* or woman's house (Fienup-Riordan 1983, 1986b; Menager 1962; Nelson 1882, 1983 [1899]; Oswalt 1963a, 1963b, 1967, 1979, 1990; Oswalt and VanStone 1967; Ray 1966; VanStone 1967). Residence in the men's house depended on age (Fienup-Riordan 1983:43; Oswalt 1963a:123); young boys (5 to 10 years of age) and single men most often stayed in the *qaygiq,* whereas married men spent time in both village spaces.

The *qaygiq* served a multitude of functions including the men's fire bath, workshop, community ceremonial space, and a place for male visitors to stay (for more on gendered use of space and what it means, see Chapters 3, 5, 6, 9, 11, 12, this volume). The *ena* was considered a female space, where women and their children resided. Grandmothers, mothers, and daughters worked, cooked, ate, and slept in these smaller "complex households" (Blanton 1993:5; Chapters 5, 6, this volume) that could house three families and twenty individuals (Menager 1962; Nelson 1983 [1899]:288; Ziff, Pratt, and Drozda 1982).

EUROPEAN CONTACT

Attesting to the ecological productivity of western Alaska, populations were among the highest in Alaska at contact (VanStone 1984b). European influence in the lower Yukon region was kept to a minimum for several reasons (Fienup-Riordan 1994; Oswalt 1990); because of the low Bering Sea shelf this "damn'd unhappy part of the world" was difficult to travel (Oswalt 1990:11). Moreover, unlike other regions in Alaska that produced timber, furs, marine fish, and the like, the Russians found no compelling economic draw in this isolated region and hence had relatively little influence on the Native groups in this part of western Alaska (Fienup-Riordan 1996; VanStone 1984a; cf. Black 1984). Native communities in the north-central Yukon delta had less contact with Russians or even early Americans than did those in the Kuskokwim area or the far northern Yukon delta (Ray 1966). In fact, although Andrey Glazunov conceivably explored further down the Yukon River in 1832 (VanStone 1984a; Ziff, Pratt, and Drozda 1982), Edward Nelson, a U.S. naturalist, traveled through the northern extent of the delta for the first time during the winter of 1878 (Nelson 1882, 1983 [1899]), collecting ethnographic data and Native material items for the Smithsonian Institution (Collins 1982; Fitzhugh and Kaplan 1982; Nelson 1882, 1983 [1899]; see also Chapter 5, this volume).

MISSIONIZATION AND DISEASE

Most major social and demographic changes in the delta region resulted from missionization and disease (Oswalt 1990). Russian Orthodox priests were present in the delta in the mid-1800s, and Catholic and Moravian missionaries began seeking converts in the late nineteenth and early twentieth centuries (Fienup-Riordan 1991; Flanders 1984; Llorente 1988; Menager 1962; O'Connor 1947; Ray 1966; Schwalbe 1951). Epidemics of influenza and smallpox continued into the early 1900s, causing tragic numbers of deaths and substantial movements of people (Fienup-Riordan 1991, 1994; Chapter 4, this volume; for an overview of early historical disease in Alaska, see Fortuine 1992). Death rates at times were staggering; for instance, in 1942 in the village of Nunaraluq (an ancestral village of Chevak), according to Father Jules Convert, seventeen children died of whooping cough in a nineteen-day period (Barker 1979:29). The disruption of disease caused major demographic shifts, especially the aggregation of village members and the incorporation of numbers of orphaned Native children into the newly formed mission boarding schools (Fienup-Riordan 1991, 1994; Llorente 1988; Oswalt 1990; Ray 1975; Woodbury 1992; see also Chapter 6, this volume).

RESEARCH PROJECT

Since 1996 I have been conducting research in the village of Chevak and its attached archaeological village sites.[4] Chevak, located 27 km east of the Bering Sea, rests on a bluff above the Ninglikfak River and is home to over 800 Cupiit Eskimos[5] (Morrow and Schneider 1995:9; Woodbury 1992:12). This region is suitable for ethnoarchaeological research, since many villagers lead a very modern lifestyle, yet traditional ways continue to be essential. For instance, although Western goods are available in this mixed-subsistence economy, they are viewed as secondary to subsistence foods; people continue to hunt, gather, and—most significantly—fish (see also Barker 1993; Fienup-Riordan 1983, 1986b; Wolfe 1984, 1989a, 1989b).

Moreover, the people of Chevak have an archaeologically unique connection to their past; Chevak is the youngest in a series of four sequentially inhabited village sites. The oldest prehistoric site, Qavinaq, is connected to the people of Chevak through oral history; however, many

Figure 7.2 Chance Hill setting whitefish net at the mouth of a slough

village elders remember living in the subsequently occupied site, Nunaraluq, a pre-proto- and historic mound site. In the 1940s people moved from Nunaraluq to Old Chevak and eventually in the 1950s to present-day New Chevak.

This community is also appropriate for gender research, since women and men practice a sexual division of labor—particularly in the collection and processing of subsistence foods. Even though this system has complexities, the general custom among this modern generation of Eskimos is that the subsistence division of labor runs along sexual lines with little task "overlap"[6] (Lepowsky 1993:113–116; Ackerman 1990a; Giffen 1930; Ray 1966). Men most often hunt birds, as well as sea and terrestrial mammals; fish with nets; and gather some foods such as berries and clams. Women gather grass, collect vegetation, dig clams, fish using lines, and—most salient to this research—are the primary processors of all food and are essential as decision makers and managers of the critical subsistence harvests.

METHODOLOGY

Data for this chapter were generated from taped interviews with ten elder women conducted during the 1998 field season in the village of Chevak. These women ranged from sixty-one to eighty-three years of age, and most lived at the previously occupied villages of Nunaraluq and Old Chevak. My interviews focused primarily on women's roles in subsistence fish processing and management and how practices may or may not have changed in these women's lifetimes. With assistance from a Native interpreter, the format was one of discussion with open-ended questions.

Additional data were collected at a herring fish camp (located on the Ninglikfak River within walking distance of the village) where I visited an elder woman (in her early eighties) while she managed her camp and cut her fish. At the early summer seasonal camp I observed, audio recorded, photographed, and participated in the processing, storage, and disposal of herring (*Culpe harengus*) and whitefish (*Coregonus* spp.). The results of this ongoing seasonal camp research suggest several critical components to understanding the role of women in Eskimo society; two are pertinent to this research.[7] First, fish processing is a learned complex skill requiring accumulated knowledge for proper processing and handling of the harvest; and second, fish handling requires advanced management skills, such as short- and long-range decision making.

DISCUSSION

Fortunately for archaeologists, a fair amount of data have been collected concerning fish processing.[8] Cutting fish, unlike what Paul Drucker and Robert Heizer (1967) recognized as fairly simple, is a learned talent requiring technical prowess and skillful decision making. Or as Robert Schalk said, processing is "not as simple as cleaning and hanging fish to dry" (Schalk 1977:232).

Given the climate of western Alaska, the temporal window for successful harvesting of fish is quite small. Many fish are processed within a short period of time; for instance, the main run of herring during the early summer lasts several weeks. The entire intensive season of fishing begins (approximately) in mid/late June and continues into August. Women must cut, dry, smoke, and store the catch in a very demanding and intensive manner. Therefore they must differentiate (according to which species of fish they are handling) and prioritize their processing activities to maximize the yield of fish harvested so that fish are not lost through spoilage. This requires knowledge about the properties of different species of fish, the condition of the fish at the time of capture, the

Figure 7.3 Ulrich Ulroan brings whitefish to his grandmother, Mrs. Angelina Ulroan.

effect of weather (humidity, temperature, rainfall) and insects on processing, and the productive capacity of the laborers available (see also O'Leary 1992; Pete 1991; Romanoff 1992; Schalk 1977)—all crucial management factors and decisions negotiated and made by women.

Processing is an intergenerational activity in which this knowledge is taught and learned through years of experience. As occurs in other Eskimo communities, grandmothers, mothers, and daughters usually cut fish together (Ellanna and Sherrod 1984; Wolfe 1989a). Similar to what Linda Ellanna and George Sherrod (1995) found with a Native Inupiaq group, elder women are active managers of the fish camp operation; for example, many elder women from Chevak establish their own camp each season, often with or near extended family.

The fish camp I visited was repeatedly referred to as the elder woman's, and all the fish her grandson caught were brought specifically for his grandmother.[9] The equipment at the fish camp—including the tent, drying rack, pits, and smokehouse—is considered the elder woman's property. The ownership of fish is an interesting issue and one I will

Figure 7.4 Mrs. Angelina Ulroan processing herring at her camp (note salmon-skin boots).

return to. During my visits to this camp I learned about several examples of decision making in the processing of fish, similar to the types of decisions James Barker (1993) observed on Nelson Island. Not all fish are processed the same way; each species is treated differently, and within individual species other factors differentiate processing techniques. For instance, herring are cut and processed differently based on size; the "larger" fish lose their heads, and the "small" fish keep theirs. Large fish are then cut on one side for gutting, whereas the small herring are completely opened up. After drying for approximately four days (weather dependent), the herring are hung using a herring braid (made of rye grass and cotton); heads are threaded on the larger fish, and tails are used for the smaller herring (Barker 1993; Pete 1991). The skill of braiding herring is deceptive; several middle-aged Chevak women were still learning to master this processing activity.

Deciding which fish should be first in the processing queue is also a complex art. Often the run of fish is so intense that decisions must be made about which species to prioritize; some demand immediate attention, whereas others can wait. For example, herring, according to my elder host, can last in a pit for up to two weeks, whereas whitefish are known to deteriorate and rot much faster and need to be cut and hung to dry in a more timely manner. The whitefish could also be eaten at camp, since they require only limited drying to be edible. Several elders also discussed the necessity, during an intensive salmon run, of deciding which individual salmon to cut first. Some of the salmon will be set aside and stored in large pits lined with grass and covered with sod blocks. The women will then decide when to return and cut these fish; in addition, further processing decisions continue after the fish have been initially processed. Each species requires specific methods and timing of processing. For example, herring are dried for several weeks and must be kept dry during the consistent rains of the delta, whereas whitefish require much less drying and can also be smoked.

Storage for hunter-fisher-gatherers in the Arctic is critical to survival. It was and is women's responsibility to store the foods properly for use by the family throughout the entire year. Traditional methods included the use of handwoven straw baskets and underground pits in which to store fish. (Today the luxury of freezers makes the job of food storage less difficult and risky.) Clearly, too little has been discussed in the literature exploring the processes by which perishable resources are stored (Schalk 1977). One notable example suggests that storage was a learned art, requiring the right positioning of items in pits, the appropriate layering of grass for circulation, and a watchful eye for the remaining stores (Lantis 1946; see also Fienup-Riordan 1983). My preliminary data suggest that women store different species in different ways at different times of the year. For instance, herring is most often stored aboveground in baskets, but needlefish—an important winter food—likely was stored in small circular floor pits within the semisubterranean houses. Again, more data need to be generated to understand the full spectrum of choices women had and have regarding proper storage.

ISSUES OF OWNERSHIP

Ernestine Friedl (1975) described Arctic women's labor as directly related to men and their economic and social success, intimating that women merely process and may not own the fruits of their labor. More recent research has demonstrated, however, that this is a simplistic understanding of women's labor and their control over the product of their work (Ellanna and Sherrod 1995; Jolles and Kaningok 1990). These data suggest the women of Chevak, like other Native northern North American women (Ellanna and Sherrod 1995; Chapter 3, this volume), not only process the bulk of subsistence products but also manage them, and this oversight extends to control over distribution and consumption as well (the full economic spectrum).

Chevak women control the daily allocation of foodstuffs. As Ann Fienup-Riordan (1986b:182, 184) found, the food caches are "owned" and managed by an extended family's elder women, who "decide what is to be eaten and when" (for more on food and ownership, see Chapter 3, this volume). This is less true today in the village; several elder women suggested that unlike today (when kids can go to the store and get snacks), when they were young their mothers had jurisdiction over all the food. They talked of their mothers' portioning at mealtimes and recalled that they would get only a certain amount of food. (One elder remembered that her brothers always got more than she.)

In making decisions concerning daily allocation, women must project long-range usage plans. A woman must decide what resources will be used for her nuclear and her extended family over the coming year (O'Leary 1985; Romanoff 1992). In addition, her planning must include nonhuman and social needs such as feasting (Fienup-Riordan 1983, 1986b; Koranda 1968; Nelson 1882, 1983 [1889]; Oswalt 1963a, 1963b, 1967, 1979, 1990; Ray 1966; Michael 1967; for the importance of feasting, see Dietler and Hayden 2001). Feasting still occurs in the winter months, especially December, and requires that large quantities of food be shared. One elder woman spoke longingly of her youth and the foods that were so available during feasting periods, unlike the controls placed on her consumption during the rest of the year.

Moreover, today most families have only one dog to feed, but prior to available mechanical transportation (mid-twentieth century) women had to plan to feed the family dog team, which could range from five to eleven dogs—each requiring at least half a salmon ration per day while traveling[10] (Ray 1966:82). While at fish camp I observed that most of the heads and backbones of fish were tossed in the river; however, the elder women I spoke with remarked that this was never done in their day, when everything was used (see also Wolfe 1989a).

Women's authority over fish production is also demonstrated by the use of ownership marks. Traditionally, when a man is catching fish, they are his; but when he brings them to his sister, wife, or mother, they become hers (see also Fienup-Riordan 1986b:184). As Fienup-Riordan (1986b:184) has found for the Native Nelson Islanders, the stores "become the property of the older women of the extended-family household for processing and for distribution" within and beyond the household. As the wife does not often hunt seal, "her husband rarely goes into the

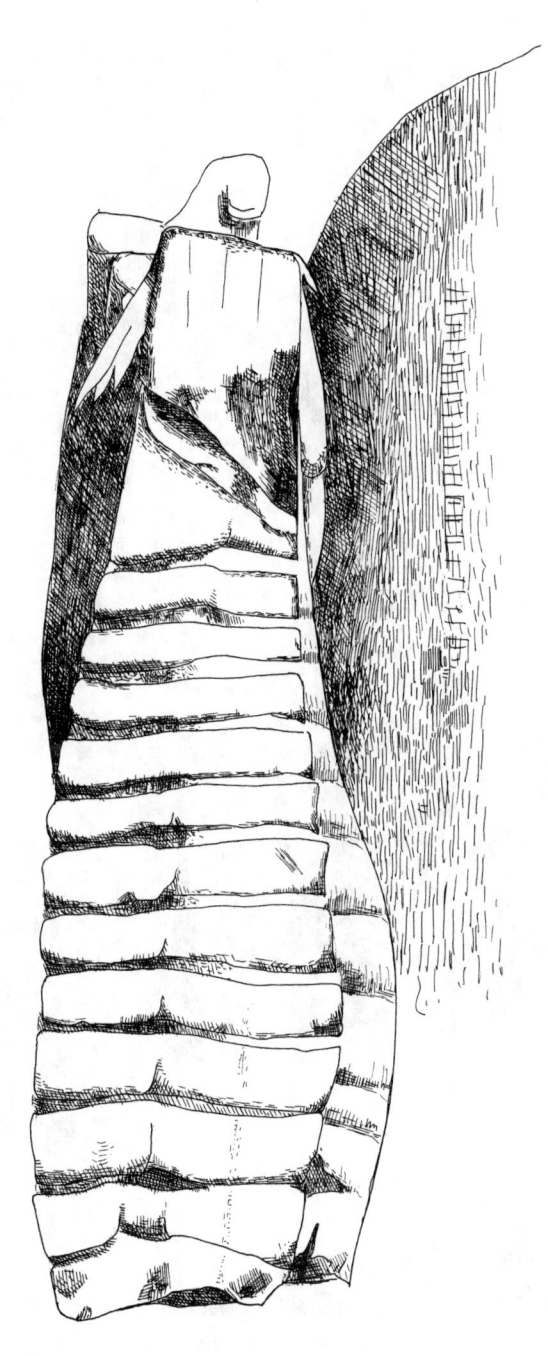

Figure 7.5 Filleted salmon (note fish mark at top); courtesy, Brian Frink, University of Minnesota, Mankato.

Figure 7.6 Dried and smoked salmon at the foot of the smokehouse and fish rack in the background

cache to bring in fish for the evening meal" (Fienup-Riordan 1986b:184). As previously discussed, however, this all-encompassing authority over food distribution is likely diminishing over time.

A physical declaration of ownership is the Chevak women's ownership mark, which several elder women described during the village interviews. These marks are simple cuts placed on both sides of the fish flesh near the tail (see Figure 7.5). I was told most women do not do this anymore (however, one elder continues to make these marks when she remembers) and do not know when the practice stopped, but one elder woman suggested it may have ceased in the 1950s when the village moved to its current location.

The fish marks are suggestive concerning ownership. According to my elder consultants, the marks are considered feminine designations of ownership (see also Romanoff 1992) and are unlike the impressions men place on their catch or material items (see Nelson 1983 [1899]); instead, these marks were passed on in a woman's line from mother to daughter. It is interesting that these female designations of ownership were a complete surprise to several middle-aged Chevak women, making it likely that the transmission of this practice has ceased. More data need to be collected concerning the use, complexities, and relevance (especially for the archaeological record) of this provocative practice of marking fish.

ARCHAEOLOGICAL IMPLICATIONS

Food production is a critical research focus for archaeologists. Fish processing in present-day Native western Alaska is no exception, and new questions born from these data abound for archaeologists. For instance: How has technological change affected efficiency and so harvest capabilities? Can archaeologists detect past fish camp activities using soil chemistry analysis? How will envisioning women as resource managers and active producers inform our theoretical models of hunter-fisher-gatherer communities and social change? With more complete documentation and appreciation of the complexity of women's productive activities, we can continue to more completely understand modern, early historic, and prehistoric production capabilities; more accurately represent women's roles; and increasingly apply these data to the interpretation of archaeological assemblages.

CONCLUSION

This research adds new and vital observations concerning Native western Alaskan women and their processing and management of fish and has critical implications for archaeological investigations, especially concerning women and their roles in a hunter-fisher-gatherer society. These data illuminate the fact that women's direction of production activities is a highly skilled craft; it requires a knowledge of processing, storage techniques, and management skills that have been critical to survival in the harsh Arctic environment and must be learned over an extensive period of time. New insights and documented data concerning the complexities of economic roles, including women as not only processors in a subsistence economy but as resource managers and producers, will increasingly broaden our recognition of the economic and social contributions of women in the present and past.

ACKNOWLEDGMENTS

I wish to thank the Elders of Chevak and the Elder Advisory Council for sharing their knowledge with me. I also am grateful to the Chevak Traditional Council and the community of Chevak for their interest in and support for this work. This research could not have been accomplished without the financial and logistical support of the United States Fish and Wildlife Service and Debbie Corbett (Anchorage Office), Mike Rearden, and Paul Liedberg (Bethel Office). Also, many thanks to Mary Berthold, Hetty Jo Brumbach, Brian Hoffman, Bob Jarvenpa, Phyllis Morrow, Mary C. Nanuwak, Greg Reinhardt, and Rita Shepard for intellectual engagement and remarks on the manuscript and to three anonymous reviewers (of course, this chapter is singly my responsibility). My heartfelt thanks also go to Brian Frink for his artwork. Finally, much gratitude goes to Kate for her continuing observations, unwavering support, and enduring partnership.

III
MATERIAL AND SPATIAL ANALYSIS

8
CHILD AND INFANT BURIALS IN THE ARCTIC

BARBARA A. CRASS

THE ARCHAEOLOGY OF GENDER INCLUDES ALL "INVISIBLE" PEOPLE (e.g., Moore and Scott 1997), not just women or gender transformers. Gender is not based solely on cultural definitions of male and female but is age associated as well. Children are currently one of the foci of gender research, especially in Europe (e.g., Baker 1997; Meskell 1994, 1996; Siemoneit 1997; Sofaer Derevenski 1994, 1997). The Arctic also provides a rich basis for looking at children and infants in the past.

Children and infants have been described as one group of invisible people in the archaeological record (e.g., Moore and Scott 1997). Although children undoubtedly left their mark in the past, as they certainly do in the present, these marks are rarely obvious archaeologically. One area where these marks may be more apparent is in mortuary contexts.

In an extensive survey of burials in the Arctic (Crass 1998), 305 infants and children were identified in pre-Christian Inuit burials. These infants and children will be compared with 1,459 adults. Since the reports were written and the archived material collected over the past century by various individuals, the data are not always complete. The numbers are large enough, however, that general trends should be apparent.

Data were gathered from fifty sites located across the Inuit range from northeastern Siberia to Greenland.[1] The sites vary from large, permanent settlements with associated cemeteries providing hundreds of burials,

Table 8.1—Sites With Infants, Children, or Both

Site	References
Siberia	
Ekwen	Arutiunov & Sergeyev 1975
Uelen	Arutiunov & Sergeyev 1969
Alaska	
Cape Krusenstern	Giddings & Anderson 1986
Cook Inlet	DeLaguna 1934
Dovelavik Bay, St. Lawrence Island	Hofman-Wyss 1987
Gambell, St. Lawrence Island	Bandi 1984
Kitnepaluk, St. Lawrence Island	Hofman-Wyss 1987
Naknek	Dumond 1981
Point Hope	Larsen & Rainey 1948; Rainey n.d.
Prince William Sound	DeLaguna 1956
Tulaagiaq	Anderson 1978a, b
Uyak, Kodiak Island	Heizer 1956
Canada	
Kamarvik, Chesterfield Inlet	McCartney 1971; Merbs 1967, 1968a, 1968b
Kulaituijavik, Chesterfield Inlet	McCartney 1971; Merbs 1967, 1968a, 1968b
Naujan	Mathiassen 1927; Fischer-Møller 1937
Niutang, Baffin Island	Salter 1984
Saglek Bay, Labrador	Way 1978
Silumiut, Chesterfield Inlet	McCartney 1971; Merbs 1967, 1968a, 1968b
Southampton and Walrus Islands	Collins 1955, n.d.; Collins & Emerson 1954; Emerson 1954
Tasioya, Baffin Island	Salter 1984
Greenland	
East Greenland	
Dødemandsbugten	Larsen 1934
Imertiit, Illuluarsuk Region	Felbo et al. 1993
Kangerlussuaq	Mathiassen 1936b; Degerbol 1936
Qoornoq, S. Skjoldungen Sound	Felbo et al. 1992
Skærgårdshalvø, Knud Rasmussen Land	Larsen 1938
Suess Island, Clavering Island	Glob 1935
Suukerti	Mathiassen 1933
Timmiarmiut, Frederick VI's Coast	Mathiassen 1936c
West Greenland	
Ammaasaq, Upernavik	Hjarnø, Jorgensen, & Vesely 1974
Illorsiut, Disko Bay	Mathiassen 1934
Illutalik, Disko Bay	Mathiassen 1934
Illutalik, Julianehåb District	Mathiassen 1936a
Kangaamiut Area	Mathiassen 1931
Narsarsuaq, Julianehåb District	Mathiassen 1936a
Saattoq Island, Upernavik	Hjarnø, Jorgensen, & Vasely 1974
Tuttutuup Isua, Julianehåb District	Mathiassen 1936a
Upernaviarsuk, Upernavik District	Hjarnø, Jorgensen, & Vasely 1974

Table 8.2—Individuals

	Infant	Child	Adult
Graves	16	170	759
Cairns	25	74	629
Other	7	13	71
Total	48	257	1,459

Table 8.3—"Other" Burial Types

	Infant	Child	Adult
House	1	5	10
Fissure	2	3	20
Midden	4	2	9
Surface	0	1	10
Cave	0	1	14
Pit	0	1	8
Total	7	13	71

such as Ekwen in Siberia and Point Hope in Alaska, to a handful of houses and a few associated cairns providing less than ten individuals, such as Narssarssuaq or Sûkersit in Greenland. Infants and/or children were found in thirty-five of these sites, as shown in Table 8.1. For this chapter, infants are defined as 0–3 years of age and children as 3–12 years.

The burials are divided into three types: graves, cairns, and other. Graves are in-ground burials found primarily in Siberia and Alaska. Cairns are aboveground stone chambers and are common in the Canadian Arctic and Greenland. The majority of the burials are either graves or cairns. The "other" category consists of less common burial methods including burials in inhabited houses or pits; placement in rock fissures, middens, or caves; and surface burials. The distribution of the 48 infants, 257 children, and 1,459 adults in these three burial types is provided in Table 8.2. A further breakdown of the distribution of infants, children, and adults in the "other" category is given in Table 8.3.

From these two tables, it is clear that child burials are infrequent compared with adult, and infant burials are rarely found. Of the 1,764 individuals, 82.7% are adults, 14.6% are children, and only 2.7% are infants. Many of the these individuals are interred together in multiple burials. Individuals are discussed instead of burials because about a third of the individuals are found in multiple burials: 30.7% (290 of 945) of the individuals in graves, 36.4% (265 of 728) of the individuals in cairns, and 28.6% (26 of 91) of the individuals in other burial types (Table 8.4).

Whereas the adults are often buried with other adults, infants and children are usually buried alone or with one or more adults (Table 8.5). Although the sex of all the adults is not known, a trend is apparent. In graves, children are buried with adult males more often than with adult females (13 versus 10). The reverse occurs with children in cairns, with 11

Table 8.4—Individuals in Single and Multiple Burials

	Infant	Child	Adult
GRAVES			
Single	14	113	538
Multiple	12	57	221
CAIRNS			
Single	20	53	390
Multiple	5	21	239
OTHER			
Single	6	10	49
Multiple	1	3	22

Table 8.5—Multiple Burial Associations

	M	F	M/F	A	*[1]
GRAVES					
Infant	0	0	1	5	6
Child	10	13	3	24	7
CAIRNS					
Infant	3	1	0	0	1
Child	8	3	2	7	5

[1]Burials contain either both an infant and child or more than one infant or child.

being buried with females and only 4 with males. Some of the multiple burials, as seen in the last column, contain either both infants and children or more than one infant or child, with or without adults.

The ethnographic record offers some explanation for the number of burials of infants and children with adults of both sexes. Most early ethnographers agree that when the mother died, infants and any children who were not weaned were killed—usually by strangling—and buried with their mother (cf. Boas 1907:117; Bogoras n.d.:26; Crantz 1767:238; Gosling 1910:213; Hawkes 1916:139; Holm 1914:62; Kroeber 1900:31; Lyon 1825:276, 380; Oswalt 1963a:144, 1979:133; Peary 1898:506; Rasmussen 1929:159). Older children not yet able to fend for themselves were also sometimes killed (Cook 1894). Exceptions were made if a woman could be found who could nurse the child or if the child was particularly strong and struggled against death (Day 1973; Steensby 1910:377). A child who fought was seen as an individual who would likely survive. Strangling small children was seen as kinder than letting them slowly starve to death because of lack of proper food. Similarly, sometimes small children were strangled and buried with their father, since there would be no one to provide for the family (Cook 1894; Day 1973; Oswalt 1979:133). The mother's chances of remarrying would be better if she was not accompanied by small children. Again, the logic was that a quick death was preferable to starvation.

Another possibility may be that small children were buried with adults or older children so they would have someone to help them get to the afterlife realm. In Greenland, small children are said to have been buried with the head of a dog so the dog could lead them to the afterlife, since small souls could not find their way alone (cf. Birket-Smith 1924:66; Crantz 1767:237; Egede 1818:153: Schultz-Lorentzen 1928:245). Unfortunately, most child and infant burials from Greenland in the study were excavated in the first half of the twentieth century when animal bones were ignored. Six single infant or child burials were excavated in the 1990s, however (Felbo et al. 1992, 1993), and one—a child—does contain the mandible of a dog.

Although graves and cairns are the most common burial type, infants and children are frequently found in the other burial methods. Some of these types are difficult to find archaeologically, such as surface burials. Others, such as burials in occupied houses, are not usually found when excavating burial sites. The majority of the house burials are from sites in Greenland, where random houses were excavated and the associated visible cairns were investigated (cf. Degerbol 1936; Larsen 1934, 1938; Mathiassen 1936a, 1936b).

If we compare the number of infants with the number of adults found in burials other than graves and cairns, we find significantly more infants (chi^2 = 8.83, p>0.005). We even find that infants are found more often than children in these alternative burials (chi^2 = 6.2, p>0.025). Since the middens and fissures are the most common types for infants, this may indicate a preference for a quick or easy disposal. The midden burials had no indication of interment in the area surrounding the infants, whereas the infants found in fissure burials were accompanied by a few burial goods. Curiously, no significant difference exists between children and adults in these other burial types (chi^2 = <1.0).

We can conclude from this that not all children and infants are buried in the same locations or burial types as adults. The numbers are small for infants in general and for children in the nongrave and noncairn burial types (Table 8.4). We may be looking at the chosen few. But then, that may very well be said for the adult burials, since the number of individuals in this study does not constitute the entire adult population over time at all of the sites. Some questions may never be resolved.

Another aspect of burials that can be examined is burial goods. The Inuit are known for having a plethora of distinct artifacts, and 188 different types of items were found in these burials. Each of the items was tallied in a present/absent fashion for each individual and tested for significance by chi-square. The majority of items were found only occasionally, and no significance was found with two exceptions that will be discussed later. To increase the numbers, items were grouped into categories.

The burial goods were divided into five discrete categories based on presumed function or composition: specialized subsistence implements, general or multipurpose tools, personal ornamentation, magic/ritual/recreation, and raw material, as well as a miscellaneous category (Crass 1998). Burial goods were placed in the most specialized category possible, so each item logically fit into only one category. For example, although a seal scratcher is a tool, it is used only in subsistence activity and is therefore placed in the subsistence category. A kayak, which can be used in subsistence activities as well as in others, is classified as a multipurpose tool.

The subsistence category includes items used only for hunting and fishing. All other tools, including tools for gathering and tools for making hunting implements, are placed in the tool category. This is the largest category. Personal ornamentation includes items that are decorative, such as jewelry, and items that are functional, such as buckles. Magic/ritual and recreation is the most complicated category. Items such as drums, rattles, dolls, and small items that may be toys, amulets, or miniature representations of full-sized burial goods have all been described in various contexts as objects of magic, ritual, and recreation. As Kaj Birket-Smith wrote, "It is now scarcely possible, with any certainty, to draw the line between amulets and playthings" (1924:419). Putting them all into one category eliminates the necessity of drawing that line. The last category, raw material, is self-explanatory.

In looking at burial goods, infants were not included because, among the few who had burial goods, the numbers were too small to test for significance. Only single burials were used so the goods were clearly associated with the individual. All five discrete categories were represented by at least five or more children in graves and two or more children in cairns.

No significant difference was found for the occurrence of any individual item in child and adult graves. As seen in Table 8.6, however, for the tool category, significantly fewer than expected children had any tools ($chi^2 = 9.57$, $p > 0,005$).

Fewer children than expected had tools in cairns as well ($chi^2 = 5.8$, $p > 0.025$), although to a less significant degree. A trend for children to have more miniature items than adults was also found ($chi^2 = 5.05$, $p > 0.025$), although the numbers are small (2 of 18 for children and 4 of 206 for adults). The numbers are also small for pendants (3 of 18 for children and 6 of 206 for adults), but a much more significant number of children had pendants than adults ($chi^2 = 8.35$, $p > 0.005$).

The amount of goods can also indicate variation in burial treatment. Approximately half of the child and infant single cairn burials did not have goods. When compared with adult single cairn burials, a signifi-

Table 8.6—Significant Goods

		Chi^2	p
Grave	Tool category	9.57	>0.005
Cairn	Tool category	5.80	>0.025
	Miniature/toy	5.05	>0.025
	Pendant	8.35	>0.005

cant difference was found (chi^2 = 8.46, p>0.005). Graves, on the other hand, did not have a significant difference between burials with goods and those without (chi^2 = 2.24). A particular problem exists when looking at goods in cairn burials, as cairns are often conspicuously visible and can be opened and closed. This made them an easy target for collectors, and many cairns were noted by the investigators as obviously disturbed (Crass 2001). The problem is compounded when one takes into consideration the Inuits' practice of borrowing or exchanging items from cairns as needed (cf. Hawkes 1916:136; Jenness 1922:176; Kumlien 1879:28; Rasmussen 1908:114). For example, it would be perfectly acceptable to remove a knife from a cairn and replace it with some food or a clothing item that would likely not be discernable archaeologically. Graves, however, are not so easily accessible, so items found in graves were likely placed there at interment.

Variation in the number of goods associated with individuals was tested by the Wilcox two-sample test with two-tailed probability. For cairns, p=0.17384, indicating little probability of a difference, whereas graves, with a p value of 0.01778, indicate a trend for adults to have a greater number of goods than children and infants.

One interesting pattern found in graves was the distribution of skeletal elements. Infant and child remains appear to include skulls more often than adult remains (chi^2 = 6.5, p>0.025). If remains consisting only of skulls are compared, the difference is highly significant (chi^2 = 14.24, p>0.001). This could be the result of taphonomic processes, but it is doubtful that is the sole explanation. In some areas the preservation is so good that several close-to-term fetuses have been recovered, fully articulated and in excellent condition! Again, the ethnographic record may provide some clues. Several ethnographers claimed a child's or infant's corpse was handled more freely and kept around longer than an adult's (Lantis 1946:229; Lyon 1825:369). If the child died when the ground was too frozen to dig a grave, perhaps it was stored somewhere and later buried in the grave. If the graves are in fact a secondary burial, this could explain the higher incidence of skulls. Although uncommon, a few ethnographic accounts exist describing parents whose care and love for their deceased children went beyond what we would expect. For example, Lucien Turner (2001 [1894]:29), describing the Inuit around Hudson Bay, claimed parents, when moving to another site, would sometimes take their child's corpse with them if it was not too badly decomposed. Any tendency to curate the remains of children, no matter how casual, could help explain the presence of child and infant skulls in burials.

Finally, a pattern can be seen in the skeletal orientation in cairn burials. Previously I have shown that a distinct north to east and south to west distribution is associated with beliefs in cosmology and the afterlife (Crass 1998, 2000). The Inuit traditionally have two afterlife realms, one in the sky and one under the sea or land. Unlike our heaven and hell, both of these realms are viewed in a positive manner. The destination of a soul to any one sphere is associated with how one died. People who die a violent death, such as victims of murder, suicide, and accidents, go to the Land of the Day in the sky, or east. In contrast, those who die a nonviolent death go to the Land of the Sea, or west.

Of the infants and children with a known orientation, 20 of 38, or 52.6 percent, were placed with their heads oriented from north to east. Although 44.7 percent of the adults were also oriented in this direction, 58.2 percent of the identified male adults were aligned with this orientation. The percentage of infants and children is very similar to that of adult males, the group most likely to die a violent death from causes such as accident, murder, or warfare. Interestingly, death in childbirth is also seen as a violent death, and 37.3 percent of the known females were found oriented from north to east.

Conversely, 10 of 38 infants and children (26.3%) were placed with their heads oriented from south to west, supposedly indicating a nonviolent death. Although 28.6% of the adults were oriented in this direction, for the adults whose sex is known, 36.4% were female and only 16.5% were male.

CONCLUSION

I have shown that, traditionally, child and infant burials vary in several aspects from adult burials among the Inuit. Infants and children were not always buried in the same manner or in the same places as adults. Infants and children were usually buried either alone or with adults of either sex, rather than with other infants and children. This supports the claim of ethnographers that when one parent died, small children and infants were often killed and buried with the parent rather than slowly starving to death.

The souls of these strangled individuals, who definitely died a violent death, would then go to the Land of the Day in the east. The analysis of head orientation in cairns supports a fairly high incidence of violent death, with 52.6 percent of infants and children oriented between north and east.

A significant number of infants, but not children, were found in burial types other than graves and cairns. The most common types were fissures and middens, which may represent quick and easy disposal methods.

When burial goods were examined, little significant difference was found between adult and infant and child burials. The main exception was the tool category, with adults having tools more often than infants and children in either graves or cairns, although the significance is much greater in graves. Although the numbers were small, pendants and miniature items were found more often with infants and children than with adults.

Although no difference was found among individuals in graves with goods and those without, adults in cairns had a much higher probability of having goods than children or infants. From the ethnographic record, however, we know items in cairns were often removed, exchanged, and replaced, which could easily mask what was originally deposited in the cairns. Still, one would not expect infants' and children's cairns to be preyed upon more often than those of adults.

The overall number of goods found with adults and infants and children appears fairly evenly distributed, with cairn burials having individuals with many goods. A trend for proportionally more adults to have a greater number of goods than infants and children was indicated in graves.

One of the oddest finds is that infant and child remains consisting only of their skulls were found significantly more often than adult remains of only skulls in graves. Although taphonomy may be partly responsible, some form of casual curation may also be the cause. More research needs to be done in this area.

I hope I have shown that Inuit infants and children are not invisible people. Although they resemble adults in many aspects of burial, enough differences exist that their presence should be noted. Our next problem is understanding what these difference may tell us.

ACKNOWLEDGMENTS

The research on which this chapter is based was made possible through a Dissertation Improvement Grant from the National Science Foundation,

Department of Polar Programs; a Full Fulbright Grant to Denmark; and the generous financial and editorial support of my husband, Paul R. Holzman. An earlier version of this chapter was presented at the 6th Gender and Archaeology Conference, Northern Arizona University, October 6–8, 2000.

9

PUZZLING OUT GENDER-SPECIFIC "SIDES" TO A PREHISTORIC HOUSE IN BARROW, ALASKA

Gregory A. Reinhardt

MOUND 44'S DISCOVERY AND SIGNIFICANCE

In 1982 a few Barrow townspeople inadvertently dug into a set of frozen bodies, which had been crushed to death 400–500 years earlier when their semisubterranean house caved in on them. That distinctive discovery caused a brief stir in local and national news, led to a symposium at the 1983 Alaska Anthropological Association annual meeting, and resulted in an entire issue of *Arctic Anthropology* (1984) dedicated to scientific studies of the corpses and their archaeological setting. The next notable publication about Mound 44 was an article in *National Geographic* (Dekin 1987). Three years later, having been the 1982 archaeological crew chief at Mound 44, I described its architectural elements and detailed all artifactual contents unearthed there that season (Reinhardt and Dekin 1990). Other authors presented data from Mound 44's 1983 excavation season in the same set of reports (Hall 1990).

What made Mound 44 such an appealing find was its unusual preservation history. Normally, in ethnographic times (and presumably prehistoric as well) the Inupiat people of Utqiagvik abandoned their houses in summer, in large part because the subterranean tunnel connecting the house to the outside world would fill with water thawed from winter's snow and frozen soil. After the tunnel water froze, by late September, the tunnel ice could be dug out with picks and mattocks (Murdoch 1988

[1892]:76). The occupants took most things with them when they left for the summer, especially if they chose not to return in the fall. Still, most prehistoric and contact-era Inupiat homes that archaeologists excavate contain artifacts, but not many.

Mound 44 differs, however, because this is not a case of "normal" abandonment (Cameron and Tomka 1993). Rather, the residents died inside their home, leaving scattered about them virtually all the artifacts they kept in the house plus the occupational debris they generated. Exemplifying archaeology in its most popular state, journalistic allusions to a "snapshot in time" larded the first tantalizing news reports about Mound 44, and most archaeologists would agree this was a veritable freeze-frame of daily life in a prehistoric Eskimo house. Besides illustrating the architectural remains, we mapped and point provenienced over 300 artifacts and dozens of discarded bones directly associated with the house interior in 1982. We also charted hundreds of other artifacts and waste items found buried in soil matrix beneath the house floor (indicating earlier occupation of the same house pit). In 1983 the Utqiagvik Archaeology Project extended its work to areas outside the house proper: the tunnel, the kitchen, a storage pit, and soils surrounding these house locations. This study considers only the 1982 data from the house interior, focus of the gender-space premise.

RELATING MOUND 44 TO OTHER STUDIES OF HOUSEHOLD AND GENDER

The importance of considering other household and gender studies, as applied to this one, should not be minimized. At the same time, because this work is principally descriptive and a reassessment of an earlier behavioral assertion, the thrust of discussion here is to examine select cases that have some bearing on Mound 44. I divide them into two kinds of relevance.

The first kind of study relates theoretically to processes affecting the archeological record of households. In their discourse on the formation of house-floor assemblages, Vincent LaMotta and Michael Schiffer (1999) posited three processual stages (Habitation, Abandonment, and Postabandonment) and divided each stage into two processes: accretion or depletion. Within the habitation stage, primary deposition (discarded or lost in situ) and provisional refuse deposition (removing refuse from one spot to a separate location) are accretion processes, whereas secondary refuse deposition (storage or caching instead of discarding) is a depletion process (LaMotta and Schiffer 1999:20–22).

Habitation pertains the most to archaeological circumstances surrounding the Mound 44 house. Raymond Newell (1984) dealt with both primary and secondary deposition. Abandonment does not really apply to Mound 44, but the postabandonment depletion process of scavenging probably occurred. Gregory Reinhardt and Albert Dekin (1990) described the secondary deposition and scavenging processes at Mound 44 in some detail, whereas Georgeanne Reynolds (n.d.) looked beyond toolkits at the spatial distribution of artifacts from Mound 44's house floor.

The second kind of study is specific to recent examples attempting to "discover" gender in archeological settings. In her excavations at a mid-nineteenth-century gold-mining town in Australia, Susan Lawrence (1999) sought to identify women through the various structures and artifacts found there. She was able to discriminate households exclusive to men from households occupied by both sexes (Lawrence 1999:138). In the same book Suzanne Spencer-Wood (1999:185–186) took to task longstanding "androcentric constructions of the unitary gender ideology and norms of a culture." Her wide-ranging documentary research reveals how changes in architecture and other reflections of material culture reflect communal shifts in the social structure of, and gender interaction within, mid-Victorian domestic life (Spencer-Wood 1999:185–186).

More challenged by a lack of historical documentation, but simultaneously influenced by discussions with local elders, Annette McFadyen Clark (1996) struggled to disclose female-male differences in behavior based on the household distributions of artifacts and ecofacts. She creatively analyzed a "composite plot" made up of material remains from three houses, projected onto one floor space, in hopes of determining whether the occupants were Koyukuk Athapaskan or Inupiat Eskimo. In the process, she concluded that the cultural remains found inside houses fit well with her interview results: gender-based activity areas within the idealized two-monogamous-family house conform to her composite plot of material remains (McFadyen Clark 1996:159, 199, 203, figs. 5-4, 5-11, 5-12).

RECONSIDERING THE GENDER-BASED "SIDES" PREMISE
THE PREMISE AS A "PROBLEM"

The longest article in *Arctic Anthropology*'s Mound 44 volume focused on the house's archaeological, human physical, and relative settings (Newell 1984). Unfortunately, the representation of artifact contents in the house (Newell 1984:fig. 14) and the corresponding breakdown as to "functional partitions" of those artifacts (Newell 1984:table 1) are not complete, internally consistent, or entirely correct. The distribution map (Newell 1984:fig. 14) shows a somewhat small assortment of artifacts (and no refuse) cast about the floor around a single corpse. Moreover, the accompanying data (Table 9.1), which list those objects in three columns (Men's Side, Women's Side, and Front of Iglu), were cited to further a hypothesis that "the gender-specific artifacts appeared to be clustered toward the western and eastern halves of the [house]" (Newell 1984:22). This excerpt from a single sentence—coupled with the map and tabulated list (Newell 1984:fig. 14, table 1)—constitutes the original gender-based "sides" premise. Nothing further accounts for either the entire floor-level artifact inventory or for tabulated discrepancies between the gender-based sides and the artifact types; and, importantly, none of those artifacts was actually linked to either sex (Newell 1984:fig. 14, table 1).

FLOOR DIMENSIONS AS ANOTHER "PROBLEM"

Perhaps the oddest thing to contemplate first in trying to compartmentalize the Mound 44 house into male and female areas is the space in question. From 1981 to 1983 the Utqiagvik Archaeology Project excavated four complete house floors in Barrow (all of which, like the Mound 44 floor, were rectangular). Their average dimensions were just over 3.1 x 2.2 m (about 10 x 7 ft) and an average floor area of around 6.9 m^2, or 70 ft^2 (Reinhardt and Dekin 1990:table 4-1). The Mound 44 floor was incomplete because floorboards at the sleeping platform end (farthest from the tunnel entrance, or *katak*, the ingress-egress floor hole) were decomposed, making its precise length unknown. Its minimum dimensions were 2.67 x 1.64 m (roughly 9 x 5 ft), however. Of greater interest than Mound 44's floor shape is its length relative to width. The length:width ratio of the four other Utqiagvik houses averages about 1:0.7, whereas the Mound 44 house floor, with its incomplete long dimension, must have been narrower, its ratio closer to 1:0.6.

In the early 1880s one house in Utqiagvik had thirteen regular residents (Murdoch 1892:75), but six corpses were crushed in the Mound 44 disaster (Reinhardt 1990, n.d.a). So before we even begin to contend with gender-based sides in this house, we must understand that we are considering the possibility for a very small floor area occupied by six people—close to the presumed prehistoric average household size of 6.4 persons around Barrow (Lee and Reinhardt n.d.:appendix 1). Perhaps the original gender-based "sides" premise envisioned bisecting the floor lengthwise when it posited discrete Women's and Men's Sides, or "functional partitions," to the Mound 44 house. Perhaps also the term *partition* connotes too discrete a division. In any case, the gender-based floor-halves idea must imagine the adults as having sexually segregated themselves into areas merely 0.82 m (2.7 ft) wide. To put this in perspective, if adults sat leaning against one long-axis wall with their legs extended (a common Eskimo pose) in this house, their feet would project many centimeters into the opposite gender's "partition." Still, that should not be an issue until we can confirm or refute the gender assertion by looking at the distribution of *all* artifacts, not just Newell's handpicked ones, from the house floor.

METHODS

CORRECTING FOR SELECTIVITY IN THE ORIGINAL DATA PRESENTATION

Our challenge in assessing the previously published data is that those objects (Newell 1984:fig. 14, table 1) were chosen nonrandomly and comprise only about half of the formal artifacts and about 20 percent of the full cultural assemblage related to the frozen bodies (Reinhardt and Dekin 1990). In hindsight, then, the original gender-based data presentation seems anecdotal. Toward reevaluating the gender hypothesis, Table 9.1 repeats the artifact inventory according to the previous sequence (Newell 1984:table 1). Table 9.2 then tries to clarify the earlier data by indicating which of those artifacts are (1) likely misidentified—for example, "whale bone ice pick," a harpoon part, should say "pick head," a digging tool; (2) not shown (Newell 1984:fig. 14) and possibly not present but listed (Table 9.1)—for example, "carving knife"; (3) shown (Newell 1984:fig. 14) but not listed (Table 9.1)—for example, "medial labret"; (4) probably not from the house at all—for example, "lamp supports," an identification lacking ethnographic precedent in this region but known elsewhere in Alaska (cf. Nelson 1983 [1899]:252, fig. 79); (5) incorrectly presented as having come from within the house—for example, "ivory ulu handle" came from soil outside the house—or incorrectly listed as having been found on the Women's Side—for example, "skin bag w/sewing equip."; and (6) from the Men's Side and the Women's Side—that is, those from the "Front of Iglu" column (Newell 1984:table 1). More important, Table 9.2 ascribes a gender role to those artifacts for which doing so seems ethnographically supportable.

REANALYZING THE ORIGINAL DATA

Using Table 9.2, we can statistically assess the strength of the original gender hypothesis. The issue at hand emerges from the "Gender" columns plus the "Side (Female/Male)" column relating to the undefined "Front of Iglu" (Newell 1984:table 1). Table 9.2 eliminates from analysis nearly half of the artifacts originally listed because I regard their typological identities as unclear, their gender ascriptions as uncertain, or

Table 9.1—Reproduction of table 1 from Newell (1984) "Artifact Inventories of Three Functional Partitions of the *Kataligaaq Iglu* [catastrophically abandoned house] near Mound 44"

Men's Side	Women's Side	Front of Iglu
Chert arrow point	Bird blunt	Chert flake
Slate end blade	Antler arrow point	Baleen comb
Bird blunt	Whale bone adze head with slate blade	Ivory comb
Bag of 6 bone & 1 chert arrow points	Boots	Wooden buckets
Whale bone ice pick	Boot liners	Wooden platter or dish
Adz handles	Boot soles	Ceramic pot
Bag of bolas weights, tooth ornaments, worked bone, & ivory	Skin bags	Baleen bucket
Snow goggles	Skin bag with ivory handle	Wooden plank
Block plane scraper	Skin bag with sewing equip.	Walrus hide mat
Chert endscraper	Needle case and holder	Sewn gut, from skylight
Wooden shaft	Thimble holder/belt hook	
Carving knife	Bird-skin bag	
Chert drill bit	Gut bag	
Chert scraper	Baleen cup with human hair	
Chert flakes	Fish box	
Men's trousers w/attached boots	Ivory *ulu* handle	
Hide fragments	Child's parka	
	Lamp supports	
	Slate *ulu* blade	
	Slate blade	
	Grooved stone abrader	
	Hide scraper	
	Sewn hide fragments	
	Chert flake	

both. For the remainder, totals at the bottom of Table 9.2, when combined according to house side, break down as seen in Graph 9.1.

Fisher's test (Langley 1971:292–297) is akin to the chi-squared test except that it is restricted to two classes, each with two qualities, and it deals with a total number of observations (N) between 8 and 50. Categorized artifacts appear in one of four possible cells: Women's-Side Female Objects, Women's-Side Male Objects, Men's-Side Female Objects, Men's-Side Male Objects. The original gender premise should show high quantities clustering in the upper left and lower right cells. Instead, when applied to the data here, Fisher's test yields a probability much larger than 5 percent (Graph 9.1), meaning the overall difference in numbers

Graph 9.1			Graph 9.2		
Object's Gender Ascription	*House Side*		*Object's Gender Ascription*	*House Side*	
	Women's	Men's		Women's	Men's
Female	8	4	Female	8	4
Male	9	9	Male	9	40

among the four cells is not statistically meaningful. Therefore the hypothesis (that there are demonstrable Men's and Women's Sides, based on my added gender ascriptions for artifacts found on those sides) is not affirmed by the original data (from Newell 1984). It may be that the insignificant results are simply the outcome of "sample size rather than lack of a trend" (Peter Whitridge, personal communication 2000), but that does not belie the fact that no statistical test accompanied the original gender premise.

The preceding test masks a quantification problem because it counts two packets on the men's side of the floor as one item each. One packet was a "[bundle] of . . . arrowpoints," which held seven items (Table 9.2), and the other was a "bag of bola weights [and similar items]," which contained twenty-four pieces (Reinhardt and Dekin 1990:fig. 4-20). These packets (Fig. 9.1) may have inspired the gender-based house-sides notion (Newell 1984:fig. 14). Certainly, their appearance (lying together next to the men's-side wall), as well as their occurrence twice in his text (Newell 1984:fig. 14, 4 and 5, fig. 22), makes this guess tempting. For reasons detailed later, I prefer the minimalist approach—first because the packets do not represent male activity so much as storage of male objects, and second because including them produces an entirely different effect, as seen in Graph 9.2.

Note the explosion in "male" artifacts on the men's side and the contrasting paucity of "female" artifacts (Graph 9.2), which strongly skews the previous artifact distribution (Graph 9.1). Following this approach, one could posit an incidental female presence in the house—despite its having contained at least two adult female corpses (Zimmerman and Aufderheide 1984:53). An appropriate statistic to use here is Yates's chi-squared test (Langley 1971:285–287), suitable for 2 x 2 contingency tables (four cells in all) when N is more than 50 and there are matched observations on sets of things that have two qualities. In this case the test yields a very high probability: 0.2 percent. Statistically, the "tentative assumption of no significant difference or association [between gender-linked artifact and house side] cannot be denied on the evidence presented"

Table 9.2— Additions and corrections to table 1 from Newell (1984) "Artifact Inventories of Three Functional Partitions of the [Mound 44 House]"

Men's Side	Artifact Gender	Women's Side	Artifact Gender	Front of Iglu (side not specified)	Men's/Women's Side	Artifact Gender
Chert arrow point	M	Bird blunt	M	Chert flake	M	?
Slate end blade	M	Antler arrow point	M	Baleen comb	M	?
Bird blunt	M	Whale bone adz head w/[jade] blade	M	Ivory comb	M	?
[Bundle] of 6 [antler] & 1 chert arrow points	M	Boots	?	6 wooden [tubs & 1 dish]	M4; W2 & 1	?
Whale bone [pick head]	M	Boot liners	M	Wooden platter or dish	?	?
Adz handles	?	Boot soles [& tops]	?	Ceramic pot	W	F
Bag of bolas weights, tooth ornaments, worked bone, & ivory	M	Skin bags	F	Baleen bucket	?	?
Snow goggles	?	Skin bag w/ivory handle	M	Wooden [slat?]	W	?
Block plane scraper	?	Skin bag w/sewing equip. **MS	F	Walrus hide mat		
Chert endscraper	F	Needle case & thimble holder	F	Sewn gut, from skylight	?	?
Wooden shaft	?	Thimble holder	F	*Wood endscraper handle	M	F
Carving knife	?	Bird-skin bag	?			
Chert drill bit	M	Gut bag	?			
Chert scraper	F	Baleen cup w/human hair	?			
Chert flakes	?	Fish[-shaped] box **MS	F			

Item		Item	
Men's trousers w/ attached boots	M?	Ivory *ulu* handle **O	F
Hide fragments	?	Child's parka	?
Hide scraper handle	F	*Lamp supports*	?
Flaker [handle]	M	Slate *ulu* blade **O	F
*2 polar bear hide mittens	?	Slate blade	?
Small ivory point	?	Grooved stone abrader	M
		Hide scraper	M
		Sewn hide fragments	?
		Chert flake	?
		*Float nozzle **O	M
		*Medial labret	M
		*Polar bear hide mitten	?
		*Ivory seal effigy	?
		*Split polar bear tooth **O	?
		*Walrus tooth bolas weight **O	M?

	Men's side	Women's side
TOTALS	3F,9M	7F,9M

Men's Side 1F,0M
Women's Side 1F,0M

[Brackets] = corrections to artifacts misidentified in Newell 1984:fig. 14 and table 1
Italics = items listed in Newell 1984:table 1 but not shown in Newell 1984:fig. 14, or probably misidentified, or apparently never in the house
* = items shown in Newell 1984:fig. 14 but not listed in Newell 1984:table 1
** = items shown in Newell 1984:fig. 14 but with misattributed locations in Newell 1984:table 1 [**MS = technically, shown and found on men's side based on mathematical bisection of floor length; *O = actually found outside house, in matrix unrelated to the house floor]

(Langley 1971:287). In lay terms the test confirms a heavily male-artifact–dominated men's side.

Whether we consider the small original sample size (Table 9.1) or my revision of those data (Table 9.2), either result still begs the question, can we really discern a men's side and a women's side to this house, based on all the artifacts known? If the answer is affirmative, using a larger sample of artifacts, it forces us to wonder something else. What, if anything, does this signify about gender-based proxemics—or use and perception of space—at Mound 44?

REEXAMINING SEX-BASED "SIDES" AT MOUND 44

"SEXING" THE ARTIFACTS

Testing the notion of discrete men's and women's sides at Mound 44 is simple enough as a four-step operation. One, divide the house floor lengthwise. Two, designate all artifacts, according to their recorded locations, as having been found on either the so-called women's or men's side of the house floor. Three, ascribe gender to the artifacts. Four, examine the results statistically, in this case using Yates's chi-squared test. The first two steps are easy because I created the grid system used at Mound 44 in 1982, mapped most artifacts from the house floor (as well as above and below it), and kept copies of those maps.

The difficulties with this study, of course, lie in step three. To begin with, specifying one's theoretical assumptions is paramount. The original gender premise essentially forces me to suppose (as Newell [1984] undoubtedly did) "that the activity for which a tool was designed was carried out on the very spot where the tool was found . . . [and] that prehistoric people [from Mound 44] left everything just where they used it" (Flannery 1986:322). Thus my primary supposition is that, all things being equal, most artifacts' recorded locations reflect essentially where they were when the house collapsed and therefore essentially their position of final antemortem use, storage, and disposal. This is essentially a presumption of "Pompeii effect" (see Binford 1981; Schiffer 1983) or "the Pompeii premise" (Flannery 1986:322), but Mound 44 surely satisfies "Pompeii" conditions. Furthermore, "For archaeologists interested in reconstructing social, economic, or demographic characteristics of households, an assemblage comprised mostly of objects both used in a house and deposited in that same house potentially provides the strongest line of evidence [for household activities]" (LaMotta and Schiffer 1999:21).

Another assumption is that, although many objects came from the general house area, only convincingly floor-related ones pertain to this study (Reinhardt and Dekin 1990:50). Archaeological remains from the tunnel, kitchen, and storage spaces—all outside the house proper—are beyond the scope of this study, as are ones buried in house-subfloor soil. Yet another operating idea, resulting in part from the difficulty in going back and forth between field specimen numbers and final catalog numbers (explained later), is that same-type objects (e.g., a set of bola weights or fishhooks) from a single location (e.g., from bundles, bags, a box, and the small caches) should count as only one item because they all came from a precisely defined spot. Similarly, if I excavated my own house, I would not count each button from a jar of them or every piece from a silverware set to use in a spatial distribution analysis, but I *might* count the different kinds of items in a kitchen drawer of mixed utensils.

The worst part of step three is correlating genders with particular artifacts. Not wanting to turn this study into a pan-Arctic ethnological discussion (e.g., Giffen 1930) about gender-dominated or gender-exclusive use for each thing found at Mound 44, I lean toward conservative assignations. In refraining from forcing gender assumptions onto artifact types, however, I have to relegate fully two-thirds of the Mound 44 objects to a gender-unassigned category. Pieces in Table 9.3 that I consider gender-uncertain include clothing and footwear, which might be "sexed" for the adult items (but I lack that information); wood- and baleen-walled vessels; cut leather, fur, and gut swatches; thongs and cords of varying thicknesses and lengths; worked and unworked animal bones and teeth; nondescript flakes and blade fragments, both chert and slate; and rod-shaped whetstones.

I systematically left out all unworked bones unless they were in cache-type locations, whereas animal teeth tended to have uses as charms, amulets, and fishing lures, making them more worth considering but still left as gender uncertain. Table 9.3 artifacts that I present as more related to female-dominated tasks include drying-rack parts; small bags (of gut and bird—and squirrel—skin) and a possible bag handle; *ulu* parts (women's slate knife blades and handles); jig-fishing items (lures and hooks, sinker parts, fish-shaped box, baleen line, leister barbs or blubber hooks); sewing items (needle case, bag); composite scraper parts (endblades, handles); scrapers of bone (modified scapulae and metapodials); a possible "crane" for hanging things (Newell's "lamp support" [1984:fig. 14, 56]); and a ceramic cooking pot. Artifacts in Table 9.3 that I associate more with male-dominated tasks include a different set of objects: harpoon and dart parts (possible dart point, endblades, harpoon head preform, dart shaft, ice pick, float nozzles, finger rest, foreshaft, socket piece); sandstone whetstones; adzes (heads, handle preform);

Table 9.3—Gender-ascribed and gender-sided inventory of floor-related Mound 44 artifacts

FS #	Object(s)	House Side	Artifact Gender	FS #	Object(s)	House Side	Artifact Gender
—	end blade, slate	M	M	228	"pyrite lump"	W	?
24	animal-head cane (see FS107)	W	?	229	*ulu* blade, slate	W	F
				230	human effigy, ivory	W	?
25	worked wood	W	?	231	blade frag., slate	W	?
30	drying rack slat	W	F	232	sandstone frags.	W	?
32	polar bear maxilla frag.	M	?	233	fishing sinker top piece, ivory	W	F
100	hide strip, walrus?	W	?				
101	drying rack slat, wood	W	F	235	"shaped & drilled wood"	W	?
102	dart shaft, wood	M	M	236	"shaped wood"	W	?
103	drying rack slat, wood	W	F	237	sandstone	W	?
104	vessel, baleen rim	W	?	238	chert flake	M	?
105	vessel, wood rim (see FS#202)	W	?	239	chert biface, black	M	M
				240	"notched wood"	M	?
106	leather frag.	W	?	241	"shaped wood"	M	?
107	animal-head cane (see FS#24)	—	—	242	bag, leather (see FS#590)	M	F
				243	fish-shaped box, wood	M	F
108	drying rack slat, wood	W	F	245	worked & drilled wood	W	?
200	vessel, wood	W	?	247	"mukluk, etc."	W	?
201	vessel, wood	W	?	248	"gut, mukluk, etc."	W	?
202	vessel, wood (see FS#105)	—	—	249	2 caribou teeth (fishing lures)	M	F
203	large hide frag., walrus	W	?				
204	flake, red chert	W	?	250	marcasite sinker, worked	W	F
205	mukluk	W	?	251	arrowhead, antler	W	M
206	mukluk	W	?	252	vessel, wood	M	?
207	whetstone, sandstone	W	M?	253	"heavy wood shaft"	M	?
208	drying rack slat, wood	W	F	254	2 ground slate frags.	W	?
209	vessel, baleen	W	?	255	"flake scraper"	W	F
210	adz head w/jade blade	W	M	256	flake, green	W	?
211	pendant, tooth (toy bola wt?)	W	?	257	chert flake, large gray	W	?
				263	bundle of arrow points	M	M
212	bag, gut	W	F?	265	needle case, bone	W	F
213	bag, bird skin	W	F?	266	labret, medial, stone	W	M
214	mitten, fur	W	?	267	charm (bone in leather)	W	?
215	hair	W	?	268	charm (feathers in leather)	W	?
216	mukluk liner	W	?	269	scraper end blade, chert	W	F
217	*ulu* blade, slate	W	F	270	scraper handle, wood	M	F
218	bird blunt	?	M	271	scraper end blade, chert	W	F
219	seal skin	W	?	272	sewn gut	W	?
220	*ulu* blade	?	F	273	boot sole creaser, ivory	W	F
221	bag/bucket handle?, ivory	W	F?	274	mukluk sole	W	?
				275	fox canine	M	?
223	fish lures, antler	M	F	276	bag of bola weights, etc.	M	M
224	fish-shape box lid, wood	M	F	277	leather frag.	M	?
225	mukluk	W	?	278	blade frag., purple slate	W	?
226	mukluk liner & sole	W	?	279	2 sandstone frags.	W	?

continued on next page

Table 9.3—continued

FS #	Object(s)	House Side	Artifact Gender
280	bola weight, walrus tooth	W	M
281	cut hide frag., walrus	W	?
282	*ulu* blade, black slate & tar wad	W	F
283	bird blunt, ivory	W	M
284	grooved white stone	W	?
285	face effigy from bola wt., ivory	W	?
286	bola weight, ivory	W	M
287	bola weight, ivory	W	M
290	bola preform, whale bone	W	M
291	worked bear canine	W	?
292	fishing sinker top piece	W	F
293	vessel, wood	W	?
295	chert flake	W	?
297	wood (worked?)	W	?
298	worked walrus tooth	W	?
299	hide frag.	W	?
300	sandstone	W	?
301	thongs	W	?
302	flake (chert?)	M	?
303	amber	M	?
304	drilled ivory cylinder	M	?
305	cut leather	M	?
306	gut frag.	M	?
307	gut frag.	W	?
309	hair, human	M	?
310	flake (chert?)	W	?
311	sandstone	W	?
312	sinker, brown whale bone	W	F
313	fishing sinker, ivory, marcasite	W	F
314	fishing sinker, ivory, marcasite	W	F
315	2 flakes, chert	W	?
316	end blade made into knife, slate	W	M
317	fish line leader, baleen	W	F
319	tar-sand frags.	W	?
320	leather thong & 5 cut frags.	W	?
322	wood rod	M	?
323	wood rod	M	?
324	worked & pegged wood	M	?
325	braided sinew	M	?

FS #	Object(s)	House Side	Artifact Gender
327	*ulu* frag., black slate	W	F
328	slate frag., purple	M	?
329	thong w/loop	M	?
330	vessel, wood	M	?
331	pointed stick	M	?
335	worked & charred wood frag.	M	?
336	mitten, polar bear fur	M	?
337	steatite frag.	M	?
338	sandstone frag.	M	?
339	steatite frag.	M	?
340	steatite frag.	M	?
341	sandstone frags., 4	M	?
342	pick head, broken, bone	M	M
343	arrow point, gray	M	M
345	whetstone, orange chert rod	M	?
346	worked bird bone	M	?
347	esophagus, bird	M	?
349	tooth, polar bear	M	?
350	bound bone & wood	M	?
351	cut seal leather	M	?
352	bola weight	W	M
353	vessel, baleen	W	?
354	vessel, wood	W	?
355	sinker, brown concretion	M	?
356	thong, knotted	M	?
357	leather, frags., cut, 2	M	?
358	slate frag., purple	M	?
359	leather strips, 2	M	?
360	hair mat	M	?
361	seal skin, cut	M	?
362	bird skin, cut	M	?
363	seal skin, cut	M	?
364	caribou skin	M	?
365	thong, single loop	M	?
366	thong	M	?
367	seal skin, cut	M	?
368	sandstone frags., 8	M	?
369	caribou skin frag.	M	?
370	fur mass	M	?
371	caribou fur	M	?
372	bird blunt	M	M
373	wood frag., worked & pegged	M	?

continued on next page

Table 9.3—*continued*

FS #	Object(s)	House Side	Artifact Gender
375	hair comb, baleen	M	?
376	hair comb, ivory	M	?
377	scapula scraper, caribou	M	F?
384	gut frag.	M	?
387	teeth, 1 dog & 1(?)	M	?
388	bone frag.	M	?
389	fat scraper charm, drilled ivory	M	?
391	sinew	M	?
392	fur strip	M	?
393	inserted bone	M	?
394	flake, gray chert	W	?
396	bola weight, ivory	W	M
397	tooth, seal canine	W	?
398	scraper, metapodial, caribou	W	F
399	float nozzle, ivory	W	M
400	whetstone, sandstone	W	M
401	gauged drill, bone	W	M
402	bola weight, walrus tooth	W	M
403	harpoon ice pick, antler	M	M
404	"worked bone/antler"	M	?
465	worked whale bone	M	?
466	flaker handle, ivory	M	M
467	pyrite concretion frag.	W	M
468	flake, gray chert	W	?
469	harpoon finger rest, ivory	W	M
470	wood rod	M	?
471	sled shoe, whale bone	M	?
472	gut	W	?
474	mukluk frag.	M	?
475	chert, drilled?	W	?
476	harpoon ice pick, antler	M	M
477	wood, cut square	M	?
478	foreshaft, antler	M	M
479	harpoon socket piece	W	M
480	harpoon ice pick, antler	M	M
494	bola weight	M	M
495	whale epiphysis	M	?
496	*ulu* handle, antler	M	F
497	baleen strip	M	?
498	leather frag.	M	?
499	blade frag., slate	M	?
500	wood shaft, cut frag.	M	?
501	leather, cut square	M	?
502	biface, chert	M	M
503	bola weight, seal calcaneus	M	M
504	leather, cut rectangle	M	?
505	leather, cut triangle	M	?
506	tooth, human, extracted	M	?
507	bag, squirrel skin	W	F
509	baleen strips	M	?
510	gut strip	M	?
511	bird skin frag.	M	?
512	bola weight, walrus tooth	M	M
513	flaker, antler	M	M
514	*ulu* blade, slate	M	F
515	bag, seal flipper	W	?
516	"crane"/blubber dripper, wood	W	F?
517	bead, red stone	M	?
518	boot upper, seal skin	M	?
519	scraper end blade, chert	M	F
520	blade, purple slate	M	M
521	boot lower, seal skin	M	?
523	leather, cut	M	?
524	scraper, caribou scapula	M	F
525	hide, cut	M	?
526	fur, bear	W	?
527	leather frag.	W	?
528	knife blade, purple slate	M	M
529	hide, cut	M	?
530	thongs, 2	M	?
531	fur, caribou	M	?
532	thong	M	?
533	whetstone frag., sandstone	M	?
534	leather, cut triangle	M	?
535	hide, cut	M	?
536	leather, rectangle	M	?
537	bone, caribou thoracic vertebra	M	?
538	drilled & incised frag., ivory	M	?
539	baleen strip	M	?
540	fur, bear	M	?
541	mukluk & legging	M	?
542	bird quills wrapped in wings	W	?
543	seal skin frag.	W	?

continued on next page

Table 9.3—continued

FS #	Object(s)	House Side	Artifact Gender	FS #	Object(s)	House Side	Artifact Gender
544	net, leather	W	?	595	slate frag.	M	?
545	baleen strip, broken	W	?	777	drill bit, chert	W	M
546	ladle charm, drilled ivory	W	?	779	tooth, walrus	M	?
547	netting needle, ivory	W	M	780	bola weight, ivory	M	M
548	thongs & cut leather	M	?	781	harpoon head preform	M	M
549	ice pick, antler	M	M	782	scraper, caribou scapula	M	F
550	gut frag.	W	?	783	leather frag., cut	M	?
551	caribou skin frag.	M	?	784	arrowhead, barbless antler	M	M
552	seal skin frag.	M	?	785	flake, used chert	M	?
553	buckle?, incised ivory	M	?	786	arrowhead, antler	M	M
554	blade, gray slate	M	M	787	slate frag., ground	M	?
555	bag, seal flipper	M	?	788	leather frag., cut	M	?
556	mukluk sole	M	?	790	arrowhead, antler or bone	M	M
557	seal skin frag.	W	?	791	labret preform	M	M
558	leather frag., sewn	W	?	792	flake, used gray chert	M	?
559	leather frag., cut, w/holes	W	?	793	slate frag.	M	?
560	arrowhead preform, antler	W	M	794	fur, bear	M	?
561	fur, bear	W	?	795	adz head, whale bone	M	M
562	seal skin frag.	W	?	796	arrowhead, antler	M	M
563	slate frag.	M	?	797	bird skin frag.	W	?
564	bola, 3-strand (toy?)	M	M	798	adz handle preform frag.	W	M
565	net float eyelet, ivory	M	M	799	teeth, 2 walrus, 1 bear incisor	W	?
566	slate, drilled frag	W	?	800	flakes, gray chert, 2	W	?
567	blade frag., purple slate	W	?	801	bone frag., caribou vertebra	W	?
568	slate frag., gray	W	?	802	worked rectangle, bone/antler	W	?
569	chert frags., orange, 2	W	?	803	leather strip	W	?
570	thong	W	?	804	drying rack slat, wood	W	F
571	seal skin strips, knotted	W	?	805	fishhook shanks, ivory	M	F
572	seal skin, cut triangle	W	?	806	flake, used gray chert	M	?
574	flake, gray chert	W	?	807	*ulu* frag., purple slate	M	F
575	arrow point, gray chert	W	M	811	blade frag., purple slate	M	?
576	leather frag., sewn	W	?	812	bola weight, whale bone	M	M
577	flake, gray chert	W	?	813	fur, bear	M	?
578	wood frags., fish-shaped box	W	?	814	peg, wood	M	?
579	flake, chert	W	?	817	vessel, wood	M	?
580	bag, bird skin?	W	F	818	flake, gray chert	M	?
581	bag, leather	W	F?	819	bag, bird foot	M	F
582	seal effigy, ivory	W	?	825	pick/mattock handle, wood	M	M
584	fishhook shank?	M	F	826	sandstone slab, large	M	M?
585	feather, fletching	W	?	827	pyrite concretion	M	M
589A	parka	W	?	832	pot, ceramic	W	F
589B	parka, child's	W	?				
590	bag, leather (see FS#242)	—	—				
593	tooth, fox canine	W?	?				
594	needle case, bone	W	F				

continued on next page

Table 9.3—continued

FS #	Object(s)	House Side	Artifact Gender	FS #	Object(s)	House Side	Artifact Gender
834	wood, burned	M	?	993	mattock head, whale bone	M	M
835	gut frag.	M	?				
836	pegged wood	M	?	1003	shaft frag., sharpened	M	?
839	cobble	M	?	1006	drill frag., gray chert	W	M
907	bola preform	M	M	1007	flakes, chert, 2	W	?
908	bola weights, whale bone, 5	M	M	1011	leister barb/blubber hook, ivory	W	F?
909	leister barb/blubber hook, ivory	M	F?	1013	float nozzle	W	M
				1014	shaft frag., wood	W	?
910	arrow shaft, wood, toy?	M	?	1015	leister barb/blubber hook, ivory	W	F?
911	pendant, green stone	M	?				
912	rod frag., wood	M	?	1016	whetstone frag., sandstone	W	?
913	whetstone frag., sandstone	M	?				
969	arrow point, chert—not on map	W	M	1017	flake, used gray chert	W	?
				1018	flake, used gray chert	W	?
983	harpoon head, ivory, toy?	M	?	1019	pegs, wood, 2	W	?
984	shaft frag., wood	M	?	1020	arrow point, gray chert	W	M
985	peg, wood	M	?	1021	flake, gray chert	W	?
986	dart point?	M	M	1038	worked whale bone	M	?
988	frag., ivory	M	?	1043	flake, gray chert	W	?
990	stone, white iridescent	M	?	1090	thong, knotted	M	?
991	bola weight, walrus	M	?	1092	½ jaw, squirrel, sinew wrapped	W	?
992	bird blunt blank?, whale bone	M	?				

FS#: field specimen number (distinct from Utqiagvik Archaeology Project catalog number)
House Side: M = Men's Side, W = Women's Side, — = listed elsewhere, ? = uncertain excavation location
Artifact Gender: M = presumed male-dominated task, F = presumed female-dominated task, ? = gender-uncertain task

arrow blunts (bird and small-game hunting); the hunting bundle (birdskin-wrapped antler arrowheads and chert arrowpoints); other arrow heads and arrow points; the bag of "men's" items (bola weights, preforms, scrap ivory and antler, and similar objects); a medial labret and preform; bola weights and toy bola (bird hunting); men's slate knives (not *ulus*); drilling items (gauged drill, chert drill bit); pyrite concretions (fire making); a flaker handle ("flint knapping"); netting items (needle, float eyelet); and digging items (pick handle, pick head, mattock head).

FLOOR SIDING THE ARTIFACTS

The process of siding and assigning gender to Mound 44's artifacts was easier said than done because of the way the Utqiagvik reports were published. Although I wrote an annotated catalog of all artifacts (Reinhardt and Dekin 1990), the editors deleted all catalog numbers from my text, arguing that the numbers would be captioned in the Utqiagvik reports' photo-plates. As a result, problems abounded. First, not all items got photographed, so their numbers cannot be culled from the text. Second, there was no system for correlating lab-assigned catalog numbers with the field specimen numbers previously assigned to the items upon excavation. Third, Mound 44 contained so many artifacts and architectural timbers, many of which were large enough to sketch, that I produced eleven different field maps to indicate all their locations (i.e., eleven maps on which to find specific field-numbered artifacts). Fourth, some objects were never mapped or even reported as to general location.

To produce artifact distribution maps for this study, I began by finding each field specimen number on one of the field maps and then reading the original field log's description of that artifact to discover its identity. (Map sketches made some identifications self-evident, fortunately.) If the artifact type was still not clear, I looked it up in the Utqiagvik report (Reinhardt and Dekin 1990), hoping to learn more. If I found its description, I usually knew what the object was; if not, I had to look up its catalog number by going through the report's photo-plate captions appendix. Then, to confirm that the numbers matched, I had to cross-reference that catalog number against several computer printouts (generated in 1983) that list Mound 44 artifacts sequentially by field specimen number. If they did not match I had to read other sections of my text, looking again for the right description and, I hoped, for a matching catalog number. Once I had positively identified an item (by field specimen number), I could then map it. If I felt I could ascribe gender-prevalent use to the artifact, I marked it on either the Gender-Female or Gender-Male map; otherwise I placed it on the Gender-Uncertain map (Figs. 9.2–9.4).

USING ADDITIONAL DATA TO TEST THE GENDER-BASED "SIDES" PREMISE

The data set employed here consists of 365 mapped artifacts and other cultural debris (or sets of these things) associated with the terminal occupation of Mound 44 (Table 9.3). I ascribe 119 of these, in roughly equal numbers, to tasks related to one sex or the other. Three distribution maps present the results. Figure 9.2 (Gender-Uncertain artifacts)

Figure 9.1 The "male" artifact packets: several arrow points wrapped in birdskin, center, and bola weights and other items in a bag, right, partly covered with debris; a floorboard is visible under the arrow points, the "Men's Side" wall sill is at the top (left to right), and an upright timber between floorboards is at the left (for orientation, see Fig. 9.4).

shows 246 items I could not ascribe to female- or male-oriented gender roles; it indicates a rather broad distribution of all sorts of objects spread across both sides of the house floor. Figure 9.3 (Gender-Female artifacts) bears 51 items that probably relate to primarily women's tasks; it illustrates relatively few pieces, which tend to occur about the center of the floor and concentrate on the women's side. Figure 9.4 (Gender-Male artifacts) displays 68 items I associate with men's tasks; it presents slightly more "male" objects, which assume something of a U-shaped pattern. The "male" majority also occurs fairly differentially toward the back of the house (away from the *katak*) and somewhat more toward the men's side (Fig. 9.4), compared with the greater centralization of "female" objects. Graph 9.3 shows the distribution of gender-ascribed artifacts, according to their appearance on the men's or women's side of the house floor.

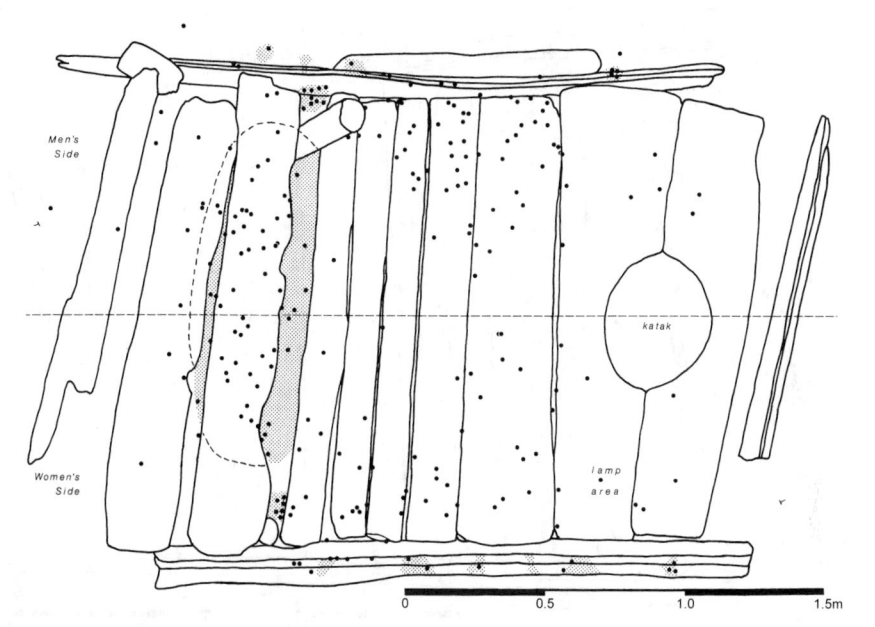

Figure 9.2 Gender-uncertain objects; shaded areas = caches (large subfloor cache also shown in dashed lines)

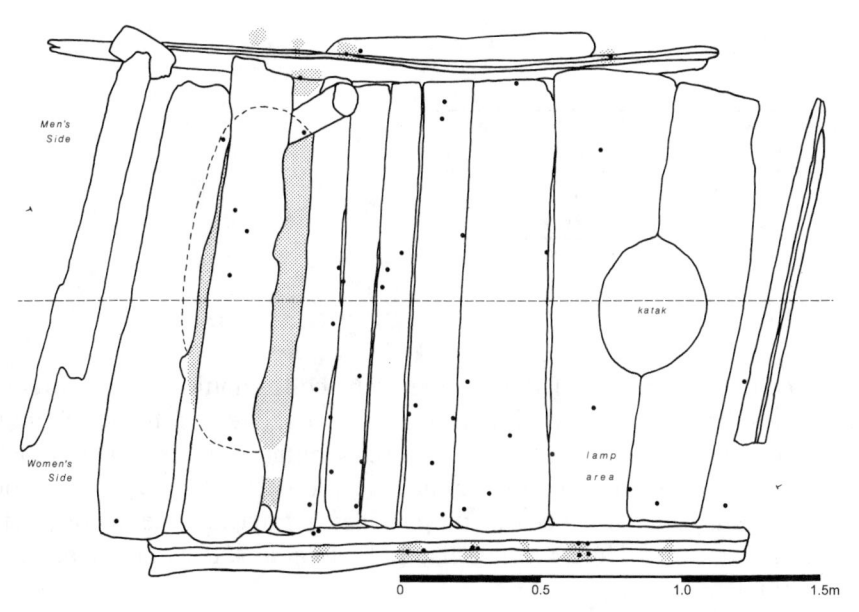

Figure 9.3 Gender-female objects; shaded areas = caches (large subfloor cache also shown in dashed lines)

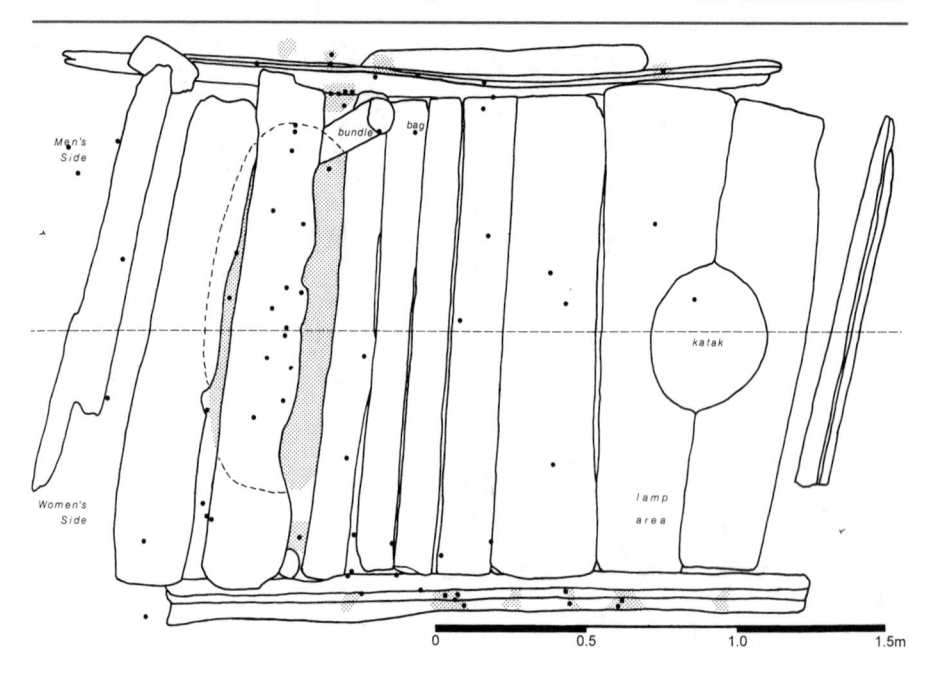

Figure 9.4 Gender-male objects; shaded areas = caches (large subfloor cache also shown in dashed lines)

Graph 9.3

Object's Gender Ascription	House Side Women's	Men's
Female	34	17
Male	28	40

Ideally, the upper left and lower right cells should contain higher quantities than those shown, but Yates's chi-squared test of the distribution data from Figures 9.3 and 9.4 still expresses significant difference: $P = 5\%$. Still, because the arrow-point bundle and the bag of bola weights (and similar items) add 31 pieces to the total, it is important to account for this larger number distribution (raising the total to 150 artifacts), as seen in Graph 9.4.

In this case the preponderance of male artifacts on the men's side far outstrips the predominance of female artifacts on the women's side,

Graph 9.4

Object's Gender Ascription	House Side	
	Women's	Men's
Female	34	17
Male	28	71

and Yates's chi-squared result is a highly significant probability of 0.2%. I prefer the first and more conservative distribution, however, as explained later.

DISCUSSION

CONTEMPLATING THE RESULTS

These statistics suggest that a measurable difference indeed exists in artifact dispersal within the house, divided lengthwise into opposing sides. Does this mean there is validity to the original notion of a women's and a men's side, if only vaguely expressed (Newell 1984:22)? Probably not, although the desire to concur seems compelling at first. True, the gender-female artifacts are twice as prevalent on the women's side (Fig. 9.3). As for gender-male artifacts, they either slightly prevail on the men's side (if we minimize the bundle and bag) or overwhelmingly occupy it (if we itemize the bundle's and bag's contents).

I nevertheless hesitate to confirm the idea of men's and women's sides, as originally proclaimed, because we need to address the rather U-shaped dispersal to the gender-male artifacts (Fig. 9.4). That is, half of the gender-male artifacts appear either in (1) the large subfloor cache (under floorboards below the sleeping platform at the back of the house, opposite the *katak*) or in (2) other peripheral storage caches (on the sill timbers [between the bases of wall planks] or below or between floorboards) (Fig. 9.4). Peter Whitridge's dissertation research at the Qariaraqyuk site (see Chapter 11, this volume) observed "a relatively widespread distribution for men's cached and discarded items, and a relatively delimited distribution for women's, with all that that might imply for the control of social space" (Whitridge, personal communication 2000). Eliminating the cached items at Mound 44—and focusing instead on the floor-surface artifacts—tends to "neutralize" the notion of gender-specific sides to the floor.

The challenging issue that emerges from this study is what male and female house sides, if they existed in emic Inupiat reality, signify about proxemics in the first place. Do Yates's chi-squared results given previously imply that men worked on one side of the house while women worked on the other? Why are there more "male" than "female" objects, particularly in the large cache? More significant, why are there not more "male" artifacts centrally located on the men's side?

Salient to these questions is the issue of sea mammal oil lamps, source of heat and light in Inupiat houses. Even though we never found it in the Mound 44 house, the main lamp (if not the sole one) had been on the women's side, which is consistent with the original gender-based-sides premise. I am certain of the lamp's general position because during excavations I noted much more lamp oil residue near the wall on that side of the house, both across the floorboards and in the soil below.

> To either side of the *katak* frame below the floor, and just north from it [i.e., toward the back of the house], are cut sods . . . those on the [women's side] being particularly seal-oil-soaked (where the seal oil seems to be most thickly accumulated under the floor). . . . Some seal oil extends to the [men's-side corner near the *katak*] of the subfloor and some is also seen in the [women's-side corner near the *katak*], but [there is] far less along the [men's side] of the house. What did appear [on the men's side] was most abundant along the [katak boards' wall edges]. (Reinhardt n.d.b)

The lamp complication is that, if men were in the house and working on things there, it would make more practical sense for their items to occur near the lamp (the women's side), where they could see better. Instead, objects such as those from the arrow-point bundle and the bola weight bag (Fig. 9.1; Table 9.1, left column) appeared about as far from the lamp as possible (Fig. 9.4)—near the wall on the presumably darker men's side of the room.

PROPOSING AN ALTERNATIVE INTERPRETATION

These results are not as definitive as they might be. I therefore propose a kind of "independent test" that another marked difference exists, in artifact distributions, according to how objects cluster on the men's and women's sides of the Mound 44 house. Let us consider two sets of gender-uncertain objects not typically regarded as formal artifact classes: sewing scraps and chert flakes (Table 9.3; Fig. 9.2). Let us assume that certain scraps (cut-up leather, gut, hide, and fur—all either stitched or not) result from tailoring and hide preparation; that is, they reflect female tasks (Giffen 1930:33–34, 87). (Sinew, thongs, and knotted leather or fur strips are potentially unrelated to sewing and might as easily relate to male tasks, thus their exclusion from analysis.) Let us also as-

Graph 9.5

Gender-linked Waste Materials?	House Side	
	Women's	Men's
Leather, etc.	22	37
Chert	16	3

sume that chert flakes result from steps in lithic manufacture; that is, they reflect male tasks (Giffen 1930:33, 87). Granting that these premises might be wrong, the test still presents itself as an intriguing counterpoint to the preceding ones that deal with formal artifacts. Paralleling previous test constructions, the outcome is seen in Graph 9.5. Yates's chi-squared test of these figures indicates a very significant difference amid the four cells: $P = 0.2\%$.

The materials just examined, leather (and other) scraps and chert debitage, are presumably by-products of basic manufacture (Figure 9.5). Together they constitute about 32% of all gender-uncertain objects from Mound 44 that relate to the house's final occupancy and about 21% of all field-numbered objects in Table 9.3. (Although some field specimen numbers—FS#s in Table 9.3—represent more than one object, I assume that the cases of multiple items per number are about evenly split between men's and women's sides of the house, making the exact quantity unimportant in this and in the preceding Yates's chi-squared tests.) Among the formal artifact classes, "female" items tended to be on the women's side and "male" items on the men's side (Figs. 9.3, 9.4). Among the analyzed "waste" objects, though, the relationship between presumed gender role and house side apparently reverses. That is, more "female" pieces ("sewing scraps") occupy the men's side, whereas "male" ones ("waste flakes") strongly favor the women's side (Fig. 9.5).

These puzzles probably relate to another simple ethnographic reality. Except in midwinter, Inupiat men and older boys in this part of Alaska spent most of their waking hours in a *qargi,* or men's house—a kind of clubhouse and workplace built elsewhere in the village—and returned to their domicile mainly to sleep (Murdoch 1892:80). This fact is rather consistent with the original gender thesis in that the Mound 44 disaster may have occurred "between early October and the end of November or between the end of April and May/June" (Newell 1984:26), which is basically outside the hard winter period.

Therefore, better than insisting on male-dominated and/or female-intensive sides to the house interior, it might be easier to suppose that

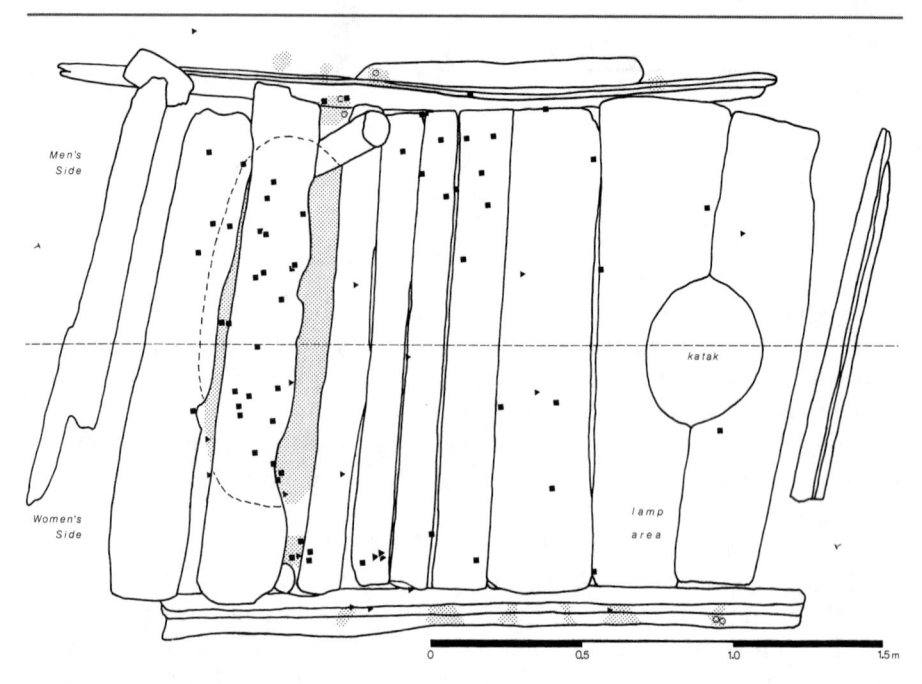

Figure 9.5 Leather (and other) scraps and debitage; squares = leather and similar items, triangles = chert debitage, open circles = used flakes, shaded areas = caches (large subfloor cache also shown in dashed lines)

women used most of the floor and usually shared it with the younger children. In this interpretation, women probably sewed by the lamp and either tossed scraps away from it or stored them in the large subfloor cache (Fig. 9.5). They also spent a good deal of time trimming the lamp wick, which kept them close to the lamp—in effect the women's workplace, a spot we could expect to be freer of debris and formal artifacts (Fig. 9.3).

The presence of chert flakes on the women's side seems harder to explain at first blush, insofar as having small, sharp objects about the floor on which adults worked and children played could pose a slight health risk. Although speculative, one might argue that women threw their work-related refuse to the other side of the room, and men did the same thing (Fig. 9.5). It could be that women did their own flaking (although this idea appeals less), or it might even have happened that children (boys?) were trying their hand at this skill. Perhaps the floor had recently been swept clean of flakes, or maybe chert was not even processed in the house but brought in for women's use (by either women or men). If so, maybe the nineteen locations for chert debitage do not particularly mirror males' stone knapping, which should generate hundreds of flakes around the house. Instead, it might reflect females' keeping a few flakes nearby as relatively "disposable" cutting tools to supplement their general use of *ulus,* which (being made of slate) are consequently duller than siliceous cherts. The appearance of visibly used flakes on both sides of the floor probably does not affect this discussion either way; in any event, all five were cached (Fig. 9.5).

We know men and older boys returned to the house to sleep, but they spent much of their waking time and did most of their tool work in a separate structure. Accordingly, they would not need their artifacts near the lamp in the house, which would clutter the women's lamp-tending area and the house floor in general. The alternatives for males were either to place their artifacts and work materials on the opposite side of the floor—by the wall, where we found the arrow-point bundle next to the bag of bola weights—or to store them below floor level in the large out-of-the-way cache or in other lateral caches. Viewed in this light, the gendered proxemics at Mound 44 clearly defy the original premise of "functional partitions," or seemingly assigned work spaces for women *and* men.

To illustrate my point, I redefine the 119 gender-ascribed formal artifacts into cache locations (those peripheral to the house floor) versus noncache locations (those more toward the central floor area) (see Graph 9.6).

Yates's chi-squared test indicates that $5\% > P > 1\%$ for the distribution in Graph 9.6. Statistically significant, the pattern is numerically almost identical to that for house sides. By a 2:1 ratio, female artifacts occur on the women's side and toward the house center, whereas male artifacts are slightly more common on the men's side and on the periphery. Adding in the 31 items from the arrow-point bundle and the bola weight bag affects the Central Location Male-Object cell, as seen in Graph 9.7.

In this case Yates's chi-squared test produces a probability greater than 10 percent, meaning the numbers in the four cells are not statistically significant. They clearly reverse the interpretation immediately previous, but they do so by falsely exaggerating the importance of two sets of parceled artifacts. Both sets, being against the far wall from where I think the lamp was located (Newell 1984:figs. 14, 22), were in a real physical sense removed from the house center. Therefore I believe my second center-versus-periphery analysis is far less valid. It confuses storage with

Graph 9.6

Object's Gender Ascription	House Location	
	Central	Peripheral
Female	34	17
Male	31	37

Graph 9.7

Object's Gender Ascription	House Location	
	Central	Peripheral
Female	34	17
Male	62	37

Graph 9.8

Object's Gender Ascription	House Location	
	Central	Peripheral
Female	34	17
Male	31	68

presumed active use of artifacts in the house. If we reverse the location of the bundle and bag contents (i.e., move them to the Peripheral-Location Male-Object cell) to distinguish curation from work, the result changes dramatically and accords better with my thesis (see Graph 9.8).

Now Yates's chi-squared probability is 0.2 percent, and both genders' pieces reflect a 2:1 ratio. Twice as many "female" items are in the center, and twice as many "male" ones are in the periphery. Furthermore, "female" formal artifacts occur around the lamp area (Fig. 9.3) more than "male" artifacts do (Fig. 9.4). Scrap materials, by contrast, tend to be either stored in the large subfloor cache or scattered far from the lamp area and toward the opposite wall (Fig. 9.5). "Male" formal artifacts (Fig. 9.4), alternatively, array themselves in a way very similar to the dispersal of scrap materials (Fig. 9.5), which I treat as added evidence for gender-based differences in the use of house space.

Peter Whitridge arrived at very similar results when he examined distributions of artifacts found in five houses and a *qargi* at Qariaraqyuk (Whitridge 1999a). In his study the parallels had to do with hide-working refuse ("'cast-offs' of various kinds, sinew, clothing fragments") at one scatterplot extreme compared with hard-material–working refuse (i.e., "ivory, antler, and whale bone debitage") at the other extreme. In other words, they tended not to co-occur, and more "male" debris appeared in the *qargi*, whereas more "female" debris was found in dwellings. In addition, "Within the dwellings female refuse tended to occur on the floor and in the kitchen, and male refuse on the sleeping platform and in the tunnel" (Whitridge, personal communication 2000).

CONCLUSION

No scientific study should ever be considered either complete or irrefutably conclusive. If it were, there would be no more questions—nothing left to say about that topic or, ultimately, about the science under which rubric the study appeared. In examining gender at Mound 44, more could have been done. For instance, I might have tried to create isopleths of house-floor artifact density to expose more visual representations of female and male household activity (Reynolds n.d.). I might have dismissed the idea of two gender-based "sides" and looked instead for "natural" artifact and debris distributions. I might also have produced two more distribution maps (one each for gender-female and gender-male artifacts), but with the cached objects eliminated; still, these should be discernible in Figures 9.3 and 9.4. (My thanks to Peter Whitridge for suggesting these lines of further inquiry.)

A major thrust of this study concerns unexpected outcomes. I had long thought Newell's gender suppositions (1984) were unsubstantiated—at least insofar as he surmised—and that seems borne out here. It surprises me, though, to discover that there is a statistically significant difference between the so-called men's and women's sides in terms of artifact ascriptions as either male or female. It intrigues me even more to realize that yet another behavior pattern emerges for two categories of waste materials and that the center-versus-periphery test seems to clarify that difference. In other words, Newell (1984) was right about male and female "sides" at Mound 44 but for the wrong reasons, both methodologically and ethnographically.

In the final analysis, though, I am skeptical of my own certainty, with which I began this research, as to what is "male" and "female" and what we can comfortably and testably assign, based on gender, to the archaeological record. As Sara Nelson phrased it, "The dichotomies produced by our language and our categories [see Chapter 2, this volume] ntend to obfuscate what could be learned about the prehistoric past, thus preventing us from encountering the variety left by the actual users of the tools" (1997:92). Statistical probabilities might lend the data-testing here an aura of assurance about artifactual femaleness or maleness. That, however, should not supplant our intellectual responsibility to know two things first: (1) what we mean by sex-based ascriptions, and (2) whether those ascriptions have any emic validity. Still, how can we fully apprehend or accurately visualize an alternative past for an alternative culture?

The glaring gender problem surrounding Mound 44 is proving with total, or even reasonable, confidence that any adult males were actually members of this household when the roof crushed the people inside. We see "male" artifacts, but although two female corpses came archaeologically from the Mound 44 house, no identified male remains were ascertained, even though Newell (1984:35) posited a missing "Senior male." One might argue that males were in fact altogether absent, owing to the dearth of male paraphernalia on the house floor. Seen differently, maybe men were absent but one or more boys or adolescent males present. Then there is the matter of whose artifacts belonged to whom (which sex or which person), what ownership itself means, and how we might ever archaeologically establish such property rules (Barbara Bodenhorn, personal communication 1998). For instance, Barbara Crass (personal communication 1998) found no statistical difference between the sexes in the number of harpoons (an indisputably "male" artifact) in her study of pan-Eskimo burial practices.

A related consideration is the extent to which males and females might have shared their material things.

> The use by one sex of the other's equipment is not uncommon and constitutes, particularly for the archaeologist, a difficult problem in social unit identification. What is the proof of a man's or woman's presence? Men frequently camp out by themselves for a day or two in the fall. They carry with them women's gear (cooking utensils, food). In this situation, men are using women's equipment and it is difficult if not impossible at times to determine from the camp debris or the items left at a permanent camp whether a woman was present. (Ackerman 1970:40)

So even if we can distinguish male from female artifacts and debris, and even if "sex-linked spatial control [can be] marked by the storage of items specific to male or female activities" (Ackerman 1970:38), this does not necessarily mean men were present or that women did not also use men's things at Mound 44.

Another caution is that the house's collapse captured for archaeology and posterity only one precise instant in the lives of its residents, and this instant was only one phase in their annual round, and this phase affected only one household (no doubt with its own idiosyncrasies) out of an entire community and society. Archaeologists generally (if often tacitly) assume that, all things being equal, a part reflects the whole. We cannot resolutely conclude, however, that the analytical picture described here represents *all* lives in that period or *all* seasons of the Mound 44 householders' yearly routine or *all* interactions between the sexes then.

Pressing the data beyond the scope of this chapter to learn more about gender is a logical further step. In fact, "It seems that a responsible archaeologist would make the recovering of gender relationships an explicit goal, and would use all available powers to delineate specific social structures" (Nelson 1997:129). Still, caution is warranted: "While a consideration of gender in household studies will unquestionably increase the archaeological visibility of women, paradoxically it will only contribute to a further reification of the link between women and home unless there is an accompanying awareness of women's activities outside the domestic environment and of men's activities within it" (Lawrence 1999:122). Mound 44, with its unique preservation, has much to offer in these regards. If nothing else, it steers us away from simplistic interpretations of household roles for men and women among the prehistoric Inupiat of Arctic Alaska. In place of such thinking, Mound 44 evidently instructs us about two cultural behaviors, house-specific though they might be: a marginalized place for males in daily domestic activities, and a living arrangement no doubt struck by mutual consensus of both sexes.

Putting a face to those who died in Mound 44, I have to imagine a lifestyle radically removed from my own. Consistent with ethnography, the women likely lived most days apart from men and managed their houses and children alone. If so, women and men agreed to a sort of daily divorce, and children learned a principally female worldview before recognizing the perspectives of males. Yet somehow, despite the seemingly compartmentalized inflexibility of adult sex roles (Giffen 1930), these Eskimo women and men nevertheless cooperated in composing a life together. They cooked meals, shared food, banged drums, survived disasters, gamboled naked, dug roots, fought frostbite, laughed heartily, built fires, picked berries, constructed houses, nurtured children, drove dogsleds, respected elders, wore jewelry, framed kayaks, hunted seals, held feasts, buried friends, sewed clothes, feared nature, argued sharply, hooked fish, assembled tools, endured famine, sang melodies, erected tents, killed whales, made love, tended lamps, rowed umiaks, danced fervently, mediated disputes, sacrificed dreams, nursed illnesses, battled invaders, grew old, and died.

ACKNOWLEDGMENTS

I thank Lisa Frink, Tammy R. Greene, Kelly E. Guthridge, Stephen P. Nawrocki, Jeffrey A. Oaks, Christopher W. Schmidt, Rita S. Shepard, Peter Whitridge, and Matthew Williamson for insights that contributed to the thoughts in this chapter and Marijane Hetrick for assistance with remapping artifacts from Mound 44.

10

BROKEN EYES AND SIMPLE GROOVES
UNDERSTANDING EASTERN ALEUT NEEDLE TECHNOLOGY
THROUGH EXPERIMENTAL MANUFACTURE
AND USE OF BONE NEEDLES

Brian W. Hoffman

Sometime around a.d. 1000 the Unangan, or people of the eastern Aleutian Islands, switched from using bone sewing needles with delicately drilled eyes to needles with simple grooves carved on their ends for attaching the thread (Figure 10.1a). This seemingly inconsequential morphological change in a tool shape came at a time of great social and economic transformations. The Unangan of a.d. 1000 also switched from occupying relatively small single-family or extended-family homes to living in large multifamily longhouses (Hoffman 1999a; McCartney 1984). They began importing slate knives in large numbers, as well as acquiring metal tools (Holland 1988; McCartney 1988). Warfare probably increased (Maschner and Reedy-Maschner 1998), as did social differentiation and inequality (Hoffman 2002; Maschner and Hoffman n.d.; McCartney 1984). The exact timing of these changes and whether they occurred independently or as part of a package remain undetermined. What is known is that by the time Russian explorers first arrived, the Unangan were culturally complex maritime foragers with ranked lineages who engaged in long-distance trading and warfare while living in large permanent villages (Black and Liapunova 1988; Lantis 1984).

For most archaeologists the change in needle form is simply diagnostic of "Late Aleutian Tradition" assemblages with little additional behavioral significance (Desautels et al. 1970; Holland 1982, 1988; McCartney

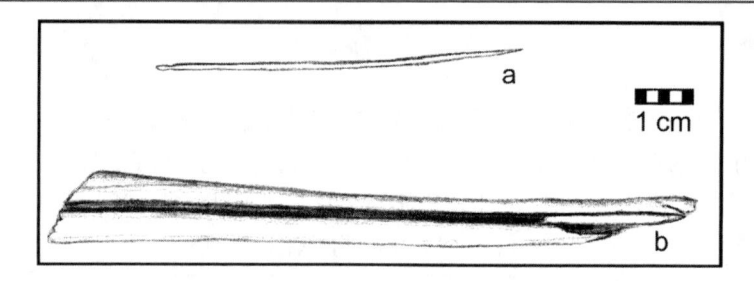

Figure 10.1 (a) Grooved needle and (b) red fox left tibia with needle blank removed via the groove and snap technique; both artifacts recovered from Agayadan Village (from Hoffman 2002)

1967). Recent excavations at Agayadan Village on Unimak Island, however, reveal sewing needles as an important material component of high-status households (Hoffman 2002). The change in needle form, far from inconsequential, helps explain the interplay among gender roles, prestige-goods production, and status differentiation in Unangan society.

This chapter explores why the Unangan changed the form of their needles by examining the manufacturing costs and functional attributes of each needle type. Experimental production and use of both eyed and grooved needles confirm that reducing needle diameter was the critical advantage gained by switching to grooved needles. Thinner needles enabled Unangan seamstresses to sew finely stitched and elaborately decorated garments. The Unangan skills with the thin grooved needles made their sewn products highly desired status symbols in their increasingly complex social world.

NEEDLES AND GENDER

Investigating gendered behavior from a society's material remains can be a difficult undertaking for archaeologists. Assigning a specific object to the activities of a single segment of a social group raises serious practical and theoretical questions, as discussed by several authors in this volume (Reinhardt, Shepard, Whitridge) and others elsewhere (Costin 1996; Hayden 1992; Owen 1999). Whether the Unangan needles were largely manufactured and used by women or by men makes little difference when answering this chapter's principal question, which is why the needles changed in form. The answer to that question, however, acquires added interest when the gendered implications of this technological change are considered (cf. Brumfiel 1991; Costin 1996). Furthermore, assigning needles and sewing activities to Unangan women is an interpretation amply supported by cross-cultural studies (Byrne 1999; Hoffman 2000) and historical records. Virtually every eyewitness account of Unangan labor practices from the eighteenth and nineteenth centuries clearly states that Unangan women made their own needles and sewed all clothing (Klichka 1988:266; Krenitsyn and Levashev 1988; Merck 1980:77, 173, 203; Sarychev 1969:8; Veniaminov 1984:285, 287). Aleut men may have carried needles to make emergency repairs on their clothing or kayak covers when traveling, but the vast majority of needles recovered archaeologically from house interiors are the residue of sewing activities by Unangan women (Hoffman 2000).

EYED AND GROOVED NEEDLES IN ALEUTIAN PREHISTORY

Bone sewing needles are a regular component of Arctic archaeological assemblages (De Laguna 1975; Holland 1982; Issenman 1997b; McCartney 1967). The earliest needles have drilled or incised eyes. Eyed needles continue to be used in most regions up until contact. Needles with a slight groove for thread attachment appear in the Aleutians, the lower Alaska Peninsula, and the Kodiak Archipelago around A.D. 700–1000. This style needle completely replaces eyed needles in the eastern Aleutian region. Western Aleutian and Kodiak Archipelago sites apparently contain a mix of needles, demonstrating contemporaneous use of both styles by the people of these regions (Desautels et al. 1970:236; Heizer 1956; Deborah Corbett, personal communication 2001).

Archaeologists have been unable to explain adequately the change in needle form. Frederica De Laguna, in her survey of Arctic artifact distributions, described the grooved needle as a "degenerate type" (1975:198). This description implies that Unangan seamstresses somehow became less skilled or lacked the motivation necessary to make eyed needles. Although no Aleutian historian today would agree that Unangan needles "degenerated" in form, many express amazement at the skill required in making the delicate eyed needles, particularly drilling the sometimes incredibly fine eye (Black 1982; Hoffman 2000). This perception led Kathryn Holland (1982:125) to hypothesize that Unangan seamstresses switched to the simpler grooved needle form because eyed needles were difficult to make. A. P. McCartney (1967:359) offers no explanation for the switch to grooved needles, but he does suggest that eyed needles were sturdier, whereas grooved needles could easily be regrooved after breaking. No one has suggested what I consider the most obvious advantage, which is that grooved needles can be made thinner because they are not limited by the size of the eye (Hoffman 2000).

Assuming one or more of these hypotheses is correct, Unangan seamstresses redesigned their needles for practical reasons. They were evidently concerned with lowering their production costs, improving needle durability, reducing needle diameter, or a combination of these factors. Experiments in the manufacture and use of replica eyed and grooved needles offer us a means for evaluating these "practical" hypotheses. Working with the False Pass, Alaska, high school class over the course of two days, we made and used both needle styles. Our experiments were designed to address three simple questions: (1) Are grooved needles quicker to make than eyed needles? (2) Which needle style lasts longer? (3) And finally, can grooved needles be made thinner than eyed needles? Needle replica experiments made by Stephanie Butler (1997) and Jeffrey Flenniken (1978) provide additional insight for this chapter. I also draw on archaeological evidence of production recovered from Amchitka Island in the western Aleutians and Agayadan Village (49 UNI [Unimak] 067), a late precontact/early contact Unangan settlement on Unimak Island (Hoffman 1999a, 2002).

MAKING NEEDLES— ARCHAEOLOGICAL AND DOCUMENTARY EVIDENCE

The first issue with our project, as with any experimental program, concerned decisions regarding the materials we employed and the manufacturing steps we followed. We used both historical accounts of Unangan needle manufacture and archaeological data to guide our decisions. Several eyewitness accounts from the late eighteenth century describe the manufacture and use of bone sewing needles by Unangan seamstresses. One of the most detailed observations comes from Dr. Carl Merck, a naturalist and physician with the Russian-sponsored Billings-Sarychev Expedition that traveled in the Aleutians between 1790 and 1792.[1] Describing Unalaska Aleut, Merck wrote that "[Unangan] women also cut seagull bones with [an iron knife] carefully. They sharpen these bits of bone on a spongy kind of volcanic rock, and so make sewing needles" (1980:77).

The commander of the expedition, Captain Joseph Billings, added that "their needles can be considered a product of accomplished craft; they are cut from the femoral bone of birds, of a large type of gull. The very smallest needles are not more than a third of a vershok long [vershok = 4.4 cm] and as thin as hair. However, they have no eye, and on the blunt end they have a very narrow cut groove, in which they fasten the thread so artfully that it follows the needle in sewing unimpeded" (in Merck 1980:203).

Table 10.1—Needle Production Steps, Materials, and Debris (*recovered at Agayadan Village, †documented in historical accounts)

Step	Materials Used	Debris Generated
1: blank production	metal knife† stone flake/knife*	a. bone cores w/blanks removed* b. "cut" ends (long bone articular ends removed from core)* c. blanks and blank fragments*
2: blank reduction	stone abrader*†	semiround needle fragments*
3: modify blunt end	acutely pointed stone	partially drilled eyes (?) flake*

Finally, Lieutenant Gavriil Sarychev (1969:8), second in command of the expedition, noted that even when given iron needles, Unangan women "immediately break off the eye, and rub it on the edge of a stone [until] they have made a notch, where they can tie the thread in their usual way."

From these observations and other eyewitness accounts (Klichka 1988:266; Krenitsyn and Levashev 1988; Veniaminov 1984:280), we can outline the basics of Unangan needle production. The preferred raw material was bird bone, with both gull and albatross mentioned specifically. These birds are strong fliers and as a result have relatively hard, dense bone, particularly in their wings. Fox and other medium-sized terrestrial mammals, along with walrus ivory, also provided suitable raw materials. The Unangan of Unimak Island at least occasionally used these alternative materials, as demonstrated by the recovery of a modified red fox (*Vulpes vulpes*) tibia found at Agayadan Village (Figure 10.1b).

Manufacturing needles involved three basic steps (Table 10.1). First, a needle blank was obtained. Next, the blank was either carved or ground to size and shape. Finally, the blunt end was drilled or grooved to allow for attaching the thread. Eyed needles were probably drilled prior to final thinning and polishing while the blunt end was still relatively thick and sturdy.

STEP 1—OBTAINING THE NEEDLE BLANK

Unangan women of the late eighteenth century, as noted by Merck (1980:77), used iron knives to "cut" the needle blanks. Iron tools, obtained either through long-distance trade networks or from shipwrecked Asian vessels, occurred in the Aleutians by or before A.D. 1000 (McCartney 1988). Sharp stone flakes or ground stone knives were probably used by Unangan women who lacked access to metal tools.

Production debris recovered from archaeological sites demonstrate that the needle blanks were not literally "cut" from the bone but removed by a "groove and snap" technique (Figure 1b; see also Jochelson 1925). This technique involves incising long parallel grooves into a bone "core" and then prying or snapping out the linear blank. The groove and snap technique is a method found around the world for working with bone and antler (Clark and Thompson 1953; Knecht 1997). This technique exploits the linear strength of long bone elements and produces thin, long blanks ideal for making needles, points, and other tool types (Scheinsohn and Ferretti 1995).

Other methods for obtaining a tool blank, not documented in historical accounts, include simply smashing or twisting a long bone to produce irregular bone splinters. Flenniken (1978) employed this method in his experimental replication of Paleo-Indian needles. Archaeological evidence from the eastern Aleutians indicates the Unangan did regularly smash bird bone. We have no evidence, however, that these splinters served as needle blanks. Instead, most modified bird-bone splinters were simply sharpened at the tip and used as awls (Czederpiltz 1997; Hoffman 2002).

Archaeologists working on Amchitka Island in the central Aleutians documented a third method for obtaining needle blanks. They recovered a bird radius "ground on two sides of the shaft leaving two, thin needle-like blanks" (Desautels et al. 1970:264). This "Amchitka" method does not appear to have been widely employed, as no other archaeologists have reported this distinctive production debris.

Whether the Unangan obtained blanks from fresh, green bone or dried bone is not recorded in published eyewitness accounts. Butler (1997), in her needle replication experiments, found dried bone difficult to groove and soaked her bone in water to keep it soft. I suspect Unangan seamstresses may also have preferred fresh bone for their needle production.

STEP 2—SHAPING THE NEEDLE

Thinning and sharpening the blanks into a needle shape is the second step in the manufacturing process. Blanks could be shaved thin by carving with a knife or by grinding on an abrasive stone. Production debris recovered from Aleutian sites indicates most needle blanks began as slim 2–3 mm wide slivers (Hoffman 2002). I suspect Unangan seamstresses did not attempt to carve these already thin needle blanks but instead ground them to shape as described earlier by Merck (1980:77). A variety of coarse to fine abraders and whetstones are typically recovered in Aleut house interiors in general association with needle production debris (Hoffman 2002). On Unimak Island these abraders included a sandstone-like tuff suitable for rough shaping and a tuffacious siltstone suitable for fine polishing and final shaping (Hoffman 2002). None of these abraders has needle-size grooves, however, like those created and described by Flenniken (1978:67) from his experiments.

STEP 3 – MODIFYING THE BLUNT END (EYES AND GROOVES)

The final step in the production process, once the needles are polished to shape, involves modifying the blunt end by either drilling an eye or inscribing a narrow groove. Sarychev (1969:8) suggested the grooves were made simply by rubbing the needle against the sharp edge of a stone. The grooves could also be cut with an iron knife or stone flake. Unangan seamstresses of the eastern Aleutians did not make eyed needles at contact, so no regionally specific accounts of this manufacturing step exist. Butler (1997) and Flenniken (1978) both used acutely pointed stone flakes to drill needle eyes. Iron drill bits could also have been used, although we have no documentary evidence of metal drills.

FALSE PASS NEEDLE PROJECT

False Pass, Alaska, is presently the only village occupied on Unimak Island. It is a small community, with a 1990 census population of sixty-eight residents. Commercial fishing dominates the local cash economy. A 1987–1988 study by the Alaska Department of Fish and Game found that subsistence harvests continue to provide substantial economic benefit (Fall et al. 1996). On average, each False Pass household used, harvested, or received as gifts nearly 1,300 pounds (usable weight) of wild foods, mostly salmon and caribou (Fall et al. 1996:79).

Students in the False Pass school are regularly involved in a wide range of Alaska Native cultural heritage studies. Many participate in traditional beadworking, weaving, and skin-sewing projects.[2] The high school class (a multigrade class of six students and one teacher during the 1999–2000 school year) and I collaborated on the needle replication project because of our mutual interest in understanding the role of needle technology and sewing activities in ancient Aleut communities.

The students and their teacher made replica sewing needles following the procedures outlined earlier (Figure 10.2). For raw material we used the femur, humerus, ulna, and tibiotarsus bones from ptarmigan (*Lagopus sp.*). We used ptarmigan because these birds were the only species hunted at the time of our study and the only fresh bone available. The ptarmigan bone is less robust than gull and albatross and was

Figure 10.2 False Pass High School class replicating needles; left to right, *Alan Hoggard, Carlin Hoblet, Teshla Freeman, Karita Freeman, Virginia Berlin (teacher), Nikki Hoblet, and Christopher Freeman*

probably rarely, if ever, used for needle manufacture in traditional situations. Chert and basalt flakes, similar to the lithic materials available on Unimak Island, provided our cutting implements. Mostly, we used unmodified flakes, although a few students resharpened their flakes with an antler pressure flaker. Abrading the needle blanks was done using a variety of locally available coarse volcanic rocks. Included in our experiments were fragments of a sandstone-like tuff abrader recovered from disturbed contexts at Agayadan Village.

The needles the students made were short and thick compared with archaeological specimens. The differences between the students' replicas and actual needles reflect the poor quality of ptarmigan bone as a raw material, the limited time available for the experiments, and to some degree the students' impatience with the needle fabrication process. One conclusion their efforts amply illustrated is that needle making is a time-consuming activity. I believe the results of our experiments would remain unchanged, however, had the students produced full-scale needles.

The only significant difference is that the production time would have been at least double the time spent on our attempts.

We treated each attempted needle/blank as a separate experiment. We recorded the time spent on each stage, whether the production was successful or not, and any reason for failure. We also measured and traced each blank/needle at each production stage. The students sewed with each successfully manufactured needle for 20 minutes or until the needle broke, recording the results of this experimental use. These data allow us to evaluate the manufacturing costs and durability of each needle type.

NEEDLE PRODUCTION RESULTS

We made our needle blanks using the groove and snap technique. We successfully removed needle blanks from seven (63.6%) of eleven experiments. Failures all occurred when attempting to snap the blank out of the bone core. Grooving the ptarmigan bone was a very time-consuming process. Each blank took an average of 27 minutes (range 10 to 40 minutes) to make. Grooving and removing longer blanks would have been even more costly. Butler (1997:8) worked for 30 to 45 minutes to make each groove in her experiments. Not included with our experiments was one student's attempt to obtain a blank using a splinter technique. This attempt produced many irregular slivers, but none was judged adequate for our needs.

Of the seven needle blanks, the students were able to grind and polish five (71.4%) into a needle shape. The two failures occurred when the needles snapped because too much pressure was applied as the tip was being sharpened. We found grinding the needles, like making the blanks, a very slow process. The students spent an average of 19.4 minutes on this stage (range 7 to 25 minutes). We could easily have ground our needles for an additional 20 minutes or more, since our finished needles were relatively thick compared with archaeological specimens.

For the final production step we had six experiments, three eyed needles and three grooved needles (including one needle regrooved after the original groove broke during use). Drilling the needle eye took between 10 and 13 minutes, whereas inscribing a groove required only a minute or two. We had no failures during this stage.

Our experiments in needle fabrication allow us to assess the hypothesis that Unangan seamstresses adopted grooved needles to reduce their manufacturing costs. Although we found drilling the eye took a little more time than inscribing a groove, this difference was negligible when considering the total time spent making the needles (Figure 10.3). Our

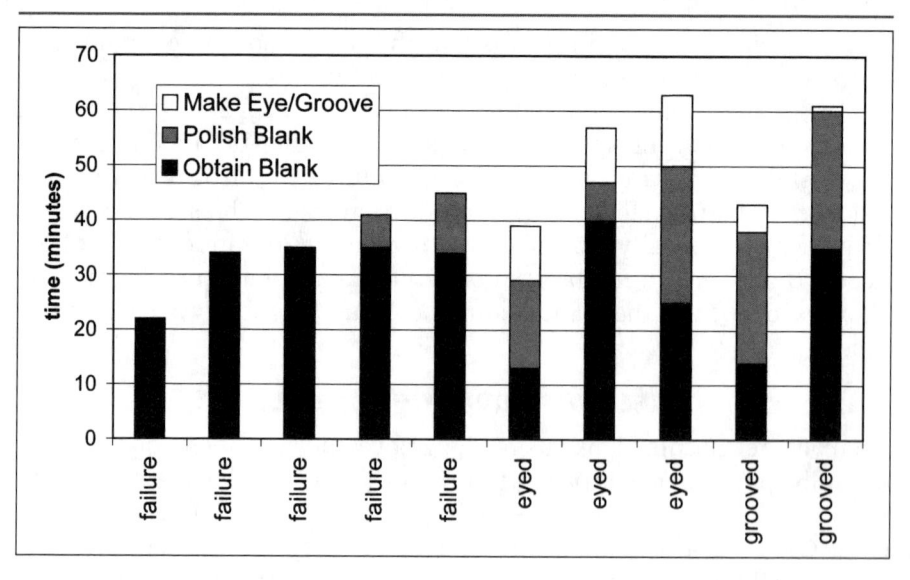

Figure 10.3 False Pass needle manufacturing experiments; total time per experiment

production costs for the three eyed needles averaged 53 minutes (range 39 to 63 minutes), whereas production costs for the two grooved needles were essentially the same, averaging 52 minutes (range 43 to 61 minutes). The vast majority of the production costs (85.2%) involved obtaining the blank and grinding it into a needle shape. These production costs, which would have been even higher had we made full-sized needles, remain the same whether making eyed or grooved needles. Switching to grooved needles would not have significantly reduced the overall time involved in needle manufacture.

Risk of failure also does not appear to differ significantly between needle styles. Most production accidents occurred when attempting to remove a needle blank from the bone core. Archaeologically recovered production debris suggests that Unangan seamstresses likewise experienced a relatively high rate of failure at this step (Hoffman 2002). We experienced no failures during the final production step, although our experiments were limited in number. Eyed needles may look impressive, but replicating them is not a particularly difficult task. The students were able to successfully drill delicate needle eyes despite the fact that none had ever worked with bone or stone tools before. Overall, our results are inconsistent with the hypothesis that grooved needles were adopted to reduce manufacturing costs or because eyed needles were more difficult to make.

NEEDLE DURABILITY RESULTS

The second phase of our experiments was to use our needles and evaluate whether either style was more durable. We had six experiments counting the regrooved needle (three eyed and three grooved). Each experiment involved stitching heavy cotton fabric with polyester thread for twenty minutes or until the needle broke, whichever came first. One eyed and one grooved needle broke before the twenty minutes were up, for a success rate of 66.7 percent for each needle style. Butler (1997) obtained similar results in her experiments sewing animal skins (deer and rabbit) using sinew thread. These experiments, although limited in number, suggest eyed and grooved needles do not differ significantly in durability. We did find it possible to regroove a broken needle, consistent with McCartney's hypothesis, but our experiments did not fully explore the potential differences in needle repair or refurbishing.

NEEDLE DIAMETER

The final hypothesis evaluated in this chapter is that Unangan seamstresses switched to grooved needles because that style could be made thinner than eyed needles. The needles made by the False Pass students do not attempt to evaluate this hypothesis, since we intentionally made relatively thick needles of both styles. Butler's (1997) replica experiments provide a better test of this hypothesis. Her eyed needles ranged between 0.75 and 4.00 mm, whereas her grooved needles ranged between 0.50 and 1.50 mm (Butler 1997:13). Butler's (1997) results closely match the diameters obtained from archaeologically recovered needles (Hoffman 2000). For this analysis I compared a sample of twenty-six eyed needles recovered from a large midden site (49 RAT 31) dated between 600 B.C. and A.D. 1000 on Amchitka Island in the western Aleutians (Desautels et al. 1970) and seventy-six grooved needles and needle fragments recovered from house interior contexts at Agayadan Village (Hoffman 2002). The Amchitka eyed needles were substantially thicker, averaging 1.67 mm in diameter compared with an average diameter of 0.98 mm for Agayadans' grooved needles (Table 10.2). Other samples of eyed needles closely match the Amchitka needle measurements (Hoffman 2000).

Both the Amchitka Island and Agayadan Village needle assemblages included relatively robust needles (>1.5 mm) suitable for heavy-duty

Table 10.2—Comparison of eyed and grooved sewing needle diameters (in millimeters)

	Minimum	Maximum	Mean	
Eyed Needles				
49 RAT 31 (n = 26)	1.00	2.28	1.67	Archaeological context
Butler 1997 (n = 5)	0.75	4.00	—	Experimental replicas
Grooved Needles				
Agayadan (n = 76)	0.52	2.22	0.98	Archaeological context
Butler 1997 (n = 3)	0.50	1.50	—	Experimental replicas

sewing tasks. The difference between the needle assemblages is that the Agayadan Village occupants also used a large number of very fine needles (< 0.75 mm). Eyed needles cannot easily be made this thin because both the eyehole and sinew thread would need to be incredibly fine. These fine needles are the principal advantage of the grooved needle style.

THIN NEEDLES, FINE STITCHING, AND LATE ALEUTIAN CULTURAL COMPLEXITY

Why thin needles? What practical purpose did thinner needles serve? Clearly, the eyed bone sewing needles used throughout the Arctic were suitable for creating all kinds of well-made garments and other skin objects, as illustrated by the impressive parkas, boots, mittens, and bags made by Native seamstresses (Buijs 1997; Chaussonnet 1988; Fitzhugh and Kaplan 1982:130–143). I suspect the Unangan could sew everything they needed to make with eyed needles. The thin grooved needles enabled them to make tiny stitches, an advantage when sewing decorative appliqué or embroidery along the seams of clothing and when sewing thin or fragile skins, like the rain parkas made from sea lion intestine and similar materials (cf. Oakes 1991:115).

Unangan seamstresses of the eastern Aleutians were renown at contact for their highly decorated and well-made clothing, especially their gut-skin parkas (Black 1982:157; Veniaminov 1984:287). The adoption of grooved needles undoubtedly factored into their ability to make these garments so exceptional. Rather than a "degenerative" needle form, I argue that the appearance of grooved needles around A.D. 1000 marked an artistic florescence in Unangan skin sewing. It is probably no coincidence that Unangan seamstresses adopted grooved needles at a time when their societies were experiencing significant social transformations. The highly decorated clothing they made would have encoded considerable social information, as well as being important status symbols and valuable trade items (Gero 1989; Hayden 1998). These qualities are all important aspects of material culture in societies that are socially and politically complex.

Admittedly, we know few details about the sociopolitical changes the eastern Unangan underwent during the late Aleutian tradition other than that they began living in large communal houses, engaged increasingly in long-distance trade and warfare, and probably experienced increased social inequality (Hoffman 2002). We know virtually nothing regarding gender relations, the organization of production, or the basis of political power during this period of critical transformation. As a result of this limited knowledge, the information gained from the experiments conducted by the False Pass students represents a significant contribution. Their results are consistent with the hypothesis that Unangan women adopted grooved needles to better sew highly decorated and finely stitched garments and not because grooved needles differed significantly from eyed needles in durability or manufacturing costs. The fact that grooved needles were adopted at a time of increased sociopolitical complexity suggests that highly decorated clothing played some role in the Unangan political economy.

These findings are a significant first step but obviously leave many questions unanswered. What were the relationships among skilled seamstresses, clothing production, and political authority? Who engaged in this labor-intensive activity—high-status households, low-status households, or all households? Who benefited from clothing production—the seamstresses and their families, or others? My ongoing research addresses these and similar questions by investigating the links among needle distributions, household status, and the prestige-goods economy during the late Aleutian tradition on Unimak Island (Hoffman 2000, 2002). The complexity of these research questions requires that we obtain a substantial body of data along multiple lines of inquiry. This chapter addresses the relatively simple issues surrounding the durability, manufacturing costs, and size of eyed and grooved needles. By better understanding the practical advantages of grooved needles, we have moved one step closer toward the larger goal of understanding gender roles and social complexity in Unangan history.

This chapter began with the archaeologically documented observation that sometime around A.D. 1000 the Unangan of the eastern Aleutian Islands switched from using sewing needles with delicately drilled eyes to using grooved needles. In trying to understand this technological change, I assume the Unangan seamstresses adopted the new needle form because of practical needs and not as the result of frivolous or idiosyncratic behavior. Three "practical" hypotheses were tested in this chapter—that the needles differed in manufacturing costs, durability, or size. The ability to make exceptionally thin grooved needles was the only practical advantage supported by the experimental and archaeological data.

ACKNOWLEDGMENTS

I thank Lisa Frink, Greg Reinhardt, and Rita Shepard for inviting me to contribute to this volume. Rita, Greg, and Nancy Hoffman provided valuable advice on earlier drafts of this chapter. Nancy illustrated the artifacts used in Figure 10.1. The Agayadan Village excavations were funded by the National Science Foundation (Grant OPP-9629992), the U.S. Fish and Wildlife Service, the Aleut Corporation, Reeve Aleutian Airways, and residents of Cold Bay, Alaska. The U.S. Fish and Wildlife Service, Regional Archaeology Office (Anchorage), financed my spring 2000 trip to False Pass, Alaska, with additional support provided by the Izembek National Wildlife Refuge. I especially want to acknowledge the contributions of the False Pass High School students—Alan Hoggard, Carlin Hoblet, Nikki Hoblet, Christopher Freeman, Teshla Freeman, Karita Freeman, and their teacher, Virginia Berlin. This chapter would not have happened without their curiosity, enthusiasm, and effort. A special thanks also goes to Lillian Bear for providing the ptarmigan bones. This project built on the needle replica experiments conducted by Randy Cooper and Stephanie Butler. I thank them for sharing their knowledge and unpublished data. I also offer my thanks to Virginia Hatfield, who generously provided the Amchitka needle data. Finally, I thank Lisa Frink, Debra Corbett, and Allison Young for their conversations on Aleutian archaeology and gender issues.

11

GENDER, HOUSEHOLDS, AND THE MATERIAL CONSTRUCTION OF SOCIAL DIFFERENCE
METAL CONSUMPTION AT A CLASSIC THULE WHALING VILLAGE

Peter Whitridge

Despite attempts to dispel the stereotype of the egalitarian band (e.g., Collier and Rosaldo 1981; Dunning 1960; Flanagan 1989; Speth 1990; Testart 1988a), the smallest-scale societies, predominantly hunter-gatherers, continue to be marginalized in archaeological discussions of the emergence of social inequality. The notion that social differentiation based minimally on gender and age is somehow consistent with "egalitarianism" and is unrelated to the differences in wealth and privilege found in ranked and stratified societies represents a naturalization of cultural categories and an ethnocentric foreclosure of interest in the social life of "simple" societies. By ignoring variability in the construction of social difference in small-scale societies, we also exclude from analysis the incipiently complex social formations that logically precede the markedly complex and inegalitarian ones that have dominated archaeological research on social change.

On closer inspection it is evident that even such epitomes of the egalitarian band as the Copper and Netsilik Inuit exhibited complex patterns of symbolic and material differentiation that include, but are not limited to, asymmetries based on gender and age (e.g., Jenness 1922:90–94; Rasmussen 1931:26, 146, 193, 195). Although potentially of great theoretical interest, the modest differences in wealth and status that occur widely in Inuit and other hunter-gatherer societies may be difficult to discern archaeologically, especially in the absence of clear analytic signposts directing us to the most worthwhile research avenues. The extremely well-preserved archaeological record of Eastern Thule culture (c. A.D. 1000–1600) is promising in this regard (for overviews, see Mathiassen 1927; Maxwell 1985; McGhee 1984b).

Between about A.D. 1200 and 1400, relatively sedentary Classic Thule communities based mainly on surplus harvesting of large sea mammals flourished in the Central Canadian Arctic. Although clearly ancestral to historical Inuit groups and sharing numerous features of socioeconomic organization and material culture with them, the greater size and permanence of Classic Thule settlements and greater productivity of the related harvesting economies appear to have been associated with greater differentiation of economic role, social status, and material wealth. Differentiation was neither as great as that typically found among groups labeled *complex hunter-gatherers* nor as elusive as what one might expect among more mobile foragers (including their historical descendants). Classic Thule thus appears to represent one of the "not-quite-so-egalitarian" (Diehl 1996) cases needed to broaden the scope of social archaeology and provide an analytic bridge to the least differentiated societies.

The present work reports part of a larger research project on the construction of social difference at the Classic Thule site of Qariaraqyuk (PaJs-2), a large winter village in the major Thule whaling region of southeast Somerset Island in the Central Canadian Arctic (Figure 11.1; Whitridge 1999a). The investigation was especially concerned with the interplay between gender and household status, on the premise that artifactual, architectural, and behavioral markers of gender difference would have been mobilized in the construction of broader social inequalities with a shift toward increasing competition and differentiation among households. The analysis reported here concentrates on one such medium of social differentiation—patterns of consumption of exotic metals—using both direct and indirect indicators of access to metal for tools and ornaments. Following a brief theoretical prelude and outline of Thule social relations, the Qariaraqyuk data are introduced, Thule metal use is reviewed, the data are presented by gender and dwelling, and the results are discussed in terms of the broader pattern of wealth consumption and social differentiation at Qariaraqyuk.

MATERIAL CULTURE AND SOCIAL IDENTITY

For many years the conventional starting point for archaeologies of gender was the observation that gender is a cultural construct rather than a natural mode of being female or male (or something else). The

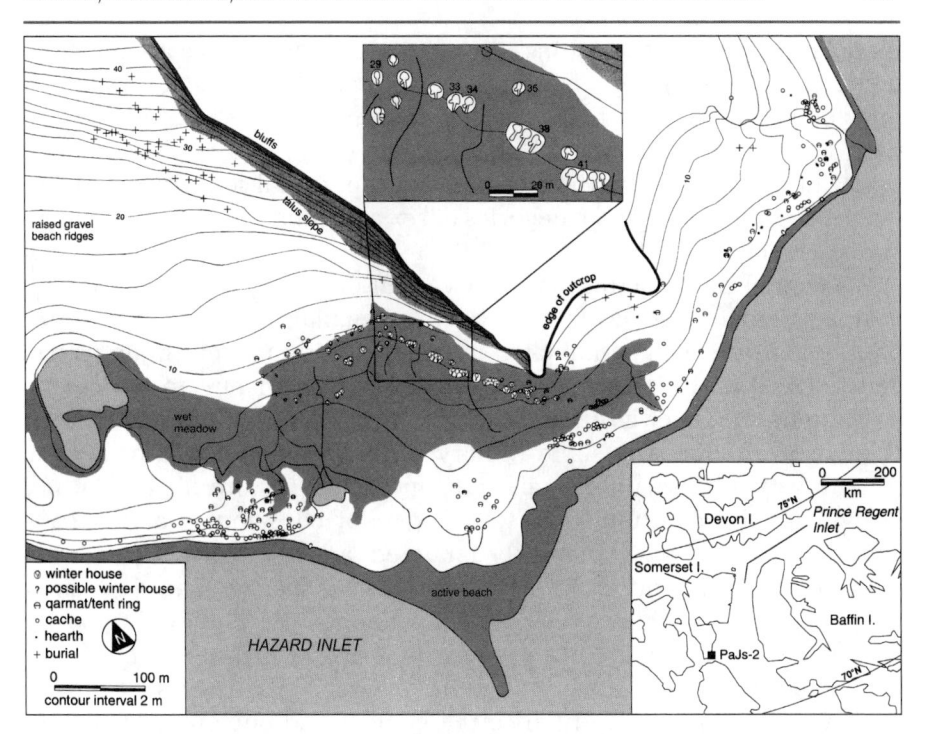

Figure 11.1 Map of Qariaraqyuk (PaJs-2), southeast Somerset Island, Nunavut, based on 1992 survey

term *sex* was reserved for the biological ground of female-male difference and was thus inadequately problematized in the rush to document past cultural variants of the gender system. It has now become apparent that this dichotomization of the cultural and the natural creates as many difficulties as it was expected to resolve. Not only cultural models of gender but also material, "biological" modes of embodiment can be considered constructed, perpetually emergent within a distinct social historical setting (see, e.g., Butler 1993; Fausto-Sterling 2000; Oyama 2000).

In retrospect it should have been obvious to archaeologists, long familiar with the interpretation of biographical information read from skeletal remains, that the social/cultural and the material/biological were so thoroughly intertwined as to be irreducible to one or the other pole. Indeed it is precisely this hybrid (Latour 1993) or cyborg (Haraway 1991) quality of social being—always simultaneously and inseparably material and ideal, subjective and objective, natural and cultural, and so on—that renders the forms and meanings of past sex/gender systems accessible to archaeologists. Sex/gender is materialized in countless ways; the skeletons and food residues and tools and architectural spaces and landscapes with which we work were all once part of living sex/gender systems, were integral to the creation of embodied personal identities and the (re)production of cultural categories of sex and gender (gender, for short, in the rest of this chapter).

One implication of this materialized plurality of gender-related things is that "gender" can never have been a singular, static phenomenon. Over a lifetime, every individual is inserted within a multitude of discourses on social difference that do not simply conspire to promote a hegemonic model of culturally appropriate gender (or ethnic or class) roles or overdetermine some unitary subjective experience of gender (or ethnicity or class) on the part of the individual (Moore 1994a). Rather, individuals are continually in the process of consciously and unconsciously constructing a complexly gendered (and ethnically marked and classed) social identity out of fundamentally disparate materials, such as speech acts, bodily postures and movements, economic roles, social interactions, material culture production, dress, adornment, and so on. The material residues encountered by archaeologists represent a wide variety of such media and hence the context and outcomes of the actions of particular individuals in the past who created and deployed material culture in the course of negotiating a situationally contingent and historically fluid social identity.

Gender is only one of the themes that inflects material culture, although it is usually one with particularly profound implications for social practice. In a given cultural context archaeologists may discern systems of correspondences—a gender field—among the expressions of gender produced within the various discursive domains, but there is no single, essential category of interior experience or social practice to which these material discourses are intrinsically and exclusively addressed. The production of a particular element of material culture—such as the decoration of a pot—as much as one's speech or actions toward others, is invariably a complex social act. The particular object or act will be perceived as conforming to some norm or perhaps as resisting or rejecting or improving upon the expected outcome, or it may not impinge upon other individuals at all. The choices an individual makes, whether unconscious or deliberate or constrained by external factors, are socially meaningful to the extent that that element of material culture, or that behavior, is in some detectable relation of difference or similarity to what others have done before. It may at once represent, however, an identification with or subversion of the types of practice expected of women or men, adult or child, rich or poor, the member of one clan or another, or one community or another. By specifying the ways in which various elements of material culture (such as the exotic raw materials discussed later) or behaviors are simultaneously implicated in several such discourses on social difference, we can begin to delineate the operation of the larger social field at a particular time and place (see Bourdieu 1984). From there we proceed to the exploration of cross-cultural patterning in the production of social difference in the past.

For example, some social theorists have suggested that sex or gender difference provides a model for other kinds of social difference, that distinctions in status or rank are somehow constructed out of gender difference, as if the latter were the prototype for all forms of social inequality (Bourdieu 1990; Collier and Rosaldo 1981; Godelier 1986). This implies that gender inequality, or at least marked gender differences, will precede or accompany the emergence of broader social inequalities. The establishment of parallels or resonances between the construction of various forms of social difference—based on gender, class, age, household, kin group, ethnicity, ritual affiliation, or whatever—should thus generate insights into the emergence of social complexity while also providing an important point of access to past systems of meaning by illuminating symbolic homologies among different conceptual domains.

A number of domains of Thule material culture and practice in which gender and household status were demonstrably intertwined are found at Qariaraqyuk, such as the use and marking of dwelling and community space, participation in ritual, and access to raw materials (Whitridge 1997, 1999a). Especially noteworthy, given the site's distance from known sources, metals of both Native and Norse extraction are unusually abundant in Qariaraqyuk dwelling assemblages and point to the strategic importance of exotic trade goods in the largest and wealthiest Classic Thule communities (see McCartney 1991 for a far-reaching analysis of the socioeconomic context of Thule metal exchange). Even among their purportedly egalitarian Netsilingmiut descendants, metals and other exotic or scarce raw materials figured in the material demarcation of social position: "there was a sort of halo about the man who owned a knife [of iron] or a sledge of wood, and the woman who could sew her husband's clothing with a needle of iron or steel was the envy of all her sisters" (Rasmussen 1931:26–27). Raw material utilization provides an archaeological vantage on the field of Thule social differentiation.

ANALOGIES FOR THULE SOCIAL RELATIONS

The Classic Thule colonists of the eastern Arctic differed from their modified Thule and historic Inuit successors in the degree to which they relied on communal harvesting of large mammals to generate a storable surplus that subsidized sedentary winter settlement (Whitridge 2002). With the onset of the Little Ice Age at about A.D. 1400 (Kreutz et al. 1997), many groups abandoned large-scale storage and land-based winter villages for mobile ringed seal hunting from temporary snow house camps on the sea ice, a shift in subsistence-settlement systems identified with the Classic-modified Thule transition. One of the best illustrations of this economic reorganization is found along the channels of the Central Canadian Arctic, which were densely settled in Classic Thule times. Winter villages with dozens of sod houses are associated with flensing beaches that stretch for kilometers, lined with caches for storing whale products and littered with the bones of hundreds of bowhead whales (see Savelle 1996; Savelle and McCartney 1994, 1999; Whitridge 2001 for some recent overviews of Classic Thule whaling). During modified Thule times the area was progressively abandoned to permanent settlement and by the historic period had been transformed into a little-used frontier (Savelle 1981). Even in Low Arctic regions where sporadic bowhead whaling continued, the scale of Classic Thule settlement and whaling success was never equaled. Economically, many Classic Thule groups are more akin to the historic Inupiat whalers of North Alaska (with whom Classic Thule shares an early Western Thule ancestor) than historic Canadian Inuit, and in important archaeological details they also appear to have had patterns of community organization similar to the North Alaskan (McCartney 1991).

One of the hallmarks of North Alaskan social relations was the role played by wealthy individuals, called boat owners, or *umialit* (singular *umialik*), in sponsoring and coordinating the cooperative harvesting of whales and walrus, and caribou in the interior (Burch 1975, 1981, 1988; Cassell 1988; Murdoch 1988 [1892]; Rainey 1947; Sheehan 1985, 1997; Spencer 1959, 1972). Coastal *umialit* assembled boat crews for sea mammal hunting, rewarding crew members with commodities obtained through the interregional trade network and a share of the harvest in what amounted to a swap of resources for labor. *Umialiks* accumulated substantial surpluses of food, fuel, and other commodities in the process, which they were expected to distribute generously within the community.

The unequal flows of resources from wealthy *umialiks* and crew members to poorer households resulted in differential relations of gift-incurred debt and ultimately grades of status. Big Man-like *umialit* occu-

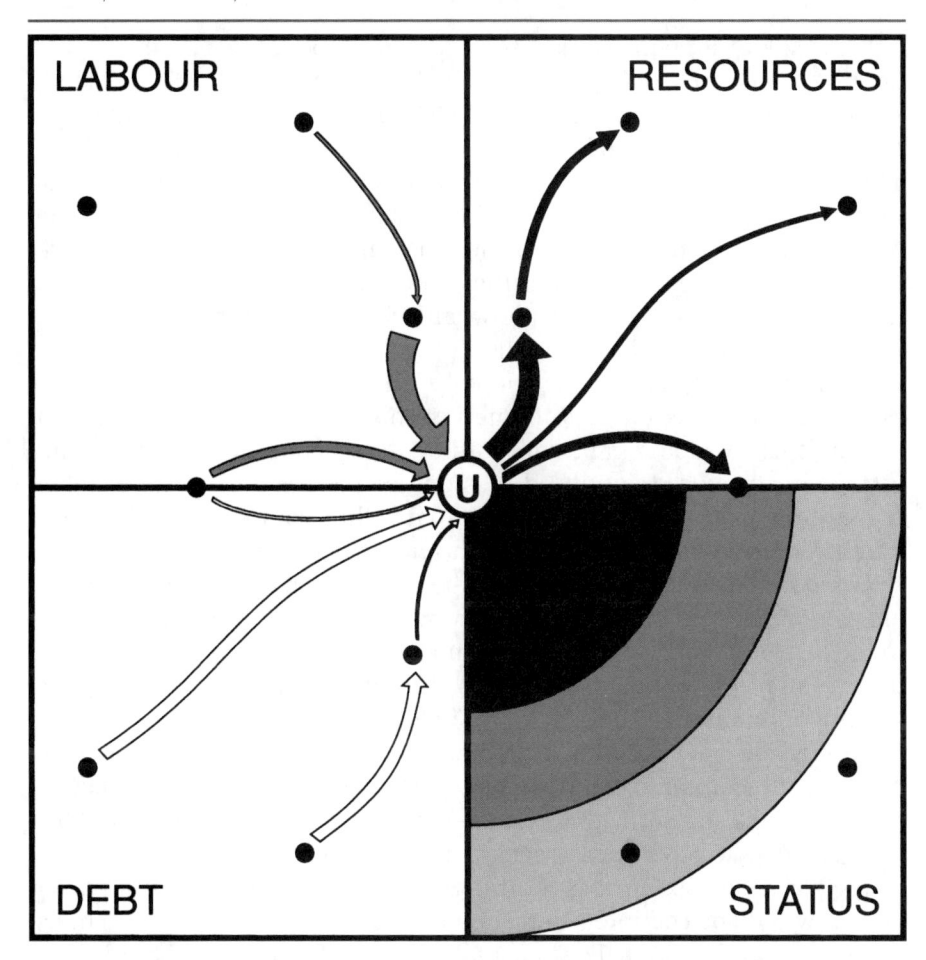

Figure 11.2 Model of Thule social relations; gradients of social status (bottom right) based on differential participation in the umialik-*sponsored whaleboat crew (top left), differential access to harvest shares and exotic commodities distributed by the* umialik *(top right), and differential accumulation of symbolic debt/capital consequent on receipt/disbursement of "unearned" resources*

pied the pinnacle of this system of informal wealth- and prestige-based ranks (Figure 11.2). The architectural expression of the whaling crew was the *qargi,* or men's house, in which crew members assembled to socialize and gear up for the whaling season and in which all important community feasts and ceremonies were held (Larson 1995). (For more on the use of the men's house, see Chapters 3, 5, 7, this volume.) Functionally analogous structures occur widely in large early Classic Thule settlements (e.g., Habu and Savelle 1994; McCullough 1989), so the *qargi* complex appears to have been part of the original cultural repertoire of Thule migrants. There is also evidence for extensive long-distance trade in Classic Thule times and, as discussed later, differential access to the exotic or locally scarce commodities that moved through the network. Classic Thule whaling communities were as dependent as their North Alaskan counterparts on flows of wealth for underwriting the entrepreneurial, *umialik*-led whaling system.

This model of the social economy of whaling has numerous archaeological implications for settlement systems, site structure, and feature assemblages. Whale-reliant communities are expected to be large and internally structured and to possess one or more *qariyit* used for whaling ceremonials and preparations. Multi-dwelling compounds, or *upsiksui*, may be present and associated with *qariyit*. Dwellings should vary in size and complexity, and the corresponding assemblages reflect differences in whaling activity, access to scarce and exotic materials, deployment of symbols of social status, and involvement in ritual. Many of these dimensions of household status differentiation are expected to have a complementary expression in the field of gender difference.

Alongside new social and ideological mechanisms legitimating the differential accumulation of wealth, an increasing cultural preoccupation with whaling from the Birnirk-Thule transition, around A.D. 900–1000, appears to have been associated with a reorganization of domestic labor (Whitridge 1997). The central hearth typical of late Birnirk winter houses was displaced into a detached kitchen wing in early Thule times, concealing and marginalizing a major locus of women's activities. Simultaneously, the *qargi* replaced the family dwelling as the major architectural locus of men's activities, much as the *qargi*-based boat crew replaced the household as the core socioeconomic institution in the new social order. This co-optation of domestic symbols and practices may have resulted in a decline, or at least a realignment, of women's status and authority (for a differing view of status and the use of a primarily male space, see Chapter 3, this volume). Evaluations of power relations between women and men in historic Inuit and Inupiat societies, however, vary enormously (see, e.g., Ager 1980; Bodenhorn 1990; Briggs 1974; Ellanna and Sherrod 1995; Giffen 1930; Guemple 1986, 1995; Kjellström 1973; Matthiasson 1979; McElroy 1979; Reimer 1996; for Yupik gender relations see Ackerman 1990a; Jolles 1997; Jolles and Kaningok 1990; Lantis 1946; Chapters 4, 7, this volume).

There are some compelling indicators of gender inequality or hierarchy in Inuit societies, the most often cited being the control exercised over women's sexuality through spouse-exchange partnerships contracted between men. Ethnographic reports also exist of marriage by abduction or purchase, rape, polygyny, wife beating, restrictive behavioral taboos related to menstruation and childbirth, predominantly male inheritance, female infanticide, and preferential treatment of male children. Balancing this are reports of an overall parity of authority within the household, occasional polyandrous marriage, female shamans, women's participation in trading and hunting, and the important symbolic role accorded women in procuring the harvest. Economic complementarity of women's and men's roles appears often to have been explicitly recognized, and in most groups women exercised significant authority with respect to the household's stores. According to Diamond Jenness (1922:162): "Marriage involves no subjection on the part of the woman. She has her own sphere of activity, and within that she is as supreme as her husband is in his." This condition of gender heterarchy among the Copper Inuit is generally consistent with reports from other Inuit and Inupiat groups (Briggs 1974; Guemple 1986, 1995), although men seem to have possessed greater overall decision-making authority, thus exercising, in Ernest Burch's (1975:91) words, a "benevolent despotism."

The complexity of Inuit gender relations should lead us to expect complex patterning in the Thule archaeological record. The existence of distinct spheres of activity and power may be expressed in the nature and degree of architectural segmentation at the dwelling and community levels, the segregation of gendered refuse, and divergent patterning in the organization of men's and women's material culture assemblages (toolkits, dress and adornment, ritual paraphernalia, and similar items). A hierarchical inflection to gender relations might be expressed in such things as differential access to raw materials for tools and dress; asymmetries with respect to the size, location, and symbolic marking of gendered dwelling and public spaces; and differential participation in core community ritual—all of which can potentially be assessed through the nature and distribution of gender-specific artifacts and refuse. These were among the expectations that shaped the collection and analysis of data at Qariaraqyuk.

RESEARCH AT QARIARAQYUK

Qariaraqyuk is situated near the southeastern tip of Somerset Island on the north shore of Hazard Inlet. Although several kilometers from the extensive flensing beaches of the open Prince Regent Inlet coast (see

Savelle and McCartney 1988), the site is sheltered from winter winds and has commanding access to productive fast ice and polynya environments for ringed seal hunting (Finley and Johnston 1977). Based on a 1992 survey, the site consists of a row of at least fifty-seven semi-subterranean winter house (including *qariyit*) depressions, the remains of dozens of less substantial tents and *qarmat* that would have been occupied during the warm seasons, and numerous caches, exterior hearths, burials, and isolated artifacts (Figure 11.1). Close to 3,400 bowhead whale bones are scattered across the 30 ha survey area, most in close association with the winter houses, representing a bowhead Minimum Number of Individuals of 261.

A *qargi* (House 41) and five dwellings (Houses 29, 33, 34, 35, and 38) were excavated in 1993 and 1994 within a restricted portion of the site, with the dwellings selected to maximize morphological variability in the sample. The easternmost excavated house (38) and the *qargi* (41) are directly adjacent to a sheet midden that contained elevated frequencies of bowhead elements derived from ethnographically prized carcass portions (Whitridge 2002). Based on calibrated ^{14}C dates and artifact seriation, occupation of the excavated portion of the site spanned approximately 250 years, with feature construction beginning around A.D. 1200 and abandonment beginning shortly after A.D. 1400 and progressing throughout the fifteenth century. The evidence is consistent with substantial occupational overlap of the excavated houses during the fourteenth century and perhaps also the late thirteenth and early fifteenth centuries.

THULE METAL USE

METAL SOURCES AND TRADE

A variety of materials with restricted sources and wide archaeological distributions in the eastern Arctic indicates extensive trade networks in Classic Thule times (McCartney 1988, 1991; for accounts of late prehistoric and early historic trade, see Anderson 1974–1975; Burch 1970, 1988; Morrison 1991; Savelle 1985; Stefansson 1914). Besides the native and Old World metals discussed later, amber, soapstone, slate, nephrite, and pyrite all appear to have been exchanged over long distances. Possible occurrences of exotic pottery and coal may represent items that accompanied early Thule migrants from Alaska (Arnold and Stimmel 1983; Kalkreuth, McCullough, and Richardson 1993; Kalkreuth and Sutherland 1998). The commodities that traditionally accounted for the majority of intersocietal trade—especially sea mammal oil, caribou hides, walrus or bearded seal hides, and wood (and to a lesser extent ivory and horn)—

were actually quite widely distributed but might be locally scarce or difficult to procure in quantity because of scheduling conflicts. Unfortunately, these materials also have relatively low archaeological visibility and are difficult to source. Trade between neighboring regions in these bulky goods was almost certainly important prehistorically but requires much additional research. Metal, however, survives reasonably well in Thule deposits and is easily identified as of nonlocal origin.

Although native copper and meteoritic iron were utilized prehistorically in several parts of North America, Classic Thule groups were exceptional in their degree of reliance on metal for a wide variety of implements and ornaments (McCartney 1988, 1991; Morrison 1987). Numerous sources of native copper are found in the eastern Arctic, but large drift deposits on Victoria Island and the adjacent mainland (Franklin et al. 1981; Morrison 1987) appear to have been the most important prehistoric sources (Figure 11.3). The Cape York meteorite in northwest Greenland has been an important source of extraterrestrial iron since at least late Dorset times, and telluric iron, which occurs naturally as nodules in basalt flows in West Greenland, was used by local groups but probably not traded widely (Buchwald and Mosdal 1985; McCartney 1991; McCartney and Mack 1973). Asian iron has been traded east across Bering Strait for as much as 2,000 years (e.g., Collins 1937; Larsen and Rainey 1948) but has not been specifically identified at sites in the Canadian Arctic. Smelted iron, copper, and occasionally bronze do occur on a large number of Classic Thule sites but were most likely obtained from the Norse colonies in Greenland, with which Thule groups are known to have interacted (McGhee 1984a).

ARTIFACTUAL EVIDENCE

Metal occurs in small quantities in most large Thule assemblages but was highly curated and so is usually abundant only at sites adjacent to major sources, such as those on Coronation Gulf and southwestern Victoria Island (McGhee 1972; Morrison 1983). Based on the actual metal pieces recovered, copper and iron were substituted for ground stone (usually slate) for the bits of gravers, adzes, and drills; the blades of side- and end-slotted men's knives and women's *ulus*; and the end blades of harpoon heads, lance heads, and arrowheads (bone was sometimes used for harpoon-head end blades). Metal was also occasionally used for needles, fishhooks, leister prongs and barbs, and gaffs and for ornaments such as bracelets and brow bands (Morrison 1987).

The extent of metal use by Thule and other prehistoric Arctic peoples is even more frequently indicated, however, by the occurrence of very

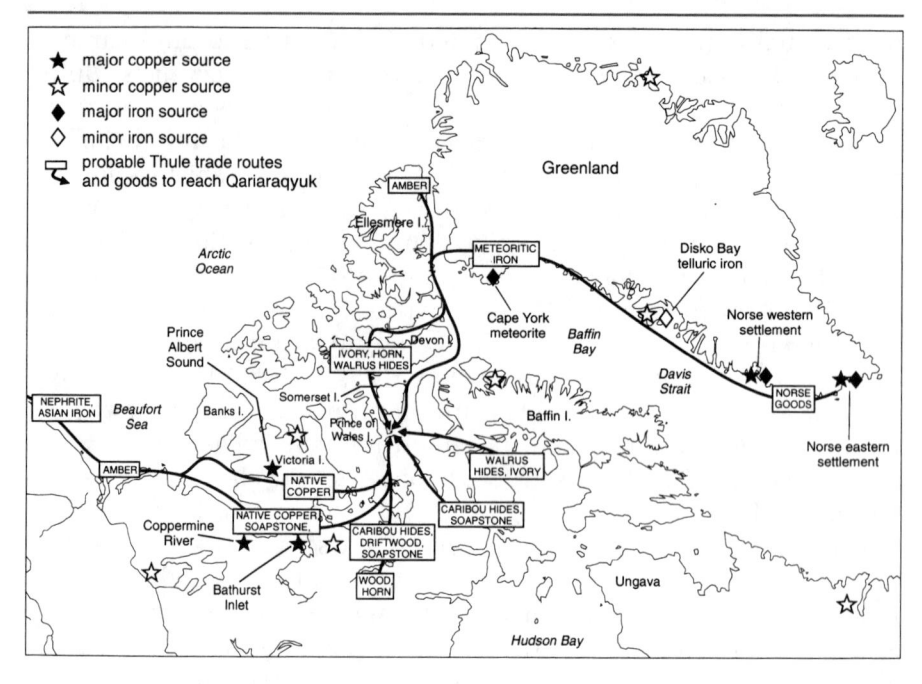

Figure 11.3 Map of Eastern Arctic showing metal sources and probable routes by which trade goods reached Qariaraqyuk during Classic Thule times

thin slots in the surviving bone, antler, or ivory portions of composite tools (Blaylock 1980; McCartney 1988, 1991). Tools that likely once held metal blades are commonly recovered with very narrow, but empty, blade slots or sockets, and sometimes the slot area is damaged from the original blade having been pried or cut away. These blade or bit hafts were discarded at a greater rate than the metal they contained, and so they potentially provide a more accurate picture of metal use than the metal artifacts themselves, to the extent that metal- and stone-bladed hafts can be discriminated. In addition, recovered metal pieces are often too fragmentary to be functionally identified and so may be relatively uninformative. Of 98 metal specimens recovered in excavations at Qariaraqyuk, only 33 (34%) could be identified to a functional class more specific than "blade." In contrast, 226 measurable blade or bit sockets occurred on functionally identifiable whale-bone, antler, and ivory artifacts.

SLOT WIDTH ANALYSIS

Slot widths have been inconsistently reported by Arctic archaeologists in the past, beyond the observation that some blade slots are very narrow and some are relatively wide. Measurements of some slots from a collection, or mean widths for entire collections, have been reported, but data on all individual specimens are rarely found. Slot widths of about 1 mm (Collins 1937:145–146; Larsen and Rainey 1948:82; McCartney 1991:30) or sometimes 1–2 mm (Blaylock 1980:171; McCartney 1977, 1988:59) have been considered diagnostic of metal blades, with some variation in reported width modes likely resulting from variability in artifact function (i.e., a metal adze bit must be thicker than the blade of a fine engraving tool). A. P. McCartney (1988:71, 1991:30) suggested that knife handles (the most common thin-slotted artifacts at Qariaraqyuk and elsewhere) with slots between 0.5 and 1.5 mm likely held metal blades, whereas those about 2.0 mm and greater held ground stone blades. Although borne out by the present analysis, this proposition is difficult to evaluate against published Thule assemblages, which tend to be reported to the nearest whole millimeter when any slot measurements are provided.

Slot dimensions were recorded to the nearest 0.05 mm for the 226 measurable slots from Qariaraqyuk. Maximum and minimum measurements were taken, and an average value was calculated for each slot, but patterning turned out to be strongest for the maximum slot width. It appears that this is the result of both the design of slots and postdepositional deformation. Some hafts have become desiccated and the slot prongs warped, with the result that minimum measurements are occasionally close to zero. This is consistent with the anecdotal observation that slots possessing in situ blades tend to be wider than slots lacking blades. This is occasionally because of the formation of an oxidation rind around iron blades but is likely also attributable to the contraction of the thin distal portions of the prongs of bladeless slots.

Many tools, however, appear to have been intentionally designed to hold blades that were thicker than at least the distal portion of the manufactured slot, the blades being inserted by prying the prongs apart or heating the haft so the slot expanded. Franz Boas (1964 [1888]:110) described the latter procedure: "the bone is heated and the blade is inserted while it is hot. As it is cooling the slit becomes narrower and the blade is firmly squeezed into the bone handle." To accomplish this more easily, some complete blades—particularly of ground stone—have wedge-shaped stems that could have been jammed into a relatively narrow slot

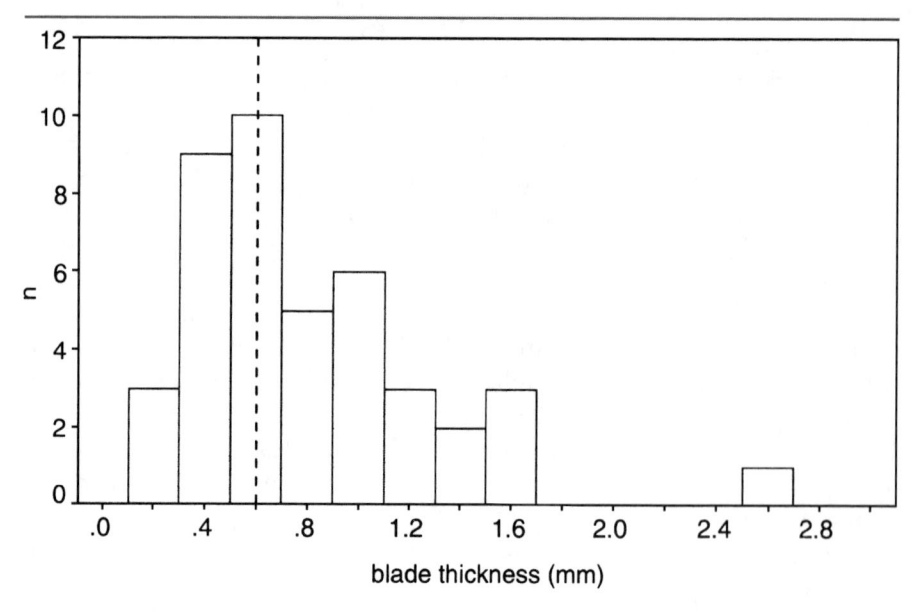

Figure 11.4 Distribution of blade thicknesses for 42 Thule blades (39 copper, 3 iron) from Qariaraqyuk, Deblicquy (Taylor 1981), Brooman Point (McGhee 1984c), and Skraeling Island (McCullough 1989)

to more effectively hold the blade in place. The less efficient alternative is to wedge packing material (wood chips, hide, baleen, and similar substances) into the space between the blade and the prong, or to tie the blade to its haft through lashing holes, both of which are observed on some specimens with in situ blades and relatively wide slots. Use of the packing technique, perhaps in combination with others mentioned earlier, may be indicated by the measurements on forty-two actual metal blades from Qariaraqyuk and other Thule sites (Franklin et al. 1981; McGhee 1984c; Taylor 1981). Blade thickness has a right-skewed distribution with a mode at about 0.6 mm, which is thinner than virtually all measured slots (Figure 11.4). It thus appears both that relatively narrow slots sometimes held thicker blades and that wide slots sometimes held thin blades. It is assumed here, however, that there would have been a tendency to manufacture relatively narrow slots for thin (i.e., metal) blades and wide slots for relatively thick (stone or, more rarely, bone) blades, since very narrow slots could not hold most stone blades and very wide slots would be highly inefficient for fastening thin metal blades.

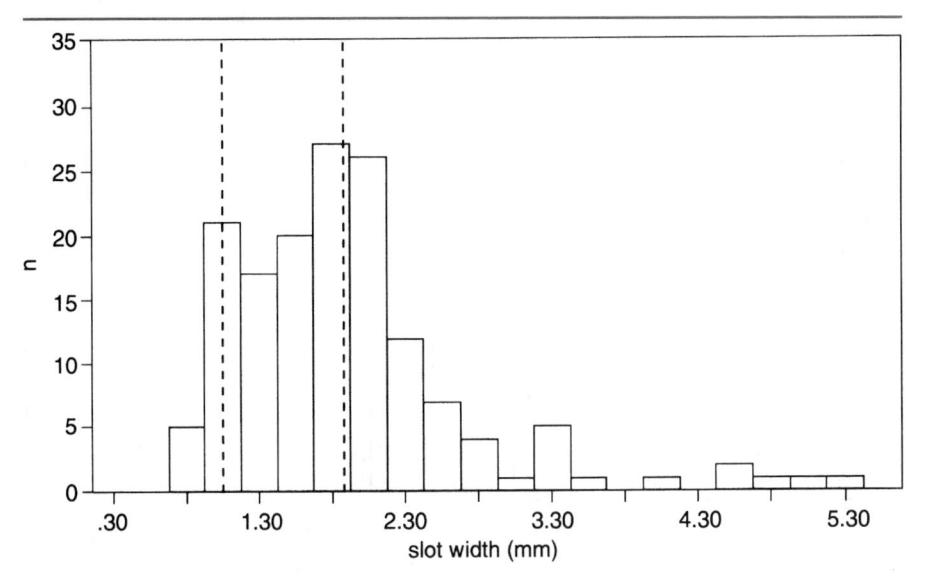

Figure 11.5 Distribution of slot widths for all knives from Qariaraqyuk (n = 152)

The ideal expression of such a tendency would be bimodal slot width distributions.

In fact, the Qariaraqyuk slot width distributions are consistently bimodal for all classes of tools, although the specific modal widths are not identical across artifact types. The tools can be divided into three groups based on slot width modes. Knife slots—including end- and side-slotted men's knives, composite knives used for grooving bone and antler, and crescent-bladed women's knives, or *ulus*—have modes at about 1.0 and 1.9 mm (Figure 11.5), corresponding closely to McCartney's suggested 1 and 2 mm modes. End-bladed "projectiles," consisting of lance heads, harpoon heads, and arrowheads, have the strongest modes at 1.45 and 1.80 mm (Figure 11.6). A small sample of twenty-two gravers and adzes has modes at 2.65 and 4.65 mm (Figure 11.7). These patterns hold up for individual artifact types within these three classes, such as for the three major types of men's knives in Figure 11.8—each of which exhibits modes, albeit of different shapes and sizes, at about 1.0 and 1.9 mm. A crude prediction of the intended blade material for each specimen can thus be produced by assigning each slot to one or the other mode, based on splitting the distribution at the midpoint: 1.45 mm for knives, 1.63 mm for projectiles, and 3.65 mm for heavy-duty manufacturing tools.

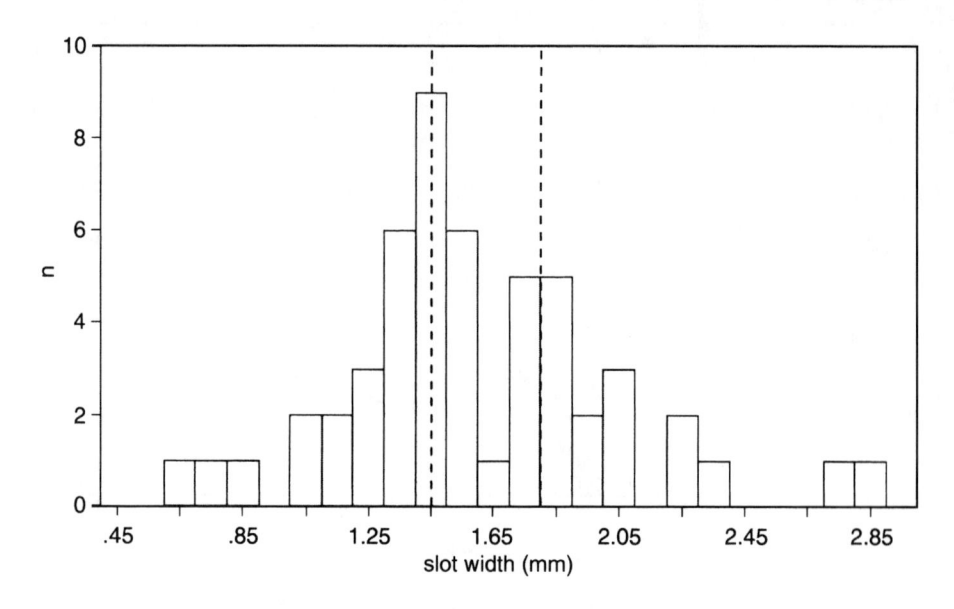

Figure 11.6 Distribution of slot widths for all projectiles from Qariaraqyuk (n = 52)

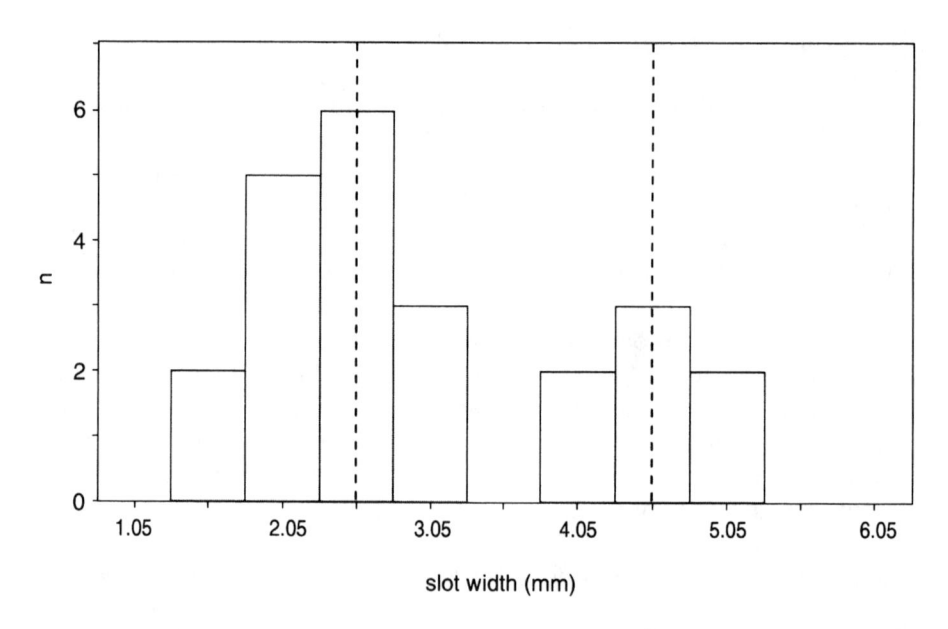

Figure 11.7 Distribution of slot widths for all heavy-duty manufacturing tools from Qariaraqyuk (n = 22)

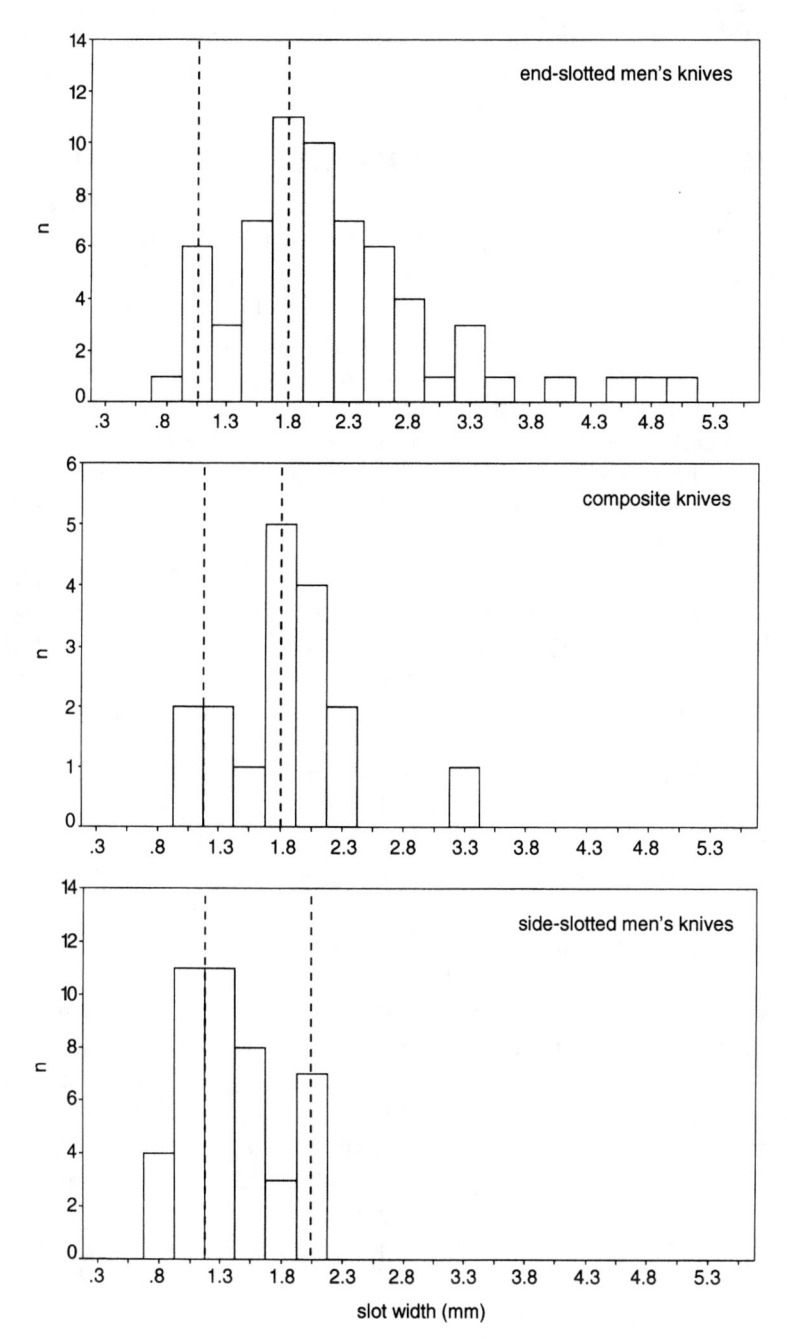

Figure 11.8 Distribution of slot widths for men's end-slotted (n = 64), composite (n = 17), and side-slotted knives (n = 44) from Qariaraqyuk

Overall, 43 percent of tool slots fall toward the thin mode in their respective category and can tentatively be considered to have held metal blades.

HOUSEHOLD METAL CONSUMPTION AT QARIARAQYUK

As a result of variable preservation of some organic materials, especially such perishables as feathers and hide, relative frequencies of metal are best evaluated with respect to other inorganic artifact finds. The distribution of these finds by house is presented in Table 11.1 (excluding chipped stone material likely of Paleoeskimo origin). Metal accounts for 16 percent of all inorganic materials in the Qariaraqyuk assemblage, with copper making up just over three-quarters of this total. Based on overall metal frequency, the House 41 *qargi* appears to have been the most important locus of metal artifact production, loss, and discard; dwellings, on the other hand, fall into two groups: those with values close to the sitewide mean (Houses 33, 34, and 38) and those with much lower values (Houses 29 and 35). Unfortunately, the House 35 sample size is inadequate; based on binomial probabilities, the frequency of metal items is not significantly less than that expected by chance ($p = 0.165$). The slot width results are slightly different (Table 11.2). Houses 33, 34, and 38 again fall above the sitewide mean, House 33 markedly so, whereas House 29 falls well below. House 35 is well above the mean, but this is impossible to evaluate on a sample of only four measurable hafts. Hafts discarded or lost in *qargi* contexts are less often thin slotted than expected, perhaps reflecting the use of this facility by individuals with and without privileged access to exotic trade goods.

Houses 29 and 35 are both small and lightly constructed and do not belong to a shared mound house group, or *upsiksui*. House 29 is spatially isolated and relatively remote from the high-status/ceremonial neighborhood centered on House 41 that was revealed in the surface whalebone distribution, suggesting reduced access to the community surplus consumed there and social distance from the *qargi* owners or sponsors. Although House 35 is also freestanding, it is not far from the House 33–34 pair and an *upsiksui* that may contain a *qargi*, and it abuts the high-status/ceremonial sheet midden. House 29 had little whaling-related gear, elevated frequencies of terrestrial hunting and fishing gear, and low frequencies of bones from prized bowhead carcass portions, whereas House 35 had no whaling gear (complicated again by small samples) but fairly abundant prestige whale bone.

It is possible that superficial architectural similarities between Houses 29 and 35 are masking important social differences. Although both house-

Table 11.1 – Distribution of inorganic finds at Qariaraqyuk, by house

	H. 29 count	H. 29 %	H. 33 count	H. 33 %	H. 34 count	H. 34 %	H. 35 count	H. 35 %	H. 38 count	H. 38 %	H. 41 count	H. 41 %	TOTAL count	TOTAL %
amber	–	–	–	–	–	–	1	5.3	3	1.3	1	0.5	5	0.8
chert (Thule)	–	–	–	–	1	1.4	–	–	3	1.3	–	–	4	0.7
clay	–	–	–	–	–	–	–	–	8	3.4	–	–	8	1.3
copper	2	3.4	–	–	7	10.0	1	5.3	30	12.8	35	17.4	75	12.5
diabase	9	15.5	1	5.3	8	11.4	5	26.3	12	5.1	43	21.4	78	13.0
dolostone	2	3.4	–	–	1	1.4	–	–	–	–	1	0.5	4	0.7
gneiss	1	1.7	–	–	–	–	–	–	–	–	–	–	1	0.2
iron	2	3.4	3	15.8	3	4.3	–	–	2	0.9	13	6.5	23	3.8
limestone	3	5.2	–	–	3	4.3	–	–	7	3.0	3	1.5	16	2.7
mica	3	5.2	7	36.8	7	10.0	1	5.3	60	25.6	50	24.9	128	21.3
misc. ground stone	9	15.5	2	10.5	1	1.4	–	–	8	3.4	3	1.5	23	3.8
misc. stone	10	17.2	–	–	6	8.6	1	5.3	13	5.6	4	2.0	34	5.7
nephrite	–	–	–	–	–	–	2		0.9	–	–	–	2	0.3
phyllite	–	–	–	–	–	–	–	–	1	0.4	–	–	1	0.2
pottery	3	5.2	1	5.3	14	20.0	1	5.3	55	23.5	27	13.4	101	16.8
pyrite	–	–	–	–	–	–	2	10.5	–	–	–	–	2	0.3
quartz	1	1.7	1	5.3	–	–	–	–	–	–	2	1.0	4	0.7
quartzite	2	3.4	–	–	4	5.7	–	–	1	0.4	1	0.5	8	1.3
sandstone	1	1.7	2	10.5	7	10.0	3	15.8	14	6.0	9	4.5	36	6.0
sandstone (Norse?)	1	1.7	–	–	–	–	–	–	–	–	–	–	1	0.2
schist	3	5.2	–	–	–	–	–	–	–	–	–	–	3	0.5
shale	1	1.7	–	–	–	–	–	–	–	–	–	–	1	0.2
siltstone	–	–	–	–	1	1.4	–	–	1	0.4	–	–	2	0.3
slate	1	1.7	–	–	4	5.7	2	10.5	13	5.6	6	3.0	26	4.3
soapstone	4	6.9	2	10.5	3	4.3	2	10.5	1	0.4	3	1.5	15	2.5
TOTALS	58	99.7	19	100.0	70	99.9	19	100.1	234	100.0	201	100.1	601	100.1

Table 11.2 Inferred blade/bit material for Qariaraqyuk hafts based on slot width analysis, by house and artifact class (M = metal, S = stone)

Artifact Type	House 6 M	House 6 S	House 29 M	House 29 S	House 33 M	House 33 S	House 34 M	House 34 S	House 35 M	House 35 S	House 38 M	House 38 S	House 41 M	House 41 S	Site M	Site S	% Metal
arrowhead	—	—	—	1	2	—	1	—	—	—	—	—	1	—	4	1	80.0
harpoon head	—	—	1	1	2	1	4	5	2	—	4	3	4	4	17	14	54.8
lance head	—	—	1	—	6	—	—	—	—	—	1	1	2	5	10	6	62.5
men's knife, end slotted	—	—	7	2	2	1	3	—	1	—	1	7	9	31	13	51	20.3
men's knife, side slotted	—	—	2	8	1	2	2	—	—	—	6	1	14	8	30	14	68.2
composite knife	—	—	—	—	—	—	1	1	—	—	3	—	—	12	4	13	23.5
ulu	—	—	—	—	5	1	—	1	4	—	—	1	1	14	3	24	11.1
graver/drill chuck	—	—	—	1	1	—	—	—	—	—	1	—	2	3	4	4	50.0
adze head	—	—	—	—	—	—	1	—	1	—	—	1	9	2	11	3	78.6
TOTAL	0	0	2	16	22	5	11	15	3	1	16	14	42	79	96	130	42.5
HOUSE %	n/a	n/a	11.1	88.9	81.5	18.5	42.3	57.7	75.0	25.0	53.3	46.7	34.7	65.2	42.5	57.5	

holds seem to have been resident in the village on a relatively temporary seasonal basis (likely during late fall/early winter), House 35's occupants may have been relatively wealthy or high-status visitors with primary residence in another large winter village, whereas House 29's occupants appear to have deliberately pursued a nonwhaling economic strategy that likely involved high residential mobility (e.g., residence on the sea ice for most of the winter).

Houses 33 and 38 are large and complex dwellings and produced elevated frequencies of whaling gear and prestige bowhead elements, whereas House 34 is intermediate in these respects. All belong to a shared mound house group and are reasonably close to one or more *qariyit*. These houses were occupied by individuals who participated actively in bowhead whaling, perhaps including *umialit* at times during the dwellings' use lives. The assemblages tended to contain high relative frequencies of items of bodily adornment (beads, pendants, brow bands, and similar items), suggesting wealth display or heightened involvement in ritual or festive occasions that called for elaborate dress. Consumption of exotic metals is thus correlated with other markers of household wealth, status, and economic orientation.

GENDER AND METAL CONSUMPTION AT QARIARAQYUK

The distribution of metal artifacts by functional class is provided in Table 11.3. These have been provisionally divided into types predominantly associated with women, with men, or of uncertain gender affiliation based on ethnographic patterns of tool use and adornment. Although most of the assignments can be considered very strong conjectures based on direct historical analogy and marked cross-cultural regularities in the gender division of activities among Inuit and Yupik groups from Siberia to Greenland (e.g., Ager 1980; Bodenhorn 1990:59; Guemple 1986; and see especially Giffen 1930 for a thorough review of ethnohistoric and early ethnographic data on gendered activities), they are open to modification by future archaeological research. Further, women and men might have used each other's tools and performed each other's conventional tasks as circumstances dictated (e.g., Jenness 1922:88). This does not, however, efface the fact that many elements of Inuit material culture were so intimately bound up with gendered practice that they had acquired a kind of iconic status, such as the lamp, pot, *ulu*, scraper, and sewing kit associated with women and the harpoon, bow and arrow, bow drill, kayak, and men's knife for men.

Twice as many of the identifiable metal objects from Qariaraqyuk fall into the men's group as into the women's group. If the unidentified

Table 11.3—Distribution of metal finds at Qariaraqyuk, by artifact class and gender category

	Iron	Copper	Total Metal
WOMEN'S ARTIFACTS			
bracelet	—	1	1
brow band	—	2	2
needle	—	2	2
scraper	—	1	1
ulu blade	3	2	5
TOTAL	3	8	11
MEN'S ARTIFACTS			
adze bit	2	1	3
arrowhead end blade	1	—	1
baleen shave blade	2	—	2
end-slotted knife blade	5	1	6
engraving tool bit	1	—	1
graver bit	1	1	2
harpoon head end blade	—	1	1
rivet	—	2	2
side-slotted knife blade	4	—	4
TOTAL	16	6	22
GENDER AFFILIATION UNCERTAIN OR NEUTRAL			
miscellaneous blade	2	27	29
miscellaneous slotted object	1	—	1
nugget	—	5	5
sheet	—	1	1
unidentifiable fragment	1	28	29
TOTAL	4	61	65

blade fragments were assigned proportionately to the identified blade categories, this imbalance would be accentuated. Furthermore, metal was one of the "hard" raw materials that traditionally fell within the male manufacturing sphere (Birket-Smith 1929:235). Since the uncertain category likely consists mainly of by-products from manufacturing and repair, most of these items can plausibly be considered men's refuse, further skewing the gender proportions. Qualifying these results is the fact that far more artifact types and specimens of all materials are associated with men than with women. Although it is interesting that men apparently consumed a greater *quantity* of a precious commodity, it is difficult to ascertain from these data alone whether they consumed metal at a higher per artifact *rate* than women, since tools or tool parts made of substitute materials will often have followed different taphonomic pathways.

Theoretically, rate of consumption can be inferred from the slot width results, since taphonomic factors are effectively held constant (i.e., the only thing distinguishing metal- and stone-bladed handles is slot form). Since women and men traditionally used different styles of knives, rates of metal consumption can be compared directly for these functionally equivalent tool classes (Figure 11.9). Only 11 percent of twenty-seven *ulus* had narrow slots, the lowest rate for any slotted tool type. About twice as many of the men's end-slotted and composite knives and over six times as many of the side-slotted knives held thin blades. Overall, 38 percent of 125 slots on men's knives (and 47% of all 199 slots on men's tools) fell toward the narrow mode, or significantly more than women's *ulus* ($X^2 = 7.06$, $p = 0.008$). Since some Thule *ulus* have in situ metal blades and metal was rapidly adopted for all *ulu* blades at contact, it is unlikely that this is the result of functional constraints.

The association of *ulus* with ground stone blades and of men's knives with metal blades receives striking semantic support. The word *savik* refers simultaneously to various types of men's knives (most often the side-slotted "crooked knife," but also to men's knives in general) and to iron in a number of dialects of Inuktitut (Murdoch 1988 [1892]:157; Rasmussen 1930:70; Schneider 1987:348), whereas slate was referred to as *uluksa,* meaning "material for an *ulu,*" in the Barrow dialect (Murdoch 1988:60): iron is to men's knife is to man as slate is to *ulu* is to woman. This echoes the results of Robert McGhee's (1977) classic analysis of the gender symbolism adhering to the selection of antler and ivory as raw materials for Thule hunting implements.

It is also noteworthy that the relative frequencies of copper and iron are precisely reversed for men's and women's objects. Iron is rarer than copper in the Qariaraqyuk assemblage and is more "exotic" in having come from a greater distance. It is also functionally superior to copper, since it is harder and will hold an edge longer without needing resharpening (Morrison 1987). Demand for copper was low where access to iron was good (Morrison 1991:240; Stefansson 1914:13). Iron was thus likely more valuable than copper, lending a superordinate inflection to the pattern of gender access to metals. These substances, however, also have deeper symbolic resonances that overlap, but need not be reduced to, their functional and pecuniary qualities. Copper was considered a red metal (Schultz-Lorentszen 1927:113) and iron a white metal (Schneider 1987:280, 348), which implies a gender alignment by virtue

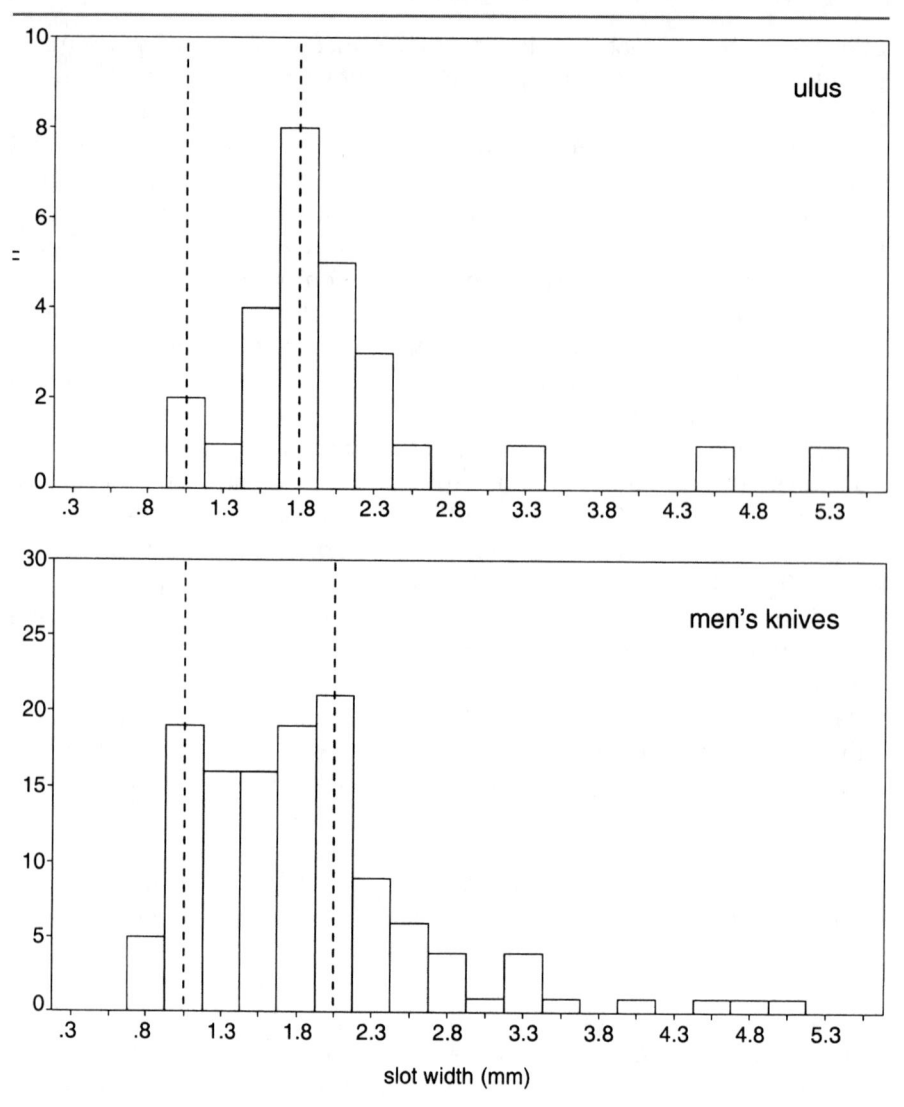

Figure 11.9 Distribution of slot widths for ulus (n = 27) and men's knives (n = 125) from Qariaraqyuk

of the association of women with the color red and men with white (Saladin d'Anglure 1977) and perhaps alludes to the bodily gender metaphors of menstrual blood and semen. An affinity between copper and blood can also be seen as a symbolic overlay on the functional disposition of metals for men's artifacts. Where copper and iron are both present, copper appears to tend to be used for the points and blades (and associated rivets) of hunting and fishing implements that come in contact with flesh and blood, whereas iron appears to be used for knives used especially to work hard materials such as antler, bone, and ivory. This was the case among the Copper Inuit historically (Stefansson 1962:249), whereas at Qariaraqyuk the ratio of iron to copper among men's manufacturing implements was 5.0, versus 0.3 for harvesting-related implements.

DISCUSSION

The results of the comparisons of metal finds and slot widths by household and gendered tool types are consistent with expectations for privileged access to the most precious trade goods by men and whaling households. Additional categories of data—such as access to other exotic or scarce materials and the size, complexity, and location of roofed spaces—indicate that a variety of material media were similarly mobilized in discourses on gender and household status; different kinds of social difference were constructed with similar symbolic resources. Just as revealing as these parallels in the material production of hierarchical difference are parallels in the way in which the latter was subverted or defused. For example, the close association of women's tools and refuse with dwelling interiors recalls the close association between women's bodies and houses reported ethnographically (Nuttall 1992; Saladin d'Anglure 1977; Therrien 1982). The house in turn is symbolically marked as a microcosm of the Inuit world (Fortescue 1988) and hence a sacred space. Furthermore, most of the kitchens at Qariaraqyuk, quintessential women's spaces, incorporated bowhead skulls in their wall construction, linking women to whaling symbolism and evoking the important role of *umialit* wives in ritually ensuring a successful whale harvest (Bodenhorn 1990). Women's manufacturing refuse and tools are also closely associated with personal objects (amulets, pendants, mica mirrors, ornaments) of potential ritual significance.

The identification of men with public ritual and celebration (because of the function of the *qariyit* as both men's workshop and the principal site of communal whaling festivals, shamanic rites, feasts, games, and performances) was thus counterbalanced by the identification of women with ritual and magic sited at the levels of the dwelling and the body. This is broadly analogous to the situation of House 29, which produced elevated frequencies of ritual paraphernalia and, although metal-poor, two out of three specimens of Norse metal (Corbeil 1995, 1996; Corbeil and Powell 1995). Although lacking elaborate architectural symbolism and remote from the major sites of community ritual, the occupants of House 29 appear to have had access to esoteric domains of ritual and geographic knowledge.

An interesting contrast also exists in the nature of the artifacts for which women and men employed metal. Two out of five metal artifact classes assigned to women and 27 percent of specimens are items of bodily adornment as opposed to tools or tool parts, whereas all nine metal artifact classes and twenty-two specimens assigned to men are elements of manufacturing or harvesting gear (a similar pattern holds for objects made from locally scarce ivory). This divergence in patterns of metal use hinders strict analytical comparison of women's and men's artifact assemblages, just as it may have helped to undermine invidious intergender comparison in past Thule social settings. Women and men deployed their preciosities in different discursive genres, competing, in effect, for different kinds of cultural capital. As Jean Briggs (1974:287) indicated, "Men and women each have their own realm . . . and prestige accrues to excellence in each." In a similar fashion, House 29's inventory of raw materials is not impoverished but rather diverse and idiosyncratic, and its harvesting gear assemblage is aligned toward a wholly distinctive resource suite.

The practical effects of these differences in women's and men's material culture, however, may not have been as dissimilar as would at first appear. With little harvesting activity during the cold and dark months of midwinter, men probably passed much time in the *qargi*, as reflected in an enormous accumulation of manufacturing refuse adjacent to House 41. On this charged social stage metal-bladed tools would have been highly visible, silently signifying the wealth and trading prowess of their possessors. Again, judging from refuse distributions, much of women's traditional work (food preparation, hide processing) occurred in relative isolation in family dwellings, although women may have gathered in groups to socialize while sewing, as described historically (Issenman 1997a; Oakes and Riewe 1995). In fact, sewing paraphernalia is the most elaborate component of women's toolkits, often including finely finished items decorated or made out of ivory, whereas other women's tools are more simply (even expediently) made out of relatively mundane materials. The greatest elaboration of women's material culture, however, occurred on the field of the body. The vast majority of the ornaments from Qariaraqyuk correspond to types usually worn by women ethnographically (rigid brow bands, bracelets, pendants, beads, combs, hair sticks) and would likely have been part of the elaborate dress put on for public events held in *qariyit*. The *qargi* thus represented a performative arena in which different genres of women's and men's material culture were displayed to the community and so contributed in parallel fashion to the demarcation of wealth- and status-based fractions of the social field.

CONCLUSION

At the height of Classic Thule bowhead whaling during the thirteenth and fourteenth centuries A.D., large Central Canadian Arctic communities like Qariaraqyuk consumed substantial quantities of metal for tools and ornaments. The abundance of metal and other exotic or locally scarce materials implies that the occupants of Qariaraqyuk were exporting goods of corresponding value, in all likelihood the surplus whale oil (and perhaps other bowhead products, such as baleen, bone, and *muktuk*) that was also the ultimate basis of wealth in traditional North Alaskan whaling villages. In fact, the year-to-year operation of the whaling economy in North Alaska and, inferentially, at Qariaraqyuk was reflexively bound up with the health of the larger trading sphere. On the one hand, the labor alliances forged by *umialit* depended heavily on prestige-enhancing gifts to crew members, supporting kin, rival *umialit*, and the community at large. Trade was necessary to obtain the useful or merely beautiful things that were used to mobilize the desire of others and so secure their labor and support. On the other hand, without a conversion mechanism for disposing of surplus whale products, no rationale would have existed for overproduction in the first place (Whitridge 2002).

Metal, at once useful, beautiful, portable, and rare, was an ideal currency of the interregional and intracommunity exchange systems—iron in particular being universally prized and traded over greater distances than any other commodity. Like other substances small-scale societies have repeatedly adopted as exchange goods in the past (shell, amber, ivory, jet, nephrite, obsidian, turquoise, fur, oil, and similar products), metal was a multivalent medium that could be inserted simultaneously into a variety of material discourses on social difference and identity. By virtue of this intertextual quality or symbolic resonance, such materials (the same applies to architectural spaces) tend inevitably to produce homologies among the different categories of social difference in which they figure. Thus, a residue of gender meanings and practices clings to metals even when they are deployed in the representation of household economic status, and vice versa. Maurice Godelier's (1986:126) suggestion that social hierarchies echo gender asymmetry "and plunge their roots into it" is apt but too narrow. In fact, the complex imbrication of a host of asymmetries based on such things as gender, age, economic role, ritual activity, and household wealth provides the fertile ground in which hierarchy takes root in small-scale societies.

ACKNOWLEDGMENTS

Research at Qariaraqyuk was made possible by permission of the Resolute Bay Hamlet Council and was supported by grants from the National Science Foundation, Wenner-Gren Foundation for Anthropological Research, and the Department of Anthropology, Arizona State University; logistical support from the Polar Continental Shelf Project, Energy, Mines and Resources Canada; and a doctoral fellowship from the Social Sciences and Humanities Research Council of Canada (SSHRC). Completion of this manuscript was made possible by a postdoctoral fellowship from SSHRC. Thanks to Max Friesen for his help during the tenure of this award at the Department of Anthropology, University of Toronto. Kate Spielmann and the other members of my dissertation committee—George Cowgill, Keith Kintigh, Allen McCartney, and Chuck Merbs—provided valuable comments on earlier versions of this analysis. Thanks also to Lisa Frink, Rita Shepard, Greg Reinhardt, Hetty Jo Brumbach, and Robert Jarvenpa for thoughtful comments on the manuscript.

IV

SYNTHESIS AND PROJECTIONS FOR INDIGENOUS NORTHERN GENDER RESEARCH

12

GENDER DYNAMICS IN NATIVE NORTHWESTERN NORTH AMERICA
PERSPECTIVES AND PROSPECTS

Hetty Jo Brumbach and Robert Jarvenpa

In reviewing this volume's stimulating chapters on Native northwestern North America, we have become conscious of two connected goals they share. First, there is a desire to produce more information on a topic that has been neglected for too long: women. Although this is admirable in itself, a second goal is even more compelling: to illuminate gender. A comprehension of gender dynamics requires penetrating analyses of women in relation to men (the latter, until recently, the de facto focus of most research), an endeavor that brings us closer to achieving one of anthropology's most worthwhile goals: to achieve a comprehensive understanding of human social life and culture. Our field's long-lived scholarly focus on men has concealed half of human experience and, in turn, given rise to some peculiar interpretations of our species' historical development and recent biocultural adaptations.

Consider a hypothetical zoologist who studies polar bears, auklets, or perhaps dung beetles but observes only males because purportedly "they are more visible" or "they are more interesting" or "they contribute more to the archaeofaunal record." Should such a research design be taken seriously? How would it affect our understanding of polar bear life? Indeed, how can we know the male polar bear or the male auklet without understanding how each fits into a social structure of females, juveniles, and elders and a complex of supraindividual behaviors and relationships that ultimately impact both the histories of individuals and the adaptability of the species? To do otherwise, the subject of research becomes conflated with the zoologist himself/herself, who admires the "majestic and ferocious" male bear rather than *Thalarctos maritimus* as it exists in the real world.

Gender research therefore involves far more than a "remedial" job of simply "adding women" to an existing data set (Conkey and Spector 1984; Wylie 1991). Not only can we achieve a more complete understanding of the human condition but also we are asking essentially new questions, designing innovative research strategies, and developing novel interpretations of the female-male nexus. Based in part on biological reproductive behaviors and in part on negotiated ideology and social relations, gender is deeply rooted in all societies. Indeed some view it as the oldest and most fundamental distinction shaping human social existence. In a related vein, Kenneth Sassaman (1992:71) argued that "gender is the primary social variable of the labor process in forager or hunter-gatherer societies." Thus when we probe the complexities of gender, we are neither celebrating the "majestic" male nor attempting to privilege a rediscovered "majestic" female. Rather, we are practicing anthropology in its most holistic sense.

In our chapter we touch on a range of themes and issues raised by this volume's authors, all of whom enrich our perspective by making gender a conscious element of the research process. Clearly, these studies go beyond the initial recognition stage of simply "seeing women" in either the ethnographic/ethnohistorical or archaeological records and also go beyond the remedial "adding women" stage. Our goal is not merely to recognize women's presence but rather to investigate the impact gender relations and gender ideology have in the construction of social landscapes and the formation of the archaeological record. In this sense an ability to "see" women or men as valid subjects of inquiry is only a starting point. The way this sightedness (or insight) generates stimulating new questions and interpretations about gender dynamics is what informs the chapters in this volume. Our discussion here is arranged to highlight several contexts in which the authors' approaches and perspectives move through comparable terrain, if not always arriving at similar destinations.

THE PERSISTENT NORTH

A notable feature of this volume on gender relations is the fact that most of its authors have been investigating societies, or archaeological populations, exhibiting significant continuities through time. The Yup'ik peoples of St. Lawrence Island, the Yukon Delta, and Norton Sound; the Deg Hit'an Athapaskans of the Kuskokwim and lower Yukon drainages; the Inupiat of Barrow, Alaska; and the Netsilik of the Central Canadian Arctic occupy some of the least accessible areas of Arctic/Subarctic northwestern North America. As such, contemporary communities are often direct descendants of archaeological populations where the late prehistoric/early historic transition emerged fairly recently. Generally speaking, this transition began in the mid-eighteenth to mid-nineteenth centuries in the Bering Strait area, the mid-nineteenth century in the interior regions of the Yukon and Kuskokwim drainages, and as recently as the late nineteenth century for communities along the coast of the Chukchi and Beaufort Seas and points eastward.

Because involvement with Europeans and the capitalist world system occurred a century or two later than in many other areas of the continent, certain indigenous economic and social institutions have remained vibrant and salient even as they have been adapted to contemporary conditions. Many historically familiar forms of food acquisition and food processing still occur in northwestern Native communities where sea mammal hunting, fishing, terrestrial hunting, and foraging are often central in the daily economic life of family households. The fact that these subsistence activities have become intertwined with cash and wage economies and with government programs and regulations in complex ways does not make the behaviors any less compelling or worthy of analysis. Women and men are still active on the landscape, utilizing materials and resources that have been significant in local economies and cultural traditions for centuries.

Behavioral/cultural persistence is not a trivial issue, especially when direct historical analogies can be used to illuminate gender relations. Archaeologists sometimes refer to the difficulty of seeing women or the residues of women's activities in the archaeological record. Yet the archaeological visibility of men is rarely questioned. We will return to this reductio ad absurdum later in the chapter. The main point here is that both women and men in contemporary northwestern communities are highly visible harvesting, processing, distributing, and consuming resources in ways that have useful analogical connections with female and male behaviors of their immediate ancestors in the recent historical past. This is readily seen in Lisa Frink's interesting discussion of Cup'ik women's ownership marks on fish tails and their prominent control of fisheries in present-day Chevak. These ongoing patterns hold potential as a guide for interpreting women's economic roles in the archaeology of this area.

In an interesting variation on this theme, Brian Hoffman enlisted the aid of Unimak Island Aleut high school students for studies of Aleut bone needles. Evidence resulting from the experimental manufacture of eyed and grooved needles becomes pivotal for interpreting women's key roles in social and economic transformation in Unangan, or eastern Aleut, society in the late prehistoric period.

THE SYNERGY OF ETHNOGRAPHY AND ARCHAEOLOGY

The recency of the prehistoric/historic transition in northwestern North America permits, if not invites, a creative interplay and corroboration between ethnographic (or ethnohistorical) and archaeological sources of information. A number of influential Northern anthropologists have conducted both ethnographic and archaeological field research in an effort to demonstrate continuities and developmental trends for particular cultures and culture areas. James VanStones's (1971, 1979a) analyses of changing settlement systems among Ingalik and Nushagak River Eskimo, Annette McFadyen Clark and Donald Clark's (1974; Clark 1996) studies of Koyukon houses, and John Campbell's (1973) concern with Tuluaqmiut territoriality and mobility come to mind. In a related vein, the "living archaeology" investigations of Lewis Binford (1978) with Nunamiut and of Robert Janes (1983) among Mackenzie Basin Slavey have sought to model the "formation processes" creating archaeological residues. Our own ethnoarchaeological research among Chipewyan, Cree, and Métis groups in central Subarctic Canada combines the use of direct historical analogies and a concern with site formation processes (Brumbach and Jarvenpa 1989, 1997a; Jarvenpa and Brumbach 1988, 1995).

Several authors in this volume have adopted ethnoarchaeological strategies for illuminating gender relations. Rita Shepard, Frink, Hoffman, and Jennifer Tobey all utilize behaviors from contemporary settings, documentary accounts from earlier historical periods, or both as frameworks for interpreting archaeological materials in their respective study areas. In a sense, these are works in progress awaiting further data and analyses to address the tantalizing issues they raise. Shepard's summary of nineteenth-century missionization in western Alaska is used to build a provocative model of linked changes in dwelling structures, division of labor, and allocation of female and male space. As Shepard notes, additional archaeological analyses of mid- to late-nineteenth-century houses, including the poorly documented *qasgi*, or men's house, will be needed to assess whether women's and men's living, work, and storage spaces indeed became smaller and more commingled through time. Such information seems well worth pursuing, as does the larger question Shepard's work poses: Do changes in ideas (missionization) produce changes in behavior (gender relations) that are identifiable archaeologically?

Frink's interesting contemporary field observations of Cup'ik women's fish management, a repertoire of skills and roles learned over time, raise worthwhile questions about the archaeological visibility of such gender-patterned behaviors—questions that remain largely untested. Tobey's review of Deg Hit'an (Ingalik) social life, drawn from Cornelius Osgood's ethnographic fieldwork in the 1930s, awaits an archaeological activity-area analysis of dwelling structures to assess the impact of missionization on the spatial and temporal patterning of households and gender roles. Thematically, Tobey's and Shepard's work shares much in common.

Hoffman refers to eighteenth- and nineteenth-century eyewitness accounts to support his argument that Unangan (Aleut) women made their own bone needles and sewed all clothing. The archaeological evidence indicates that thin, eyeless needles began to replace the older eyed form around A.D. 1000, at about the same time the people of the eastern Aleutian Islands experienced significant and fundamental transformations in social life (including changes in patterns of status differentiation and the emergence of ranked lineages), house forms, and trade.

LABORATORY OF CHANGE

Because the most devastating aspects of contact with Europeans came late compared with other areas of North America, many aspects of traditional behavior and culture in the northwestern Arctic/Subarctic remained to be documented by traders, missionaries, and early ethnographers. These earlier forms of economy, society, and culture—including relationships between women and men—can be compared with recent adaptations to shed light on what are often dramatically rapid processes of change. Although all societies change over time, the impact of Western colonial and postcolonial markets and institutions in the North has been compressed into a rather narrow band of recent history, speeding up the progression of change much like fast-forwarding a videotape. This situation presents some unique opportunities for understanding shifts in gender relations.

A wide variety of documentary sources are available, including photographs, travelers' journals, business accounts, church records, and a rich body of oral testimony and folklore. This diversity of data sets, especially when combined with archaeology and ethnography, facilitates fine-grained analysis of transformations from the early historic period through contact-traditional phases to contemporary rural village life. Archaeological interpretations of sites in the Yukon Delta, for example, may be aided by Frink's ethnographic observations of contemporary Cup'ik fish processing. Rather than modeling the past through fanciful speculation or fashionable stereotype, she is able to make meaningful extrapolations based on ongoing behaviors.

Carol Jolles's biography of her "friend, adviser, and consultant" Linda Womkon Badten dramatically underscores the rapidity of change. Linda's life story writ large is the recent history of contact and change on St. Lawrence Island and the Alaskan mainland. As a child she grew up in a traditional world of family and kin, pursuing a livelihood of hunting and trapping. Her family experienced a change in domestic structures from semiunderground dwellings, or *nenglus,* in the late 1800s to the dome-shaped two-room house of the early twentieth century. Later, trade in Arctic fox skins proved profitable enough for the family to build a large two-story wood frame dwelling. As a young girl, Linda's interest in school and her curiosity about the outside world led her first to Sheldon Jackson High School in Sitka and later to Emporia College in Kansas. She was the first from her St. Lawrence Island community to earn a B.A. degree. These far-reaching changes in economy and material culture were within the life experiences of a single individual.

As noted earlier, both Shepard and Tobey grapple with the changes generated by missionization and its impacts on family, domestic relations, and gender roles. Shepard examines how such transformations reverberated through the social and economic life of the residents of small communities in western Alaska. Describing changes in house form, she writes: "When a new lifeway supplants an earlier one, the material culture changes; so also do the tangible components of an original ideology change when a new belief system replaces an old one." Accordingly, she emphasizes how archaeological study of recent historic sites might enrich our understanding of cultural systemics. She recommends careful examination of "transitional" dwellings of the period around the turn of the twentieth century. Changes in work places and habits could be readily detected when compared with earlier semisubterranean structures of the late historic period. Tobey focuses on many of these same processes, as well as impacts on sociospatial organization.

Lillian Ackerman's chapter on gender equality on the Colville Indian Reservation in Washington state also makes effective use of well-documented changes in economy and social organization. Gender equality was the norm in Plateau life prior to the reservation period when women's foraging efforts provided half of the community's food supply. Older traditions from the prereservation period—such as the observance of first-hunt or first-gathering feasts for both boys and girls—continue to affect contemporary values, social customs, and gender relations. Ackerman poses a provocative question: "Why has female status been reduced in other parts of the country and the world by colonialism and capitalism and yet escaped that fate on the Colville Reservation and in fact in the entire Plateau area?" In answering this, she notes that whereas missionaries were successful in destroying several female leadership positions, they were not successful in reducing female status by assigning superior value to men's work. Ackerman suggests that gender equality persisted on the Colville Reservation in part because reservation confinement did not begin there until 1872 and also because large numbers of Euro-American settlers did not appear in the Plateau area until the 1890s. She also notes, however, that gender equality translates from the past to the present contemporary Euro-American reservation economy along indigenous traditions of foraging equality: equal access to all jobs, equal pay for equal work. We will return to this issue later. Ackerman's observations on the role of missionaries in attempting to restructure gender status and relations remind us of the impacts missionization had on domestic life in the communities studied by Shepard and Tobey.

THE REPRODUCTION OF SOCIETY AND THE (IN)VISIBILITY OF WOMEN

If women are hard to "see" in the archaeological and anthropological record, children are often totally invisible. Few archaeological studies even consider children unless skeletal remains are recovered. Yet without younger generations, a culture lacks time depth and soon withers. A society must "reproduce" itself, meaning both the production of new members and the process by which the society reproduces its own institutions and systems of meaning. Although the significance of children, child care, and socialization is too often missed when research is carried out in a strictly archaeological landscape, the significance is unmistakable in living systemic contexts like those investigated by Henry Stewart, Ackerman, Jolles, and other contributors to this volume. Barbara Crass's study of 305 infant and child burials from fifty sites across the Inuit range of the Arctic sheds light on the differential treatment afforded children after death. Although Crass effectively documents differences in many aspects of burial, she points out that we still must be able to interpret the meaning of these differences.

We must also investigate how reproduction and child care differentially impact women and men. For a society to reproduce itself, women must "invest" in the biological processes of gestation and lactation. As Crass's chapter makes clear, the death of the mother of an infant or very young child is perceived as leading to the infant's eventual starvation and death. Even so, these investments, which ensure the long-range viability of communities and societies, are rarely considered as such. Some anthropologists, especially archaeologists, have tended to regard pregnancy and lactation—if they are considered at all—as personal or idiosyncratic nuisance behaviors or as universal limiting factors that incapacitate women from performing the "important" work men do (Washburn and Lancaster 1968).

Ackerman's questions about gender equality—or inequality—and its causes are relevant to the foregoing issues. Is gender equality related to subsistence, or is it associated with concern for women as the producers of children? A widespread notion in anthropology purports that women's contributions to subsistence activity directly determine female power and status, even though large-scale cross-cultural studies provide little support for this idea (Levinson and Malone 1980:275). At the same time, however, some comparative research distorts the nature of men's and especially women's economic contributions by narrowly defining or viewing subsistence as a procurement process only (Barry and Schlegel 1982; Ember 1978). This perspective is myopic (that is, it creates difficulties in seeing women) because it ignores the indispensable contribution women make in processing, storing, and managing food resources, for example, as discussed by Frink and as treated in our own research (discussed later). Such myopia also marginalizes women's reproductive role, reducing it to an idiosyncratic nuisance or limiting factor. As Ackerman's work clearly attests, equality can derive from society's concern for the well-being of children and their mothers. In Colville society women are not accorded a lower status because of their childbearing, child-rearing, and lactating functions but rather are honored by men for these contributions.

HOUSEHOLDS, HOUSEHOLDERS, AND HOUSEHOLD ANALYSIS

In hunter-gatherer populations the household is more than a reflection of society. One might argue that it *is* society. For most hunter-gatherers the household is the center of resource production, and male-female relations form the core of economic, social, and political arrangements linking communities of households. As this volume attests, household analysis can be a productive research strategy in the North. The cold and sometimes dry climate and a slow accumulation of overlying sediments contribute to the preservation of houses and their archaeological residues. Gregory Reinhardt's chapter addresses the well-known (even to non-Arctic scholars) "frozen family" of Barrow who perished in an ice override. The remarkable preservation at this site has allowed very detailed studies of artifactual remains and architecture. Households and household analysis are the foci of four chapters in this volume. Yet the authors approach the topic from different vantage points, offering interpretations that are both complementary and divergent.

Shepard's study of western Native Alaskan gender roles and domestic space examines changes in household social organization and division of labor triggered by missionization. She argues that in nonstratified societies, house structures provide the clearest expression of "materialized ideology," their general design and interior layout reflecting the community's social values and ideals. Men's and women's activities in the winter settlements on the Kuskokwim prior to missionization were segregated into large *qasgi* (men's dormitory, communal center, and bath house) and small separate houses for women and children. One impact of missionization was the gradual abandonment of the *qasgi*, with the mission church becoming the focus of ceremonial life. In turn, men and women began to occupy the same domestic space, ultimately leading to a modification of dwellings and a reorientation of the spatial dimension of activity performance.

Although not focusing on household analysis in the strict sense, Ackerman's view that men's houses were not an index of male dominance in Yup'ik society has relevance for the present discussion. Contrary to other interpretations (discussed later), she suggests that Yup'ik men's houses contributed to their isolation and marginalization: "[Men] were excluded from the company of their male kin, since they were scattered over wide territory into patrilineal dispersed clans. . . . [In contrast,] women lived with their mothers, sisters, children, aunts, and cousins, which formed a support network, whereas men were isolated from their kin of both genders." Following Sergei Bogojavlensky and Robert Fuller (1973), she argues that the occupants of men's houses, thus isolated from family and kin, were more likely to be competitive, hostile, and suspicious of each other.

Tobey's study investigates the impact of missionization on Alaskan Natives, in this case the Deg Hit'an (Ingalik). Her emphasis is on households as dynamic social units with a changing spatial and temporal organization of activities. Thus she focuses less on houses as physical structures, perhaps, than on constellations of activities engaging members of social groups associated with dwellings. Particularly useful is Tobey's observation that the social composition of houses or households oscillated dramatically during the course of the day as constituent members moved across the local landscape. Among the Deg Hit'an, three households with distinct age and gender compositions can be identified. Two of these social groupings were defined on the basis of gender, and during the day they were associated with different village structures: houses and the *kashim* (men's house). Paralleling Shepard's findings, missionization spurred the demise of the *kashim* and led to other changes in household and community organization.

In a third chapter on households, Peter Whitridge identifies examples of gendered space in a Classic Thule whaling village. His interpretation of the archaeological site of Qariaraqyuk, Somerset Island, identifies a detached kitchen wing he characterizes as "concealing and marginalizing a major locus of women's activities" and a *qargi* that "replaced the family dwelling as the major architectural locus of men's activities." It is not clear why specialized male space is interpreted as evidence for higher status, whereas female space is interpreted as signaling a decline in, or at least a realignment of, women's status and authority. We offer another interpretation of these architectural changes based on our research on transformations in the use of domestic space among nineteenth- and twentieth-century Chipewyan of northwestern Saskatchewan. In that context, historical changes in the hunting economy, involving increased settlement centralization and logistical organization, were accompanied by a proliferation and specialization in processing and storage facilities by gender (*loretthe kwae,* or women's log smoking caches, and *t'asi thelaikoe,* or men's log storehouses)—changes that made women's special-purpose structures more visible archaeologically (Brumbach and Jarvenpa 1997a). It is worth noting that this historical trend toward specialized gender-segregated spaces reverses the pattern Shepard suggested for mainland western Alaskan Eskimo. The fact that the *qasgi* was not part of indigenous social structure in the central Subarctic no doubt has some bearing on these divergent patterns. From this perspective, however, the Thule kitchen and *qargi* complex could be interpreted as signs of increased specialization and separation of male and female economic roles but not necessarily marginalization of women.

Nonetheless, Whitridge assigns high status to men associated with the *qargi*. Does this contradict Ackerman? Or do the two case studies differ in terms of economic emphasis on whaling, a group effort involving crews of adult males under the leadership of *umialit* (boat owners)? Whitridge argues that men derive prestige from whaling, as well as from the trade goods obtained from the exchange of surplus whale products. But he makes several assumptions that need to be examined, including the notion that only men participated in the actual whale "hunt." If men indeed dominated the direct harvest phase of whale hunting, can we assume that women controlled much of the processing phases of hunting—that is, converting carcasses into both subsistence products and valuable trade items, as well as storing, managing, and distributing food? Ackerman observes that Yup'ik women not only directly harvested half of the community food supply but also were regarded as the owners of food, as they dominated its storage, preparation, and distribution. Could we not argue therefore that Thule women likewise gained prestige for their management of an array of harvesting and processing skills, their knowledge of complex manufacturing and storage technologies, their whale products given in exchange for valuable trade items like iron and copper, and indeed, their iron and copper supplies provided to local men who were their loyal supporters?

Although some scholars may see this interpretation as fanciful, nothing in the archaeological record demonstrates that women, any less than men, were not active participants in their culture pursuing strategies of prestige and self-realization. In this light, we encourage Whitridge to model Thule social relations from a women's perspective as a complement to his insightful Figure 11.2 illustrating men's social relations. Indeed, as we discuss later, Hoffman's study of Aleut needles employs the perspective that women, like men, actively participated in regional exchange networks.

Can we reconcile these opposing views? Ackerman views the men's house as evidence for marginalization (see also Reinhardt, this volume), whereas Whitridge presents the *qargi* as evidence for men's elevated status. Is the difference the result of favorable whaling conditions among the Thule population that offered opportunities for ambitious and competent male leaders? Different cultural ecological developments may have played a role. Yet there are other possibilities. The distinction may arise from men's and women's interpretations of what appears at first glance to be the same phenomenon. When men congregate in men's houses (or women in women's dwellings), they may see themselves as the epicenter of community life, whereas women may view the men as peripheralized. Gender-conscious or gender-informed research demands that we take seriously the notion that men and women are likely to hold divergent interpretations of gender differences within their own culture. There is also the possibility that external views can easily privilege such activities as whale killing or harvesting as more interesting and valuable than whale processing, whereas insiders understand the value and indispensable linkage of both sets of activities.

Hoffman's chapter on Aleut bone needles recovered from houses, among other archaeological contexts, is an insightful study of craft production. Inspired by changes in sewing needles from an eyed form to a grooved form, Hoffman carried out experiments in the production and use of both types of needles. Previous wisdom held that the eyed form was more time-consuming and difficult to produce, with the switch to the grooved form signaling a decline in workmanship. Yet Hoffman's experiments indicate that both types of needles require similar degrees of skill and time to produce and are equally durable.

The crucial distinction involves the diameter of the needles. Archaeological examples of the earlier eyed form averaged 1.63 mm in diameter, whereas the grooved needles averaged 0.98 mm. These data, combined with evidence for the emergence of social complexity and finely tailored clothing—especially gut-skin parkas—spur Hoffman's conclusion that the change in needle form resulted from the desire of women seamstresses to produce exceptionally fine decorated clothing. From this perspective, the decorated clothing and gut-skin parkas become important status items in aboriginal trade networks and were exchanged for prestige goods like iron and amber. Hoffman's excavations reveal concentrations of sewing needles in large houses, providing the connection between craft production and high-status households and, in turn, women's pivotal roles in sociopolitical organization. This perspective contrasts with that of Whitridge in that women are seen as taking an active and conscious role in the design and production of useful tools and the crafting of high-status trade goods. In Hoffman's view, Unangan women actively participated in trade networks and gained prestige and exotic goods for themselves and their families.

Another chapter examining households from an archaeological perspective is Reinhardt's reanalysis and reinterpretation of the prehistoric semisubterranean dwelling destroyed by an ice override in Barrow, Alaska. His chapter is strongly methodological and self-contemplative. He leads us step-by-step through his analysis, clarifying the decisions, problems, and contradictions he grappled with in converting raw archaeological materials into quantifiable "data." His chapter is not only an insightful investigation of the nature of the prehistoric Inupiat household but also a revealing glimpse at the potential pitfalls of the "scientific process" whereby residues are converted (processed?) into Western "facts." Reinhardt raises some disquieting questions. What kinds of statistical tests are appropriate for these data? Can we model Inupiat culture on the basis of such small samples? How do we decide what is "male" and what is "female" in the archaeological record? How do we assign gender usage or ownership to tools and residues? And how do we accomplish this if men use "women's" tools and women use "men's"?

Some of these questions, although troubling and perhaps unanswerable, heighten our awareness of the problems inherent in conducting research on non-Western cultures with ill-fitting paradigms from social science. These questions ask us to rethink the very nature of gender. As discussed later, we may be on Arctic "thin ice" when we employ Euro-American frameworks of gender and gender roles for interpreting other peoples' lives.

INSIDE(R) GENDER: NATIVE CONSTRUCTIONS AND EXTERNAL MODELS

Stewart's fascinating analysis of the Netsilik *kipijuituq* (young male reared in part as a female) raises questions about the prevalence of gender changing and third-gender phenomena among Inuit generally. A larger implication of his study is the danger of imposing Western dualisms and categories of "sex," "sexuality," and "gender" on other people. The *kipijuituq* defies conventional Western definitions of maleness and femaleness. Yet as a sexually inactive or presexual being, the *kipijuituq* does not easily mesh with our understandings of homosexuality or of berdache and berdachelike third-gender personae in various cultures. The full meaning of *kipijuituq* in the local cultural context requires an insider's appreciation of Inuit or Netsilik ethnobiology, worldview, and ethos—including all of the symbolic apparatus that associates males and maleness especially with polar bears.

This serves as a dramatic reminder that gender is indeed socially constructed, however much sex may be biogenetically programmed. Without an explicit acknowledgment of the gender ideology informing one's scholarship, there is always a risk that some version of Western ideology will be privileged. The familiar "man the hunter/woman the gatherer" (or "man the hunter/woman the childbearer-lactator") model (Washburn and Lancaster 1968), for example, persists as a way of interpreting domestic economies and the division of labor in many archaeological studies of nonagricultural societies. Yet this view may be less a reflection of past male and female behaviors than an uncritical imposition of American postwar values and sexual ideology on others. One might term it "Ozzie and Harriet do prehistory."

Archaeologists especially, but other anthropologists as well, have paid inordinate attention to such things as fluted points, big-game hunting, military campaigns, mortuary ceremonialism, and the emergence of more complex forms of sociopolitical organization—areas of life conventionally presumed to be dominated by men. Economic enterprise has often been reduced to ecology and the latter to caloric transfers, thereby obscuring the complexity of women's processing and transformation skills (Isaac 1990, 1995:3). Our own ethnoarchaeological work with the Chipewyan in the Canadian Subarctic reveals that women's roles are far more flexible and expansive than previously believed. Women as well as men directly harvest a variety of mammals and fish. Moreover, hunting needs to be seen in context as part of a complex system of travel, preparation, and logistics preceding harvests or kills and the intricacies of butchering, processing, and distribution following kills. This full spectrum of activity is most appropriately seen as "hunting," an enterprise that provides food, clothing, tools, and other necessities of life and that requires the interdependence of female and male labor in any foraging society (Jarvenpa and Brumbach 1995; Brumbach and Jarvenpa 1997b).

Ackerman offers a similar interpretation of Inupiat women. That is, their sewing, butchering, and meat sharing, as well as their power in "bringing animals to men," are integral to hunting as a comprehensive system of behavior. Such acts also illustrate "complementary gender equality," a theme Ackerman explores in greater depth for the Colville Indians. She suggests that the relative equality women and men enjoy in contemporary reservation life derives from historical economic experience on the one hand and a pervasive ideology of equality in Plateau culture on the other hand. Indeed, the fact that women's and men's activities and spheres of influence may be complementary rather than identical can lead casual observers and researchers alike to see social hierarchies and asymmetries of power where none exist or where they are of lesser intensity.

Whitridge's work at Qariaraqyuk, however, reminds us that the distinction between complementary gender differences and emergent asymmetries of power can be subtle. As he notes, Thule "women and men deployed their preciosities in different discursive genres, competing in effect for different kinds of cultural capital." Although this sounds like complementary gender equality, his argument about the prominent position of men in interregional systems of exchange of exotic metals points to growing differences in power and status. Whether one prefers to view this as emergent "complexity" or emergent "social asymmetry," we concur that as a fundamental structuring principle in all foraging and hunting societies, gender has been largely overlooked as a starting point for intensification and specialization in labor.

Although not an easy task, we are all challenged to capture the local or Native vision of gender roles and relationships when documenting how female and male actors actually conduct their lives. The dialectic between these forces of thought and action through history should provide clues to community-wide patterns of continuity and change. A double hurdle exists in realizing this goal, however. Not only must we prevent the gender bias of our own culture from coloring our interpretations of women and men in other societies; we also need to stand guard against gender-centric views fostered within the local cultures we are seeking to understand. For example, Shepard discusses some of the unexpected patterning of faunal remains in the nineteenth-century Koyukon houses excavated by Annette McFadyen Clark. In local magico-religious thought, premenopausal women are tabooed from contact with spiritually powerful bears, thus requiring an explanation for the presence of bear remains in house floors that presumably once accommodated families with women present. Aside from invoking exceptional circumstances, such as inhabiting the houses with female shamans or Inupiat occupants, there is also the possibility—as in most societies—that some degree of behavioral flexibility operated in spite of or in contradiction to ideal norms and proscriptions.

WHEN ACTIONS SPEAK LOUDER THAN WORDS/BEHAVIORS/DECISIONS/PROCESSES

Several authors in this volume deal pointedly with the actions, choices, or decisions women and men make in negotiating their existence. Gender is not merely an abstraction, a faceless normative structuring of society, but involves real individuals interpreting the ambiguities of life, weighing costs and benefits, and taking courses of action. This theme emerges clearly in Frink's work on Cup'ik women. As the prime managers of multigenerational fish camps, they must make complex decisions regarding the processing of fish according to species and intensity of spawning runs. Likewise, their decisions about storage of fish are affected by species and time of year. Resource management is neither simple nor automatic but involves judicious monitoring and prudent choices among alternative courses of action. Even matters such as gender identity may be determined by the interpretations and choices of others. As Stewart notes, Netsilik grandparents sometimes make decisions about who will become *kipijuituq* by interacting with and observing the reactions of their infant grandsons.

In a related vein, Jolles's sensitive portrait of Linda Womkon Badten illustrates how biography provides a rich context for understanding choices and actions linked together over the entire life history of individuals, including the motivations and means for dramatic events such as leaving one's home community. Life histories may provide some of the connective tissue for understanding how "agency" is wedded to "structure" or how the "adaptive strategies" of individuals become the institutionalized "adaptive processes" of groups (Bennett 1996; Giddens 1979). Men's decision-making patterns, whether short-term or long-run, are given less attention in this collection. Yet an ethnographically informed understanding of both men's and women's daily domestic routines, decisions, and actions might be helpful in building a model of the "formation processes" that generated the residues at Reinhardt's Mound 44 archaeological household at Barrow or, for that matter, the metal artifacts at Whitridge's Thule site at Qariaraqyuk.

This comment does not diminish Reinhardt's careful statistical reappraisal of Newell's earlier idea of male and female seating areas, nor does it detract from Whitridge's compelling arguments about the role of metal tools in supporting intercommunity/interregional systems of exchange and social asymmetry. What we are saying, and it is a point both authors recognize, is that assignment of static gender categories (e.g., "female" or "male") to archaeological artifacts may bear a misleading relationship to the way such materials were employed in the real world. At best, the assignments reflect normative patterns culled from ethnology. At worst, they are a kind of "best-guess" gender stereotyping based on internalized assumptions from our own cultural background. Fine-grained ethnoarchaeological accounts of actual implements and facilities in living context, including scrupulous tracking of women's and men's behaviors vis-à-vis these use-histories and processing cycles, are needed to interpret how gender dynamics generate the static residues in the archaeological record. As Whitridge notes, to say that a lamp is "female" and a harpoon "male" may reflect meaningful symbolic or iconic associations. Yet these associations may obscure rather than illuminate the myriad ways such materials are actually manufactured, utilized, curated, recycled, and discarded by both women and men.

ACKNOWLEDGMENTS

We would like to thank the editors, Lisa Frink, Rita Shepard, and Greg Reinhardt, for offering us the opportunity to comment on these chapters.

NOTES

CHAPTER 1

1. The geographic range this volume includes does go beyond northern North America (Siberia and Northwestern Plateau); however, the majority of the chapters encompass research in the northern North American continent.

2. For notable works see Ackerman 1990a; Bodenhorn 1990; Brumbach and Jarvenpa 1995, 1997a, 1997b, 1999; Cassell 1988; Crass 2000, 2001; Ellanna and Sherrod 1995; Guemple 1986, 1995; Jackson 1994; Jarvenpa and Brumbach 2001; Jolles 1997; Jolles and Kaningok 1991; Woodhouse-Beyer 1999.

3. Here is but a sampling of the plethora of explicitly gender-focused work in anthropology: Arnold and Wicker 2001; Behar and Gordon 1995; Berres 2001; Bordo 1999; Caplan 1987; Claassen and Joyce 1997; Conkey and Gero 1997; Delle, Mrozowski, and Paynter 2000; Devere Brody 1998; di Leonardo 1991; Gal 1991; Gero and Conkey 1991; Ginsburg and Lowenhaupt Tsing 1990; Hager 1997; Hays-Gilpin and Whitley 1998; Holtzman 2001; Kehoe 1997; Kent 1998; Klein and Ackerman 1995; Lang 2000; Lepowsky 1993; Lightfoot, Martinez, and Schiff 1998; Maynes et al. 1996; Moller Okin 1999; Moore and Scott 1997; Nelson 1997; Noss and Hewlett 2001; Schmidt and Voss 2000; Scott 1994; Spencer-Wood 1999; Sperling 1991; Sweely 1999; Walde and Willows 1991; Wright 1996).

4. The editors apologize for our inability to find a northern North American linguistic anthropologist who focuses on gender as a research inquiry for this edition.

CHAPTER 2

1. Inuit/Yupik refers to all year-round inhabitants of the North American tundra and Greenland, in preference to Eskimo Inuit—used in reference to North Alaska, Canada, and Greenland—and Yupik for tundra inhabitants of Alaska south of Norton Sound, excluding the Aleuts. In cases where the group designation for Alaskan groups is indeterminate, I use the term *Alaska Eskimo.*

2. In this chapter I use the terms *male* and *female* in a strictly Western, etic, ethnocentric sense. As I discuss later, to the Netsilik the *kipijuituq* is a *kipjuitaq* and may not fall into an either/or category.

3. According to informants, *kipijuituq* consists of the verb base *ipi* (to cut), *ui* (never), *uq* (noun ending). Further linguistic research is necessary to establish the full meaning and significance of this term.

4. It was also the custom among the Ammassilik for a young boy to cut his hair for the first time after harpooning a bearded seal (Holm 1914:49). Holm's report, however, does not mention whether this was a special situation or whether the boy was subject to other proscriptions. Therefore it is not possible to draw a satisfactory correlation between this Ammassilik phenomenon and the Netsilik *kipijuituq.*

5. In contemporary Netsilik society, male-female distinction in clothing is no longer strictly observed as it was traditionally. B did not dress in distinctively female clothing.

6. I have not been able to determine whether the Yup'ik *yuungcaraulua* corresponds to the Netsilik *tiringnaqtaq* concept—that is, being subject to special taboos. Should these two concepts correspond, it may be that special significance was attributed to hair throughout the Inuit/Yup'ik world.

7. The term *berdache* derives from an Arab term meaning male prostitute or catamite and as such is inappropriate for gender change in Native American society. In its place, two-spirit is used, particularly in reference to contemporary Native American gay or lesbian persons. In some Native societies, however, the term *two-spirit* refers to one who is neither living nor dead, or ghost. Therefore I follow Lang (1998:xii–xvi) in using man-woman to refer to males taking up a woman role and woman-man to refer to females in a man role. Lang (1998:xvii) also proposed that pronouns referring to women-men and men-women should correspond to chosen gender, or the pronoun that most aptly fits the particular circumstance. As the *kipijuituq* does not choose a gender, I shall use the pronoun referring to the *kipijuituq*'s biological sex.

8. As Murray (1994) pointed out, sex, gender, and sexuality categories as understood in many Western (or Judeo-Christian) societies may not coincide with Native North American concepts. For the sake of discussion, however, I shall use the etic terms *sex* and *gender* in this chapter.

9. Issenman (1997a) also refers to Washburne and Anauta (1940) concerning the *sipiniq.* In that publication, however, Anauta, born on Baffin Island, was named for a male hunter recently dead. It is probably for that reason that

she was dressed as a male until puberty and was not a *sipiniq* as described by Saladin d'Anglure.

CHAPTER 4

1. The word Yupik has two spellings. Y-u-p-i-k is used to denote the peoples of St. Lawrence Island and Chukotka, Russia. Formerly, these two groups were referred to as Siberian Yupik. Recently, the St. Lawrence Islanders have self-identified as St. Lawrence Island Yupik because of the cultural distinctions between them and their Yupik relatives on the Russian mainland. The second major group consists of the Yup'ik found in mainland southwestern Alaska. The spelling Y-u-p-'-i-k indicates slight differences in pronunciation as well as cultural distinctions between these groups.

CHAPTER 5

1. Oswalt based his research primarily on journals left by the Moravian missionary William H. Weinland and his own field notes recorded from 1950 to 1960.

2. Based on Thomas Correll's linguistic research in and around Unalakleet, the work *qasgi* will be used throughout this text to refer to a traditional men's ceremonial house (see Correll 1972). Linguistic variations include *kashgee, qargi, karigi, kashim,* and *qaygiq.*

3. Kang-yulit was Zagoskin's term for all Eskimo groups who occupied Kodiak Island, the Chugach Gulf, and the Bering Sea and Arctic Ocean shores (Michael 1967:108).

CHAPTER 6

1. In the literature the name Ingalik has been used to refer to these people, a term given them by neighboring Eskimos. I have chosen to use Deg Hit'an, a term used by the people themselves (see de Laguna 1995).

2. Osgood's interest was in traditional Deg Hit'an culture, presumably precontact. His ethnographic information, however, came from one informant, Billy Williams, and was conducted in 1934 and 1937—100 years after Russian explorers traveled through this area. Therefore the uncritical acceptance of his analysis as pre-Russian contact is somewhat problematic. Treating his examination as pre-American missionary and perhaps post-Russian is less problematic. I have discussed this issue in more detail in my master's thesis (Tobey 1998:51–54). For more discussions on the use of the ethnographic present, narratives, and oral history, see Stahl 1993; Tonkin 1992; Vansina 1985; Yow 1994.

3. When I use *village landscape,* I am not using the term merely to denote the physical place on which the Deg Hit'an lived. Indeed it is where activities took place, but it reflects, and to some extent is shaped by, those activities.

4. Unlike Anvik and Holy Cross, a mission was not established at Shageluk. VanStone (VanStone 1979a:84) believed the coalescence of people at Shageluk

resulted from a boarding school established there, as well as from the decline in gold prospecting.

CHAPTER 7

1. In molting season waterfowl are communally netted (Andrews 1989:256–259; Shaw 1983).

2. Historically (and certainly prehistorically), mismanagement or unsuccessful storage had been known to lead to famine (Michael 1967; Shnirlemen 1994; Testart 1982).

3. As far as I have observed, Chevak families do not catch and process this large quantity of fish. According to consultants, families project (according to each household's needs) each year how many fish are required (I have been told that this number ranges from 150 to 300 salmon per season) and subsequently work toward that goal. (Robert Wolfe [1989a:18] reported that it is customary for people to "take only what is needed.") Wendell Oswalt estimated that a "small" Eskimo family requires around 500 fish per year (1990:29). Also, I have been told that a "busy" day for a Chevak woman would be to clean 30 fish.

4. These lands are part of the Clarence Rhode National Wildlife Refuge.

5. Following Phyllis Morrow and William Schneider (1995:9), this chapter uses the singular Yup'ik and plural Yupiit (and Cup'ik and Cupiit as a regional subdialect) to indicate the language group of Native people in western Alaska.

6. Although Native women and men are clearly often perfectly capable (and at least aware of the requirements) of accomplishing many of one another's gendered tasks, the modern (and historically documented) ideology is one of sexed (and aged) task differentiation. For a thorough discussion on task overlay and what it means for gender studies, see Lepowsky (1993).

7. This chapter stems from my ongoing research in western Alaskan seasonal camps. Since this initial research, I have spent additional field seasons at summer salmon camps, documenting activities and continuing experimental research (Frink, Hoffman, and Shaw n.d.; Knudson et al. n.d.).

8. For references on Native subsistence fish cutting, see Barker 1993; Chang 1988, 1991; Fienup-Riordan 1983, 1986b; Frink, Hoffman, and Shaw n.d.; Menager 1962; Nelson 1983 [1899]; O'Leary 1992; Oswalt 1963, 1990; Pete 1991; Schalk 1977; Seitz 1996; Wolfe 1984, 1989a, 1989b; Wolfe et al. 1984.

9. The issue of camp "ownership" or identification needs to be investigated further, since some camps are identified with the elder male.

10. I have been told that most dogs today eat one fish per day; these are dogs no longer used for pulling sleds.

CHAPTER 8

1. No single term can be accurately applied to all the people commonly known as Eskimo. The term *Eskimo* is viewed by many as derogatory. To list

each group individually at every mention is awkward and impractical. When reference is made to a particular group, such as the Siberian Yupik, the appropriate name will be used. When reference is made to multiple groups, however, the term *Inuit* will be used as defined by the Inuit Circumpolar Conference Charter adopted in Barrow, Alaska, on June 15, 1977. The term *Inuit* encompasses all regional groups including Siberian Yupik and Central Yupik, Aluttiq, Inupiat, Inuvialuit, and Kalaallit.

CHAPTER 10

1. Officially known as the Northeaster Secret Geographic and Astronomical Expedition (Merck 1980:v).

2. Some of these projects are described on the False Pass School Web page at www.aesd.gcisa.net/falsep/FALSEP_2.HTM.

REFERENCES

Ackerman, Lillian A. Gender status in Yup'ik society. *Etudes/Inuit/Studies* 14 (1–2):209–221, 1990a.
———. Yup'ik Eskimo residence and descent in southwestern Alaska. *Inter-Nord* 19:253–263, 1990b.
———. Nonunilinear descent groups in the Plateau culture area. *American Ethnologist* 21 (2):286–309, 1994.
Ackerman, Robert E. Archaeoethnology, ethnoarchaeology, and the problems of past cultural patterning. In *Ethnohistory in Southwestern Alaska and the Southern Yukon: Method and Content, Studies in Anthropology 7,* ed. M. Lantis, 11–47. Lexington: University of Kentucky Press, 1970.
Adams, George R. *Life on the Yukon 1865–1867,* ed. R. A. Pierce. Kingston, Ontario: Limestone, 1982.
Ager, Lynn Price. The economic role of women in Alaskan Eskimo society. In *A World of Women: Anthropological Studies of Women in the Societies of the World,* ed. E. Buorguignon, 305–317. New York: Praeger, 1980.
Ager, Thomas. Raven's work. In *Inua: Spirit World of the Bering Sea Eskimo,* ed. W. W. Fitzhugh and S. A. Kaplan, 39–54. Washington, D.C.: Smithsonian Institution Press, 1982.
Alia, Valerie. *Un/covering the North: News, Media, and Aboriginal People.* Vancouver: University of British Columbia Press, 1999.
Anderson, Douglas. Trade networks among the Selawik Eskimos, northwestern Alaska during the late 19th and early 20th centuries. *Folk* 16–17:63–72, 1974–1975.

———. Tulaagiaq: a transitional Near Ipiutak-Ipiutak period archaeological site. *Anthropological Papers of the University of Alaska* 19 (1), University of Alaska, Fairbanks, 1978a.

———. *Tulaagiaq: A Transitional Near Ipiutak-Ipiutak Period Archaeological Site From Kotzebue Sound, Alaska.* Ms. in Ethnografisk Samling Bibliotek, National Museum, Kobenhavn, Denmark, 1978b.

Andrews, Elizabeth F. *The Akulmiut: Territorial Dimensions of a Yup'ik Eskimo Society.* Technical paper no. 177. Juneau: Alaska Department of Fish and Game, Division of Subsistence, 1989.

Arnold, Bettina, and Nancy L. Wicker, eds. *Gender and the Archaeology of Death.* Walnut Creek: AltaMira, 2001.

Arnold, Charles D., and Carol Stimmel. An analysis of Thule pottery. *Canadian Journal of Archaeology* 7:1–21, 1983.

Arutinov, Sergei A., and Dorian A. Sergeyev. *Drevnie Kul'tury Aziatskikh Eskimosov (Uelenskii Mogil'nik).* Moscow: Nauka (partial trans. by Valeria Krashenikov, ms. in possession of author), 1969.

———. *Problemy Etnicheskoi Istorii Beringo Mor'ia. Ekvenskii Mogil'nik.* Moscow: Nauka (partial trans. by Valeria Krashenikov, ms. in possession of author), 1975.

Badten, Linda, Vera Oovi Kaneshiro, and Marie Oovi. A dictionary of the St. Lawrence Island (or Siberian) Yupik Eskimo language, preliminary version, ed. S. Jacobson. Unpublished ms., 1983.

Bailey, Douglass W. The living house: signifying continuity. In *The Social Archaeology of Houses,* ed. R. Samson, 19–48. Edinburgh: Edinburgh University Press, 1990.

Baker, M. Invisibility as a symptom of gender categories in archaeology. In *Invisible People and Processes: Writing Gender and Childhood Into European Archaeology,* ed. J. Moore and E. Scott. Leicester: Leicester University Press, 1997.

Bandi, Hans-Georg. *St. Lorenz Insel-Studien. Berner Beitrage zur Archaologischen und Ethnologischen Erforschung des Beringstrassengebietes. Band I. Allgemeine Einfuhrung und Graberfunde bei Gambell am Nordwestkap der St. Lorenz Insel, Alaska.* Bern: Verlag Paul Haupt, 1984.

Barker, James H. From mud houses to wood: Kashunuk to Chevak. *Alaska Journal* 9 (3):24–31, 1979.

———. *Always Getting Ready: Yup'ik Eskimo Subsistence in Southwest Alaska.* Seattle: University of Washington Press, 1993.

Barry, Herbert III, and Alice Schlegel. Cross-cultural codes on contribution by women to subsistence. *Ethnology* 21:165–188, 1982.

Behar, Ruth, and Deborah A. Gordon, eds. *Women Writing Culture.* Berkeley: University of California Press, 1995.

Bennett, John W. *Human Ecology as Human Behavior: Essays in Environmental and Developmental Anthropology.* New Brunswick, N.J.: Transaction, 1996.

Berres, Thomas Edward. *Power and Gender in Oneota Culture: A Study of a Late Prehistoric People.* Dekalb: Northern Illinois University Press, 2001.

Binford, Lewis R. *Nunamiut Ethnoarchaeology.* New York: Academic, 1978.

———. Behavioral archaeology and the "Pompeii premise." *Journal of Anthropological Research* 37:295–308, 1981.

Birket-Smith, Kaj. Ethnography of the Egedesmindre District with aspects of the general culture of West Greenland. Trans. from Danish by Aslaug Mikkelsen. *Meddelelser om Gronland* 66. Copenhagen: C. A. Reitzels Forlag, 1924.

———. *The Caribou Eskimos: Material and Social Life and Their Cultural Position.* Report of the Fifth Thule Expedition 1921–1924, vol. 5, part 1. Copenhagen: Gyldendalske Boghandel, Nordisk Forlag, 1929.

———. *The Chugach Eskimo.* Copenhagen; Nationalmuseets Publikationsfond, 1953.

Black, Lydia T. *Aleut Art.* Anchorage: Aleutian/Pribilof Islands Association, 1982.

———. The Yup'ik of western Alaska and Russian impact. *Etudes/Inuit/Studies* 8:21–44, 1984.

Black, Lydia T., and Roza G. Liapunova. Aleut: islanders of the North Pacific. In *Crossroads of Continents: Cultures of Siberia and Alaska,* ed. W. W. Fitzhugh and A. Crowell, 52–57. Washington, D.C.: Smithsonian Institution Press, 1988.

Blackman, Margaret B. *During My Time: Florence Edenshaw Davidson, a Haida Woman.* Seattle: University of Washington Press, 1982.

———. *Sadie Brower Neakok: An Inupiaq Woman.* Seattle: University of Washington Press, 1989.

———. The individual and beyond: reflections of the life history process. *Anthropology and Humanism Quarterly* (16) 2:56–62, 1991.

Blanton, Richard E. *Houses and Households: A Comparative Study.* New York: Plenum, 1993.

Blaylock, Sandra K. A Thule bone and antler industry from Somerset Island, Central Canadian Arctic, N.W.T. Unpublished M.A. thesis, University of Arkansas, 1980.

Boas, Franz. *The Central Eskimo.* Lincoln: University of Nebraska Press, 1964 [1888].

———. The Eskimo of Baffin Land and Hudson Bay. *Bulletin of the American Museum of Natural History* 15:371–570. New York: American Museum of Natural History, 1901.

———. Second report on the Eskimo of Baffin Land and Hudson Bay from the notes collected by Captain George Comer, Captain James S. Mutch, and Rev. E. J. Peck. *Bulletin of the American Museum of Natural History* 15 (2). New York: American Museum of Natural History, 1907.

Bodenhorn, Barbara. "I'm not the great hunter, my wife is": Inupiat and anthropological models of gender. *Etudes/Inuit/Studies* 14:55–74, 1990.

Bogojavlensky, Sergei, and Robert W. Fuller. Polar bears, walrus hides, and social solidarity. *Alaska Journal* 3 (2):66–76, 1973.

Bogoras, Waldemar. *Ethnographic Introduction: The Asiatic Eskimo. Bogoras Papers,* Reel 2. Archives, Alaska and Polar Regions Department, Rasmuson Library, University of Alaska Fairbanks, n.d.

Bordo, Susan. *The Male Body: A New Look at Men in Public and in Private.* New York: Farrar, Straus, and Giroux, 1999.

Bourdieu, Pierre. *Distinction: A Social Critique of the Judgement of Taste.* Cambridge: Harvard University Press, 1984.

———. *The Logic of Practice.* Stanford: Stanford University Press, 1990.

Briggs, Jean L. Utkuhikhalingmiut Eskimo emotional expression. *Northern Science Research Group.* Ottawa: Department of Indian Affairs and Northern Development, 1969.

———. Inuit women: makers of men. In *Many Sisters: Women in Cross-Cultural Perspective,* ed. C. Matthiasson, 261–304. New York: Free Press, 1974.

Brumbach, Hetty Jo, and Robert Jarvenpa. *Ethnoarchaeological and Cultural Frontiers: Athapaskan, Algonquian, and European Adaptations in the Central Subarctic.* New York: Peter Lang, 1989.

———. Ethnoarchaeology of subsistence space and gender: a Subarctic Dene case. *American Antiquity* 62 (3):414–436, 1997a.

———. Woman the hunter: ethnoarchaeological lessons from Chipewyan life cycle dynamics. In *Women in Prehistory: North America and Mesoamerica,* ed. C. Claassen and R. A. Joyce, 17–32. Philadelphia: University of Pennsylvania Press, 1997b.

Brumfiel, Elizabeth M. Weaving and cooking: women's production in Aztec Mexico. In *Engendering Archaeology: Women and Prehistory,* ed. J. M. Gero and M. W. Conkey, 224–251. Oxford: Basil Blackwell, 1991.

Buchwald, Vagn Fabritius, and Gert Mosdal. *Meteoric Iron, Telluric Iron, and Wrought Iron in Greenland.* Man and Society Series no. 9. Copenhagen: Meddelelser om Gronland, 1985.

Buijs, Cunera. Ecology and principles of polar clothing. In *Braving the Cold: Continuity and Change in Arctic Clothing,* ed. C. Buijs and J. Oosten, 11–33. Leiden: CNWS, 1997.

Burch, Ernest S., Jr. The Eskimo trading partnership in north Alaska: a study in "balanced reciprocity." *Anthropological Papers of the University of Alaska* 15:49–80. Fairbanks: University of Alaska Press, 1970.

———. *Eskimo Kinsmen: Changing Family Relationships in Northwest Alaska.* St. Paul: West, 1975.

———. *The Traditional Eskimo Hunters of Point Hope, Alaska: 1800–1875.* Barrow: North Slope Borough, 1981.

———. Modes of exchange in northwest Alaska. In *Hunters and Gatherers 2: Power and Ideology,* ed. T. Ingold, D. Riches, and J. Woodburn, 95–109. Oxford: Berg, 1988.

Butler, Judith. *Bodies That Matter: On the Discursive Limits of "Sex."* New York: Routledge, 1993.

Butler, Stephanie. Bone needle production as it relates to social relations in Aleut society. Ms. in possession of author, 1997.

Byrne, Brian. Subsistence strategies and the division of labor by gender among clothes makers in nonindustrial societies. *Cross-Cultural Research* 33 (4):307–317, 1999.

Callender, Charles, and Lee M. Kochems. The North American berdache. *Current Anthropology* 24:443–456, 1983.

Cameron, Catherine M., and Steve A. Tomka, eds. *Abandonment and Settlements and Regions: Ethnoarchaeological and Archaeological Approaches.* Cambridge: Cambridge University Press, 1993.

Campbell, John M. Territoriality among ancient hunters: interpretations from ethnography and nature. In *Anthropological Archaeology in the Americas,* ed. B. J. Meggers, 1–21. Washington, D.C.: Anthropological Society of Washington, 1973.

Caplan, Pat, ed. *The Cultural Construction of Sexuality.* New York: Routledge, 1987.

Cassell, Mark S. "Farmers of the northern ice": relations of production in the traditional north Alaskan Inupiat whale hunt. *Research in Economic Anthropology* 10:89–116, 1988.

Chang, Claudia. Nauyalik fish camp: an ethnoarchaeological study in activity-area formation. *American Antiquity* 53 (1):145–157, 1988.

———. Refuse disposal at an Inupiat fish camp: ethnoarchaeological implications of site formation processes. In *The Ethnoarchaeology of Refuse Disposal,* ed. E. Staski and L. D. Sutro, 53–62. Anthropological Research Papers no. 42. Tempe: Arizona State University Press, 1991.

Chaussonnet, Valerie. Needles and animals: women's magic. In *Crossroads of Continents: Cultures of Siberia and Alaska,* ed. W. W. Fitzhugh and A. Crowell, 209–226. Washington, D.C.: Smithsonian Institution, 1988.

Chodorow, Nancy. Family structure and feminine personality. In *Woman, Culture, and Society,* ed. M. Zimbalist Rosaldo and L. Lamphere, 43–66. Stanford: Stanford University Press, 1974.

Claassen, Cheryl, and Rosemary A. Joyce, eds. *Women in Prehistory: North America and Mesoamerica.* Philadelphia: University of Pennsylvania Press, 1997.

Clark, A. McFadyen. Koyukon. In *Handbook of North American Indians, Vol. 6, Subarctic,* ed. J. Helm, 582–601. Washington, D.C.: Smithsonian Institution Press, 1981.

———. *Who Lived in This House?* Mercury Series, Archaeological Survey of Canada Paper 153. Hull, Quebec: Canadian Museum of Civilization, 1996.

Clark, A. McFadyen, and Donald W. Clark. Koyukon houses as seen through oral tradition and through archaeology. *Arctic Anthropology* 11:29–38, 1974.

Clark, J.G. Desmond, and M. W. Thompson. The groove and splinter technique of working antler in Upper Paleolithic and Mesolithic Europe. *Proceedings of the Prehistoric Society* 19:148–160, 1953.

Clifford, James, and George E. Marcus, eds. *Writing Culture: The Poetics and Politics of Ethnography.* Berkeley: University of California Press, 1986.

Collier, Jane F., and Michelle Zimbalist Rosaldo. Politics and gender in simple societies. In *Sexual Meanings: The Cultural Construction of Gender and Sexuality,* ed. S. Ortner and H. Whitehead, 275–329. Cambridge: Cambridge University Press, 1981.

Collins, Henry B., Jr. *Archaeology of St. Lawrence Island.* Washington, D.C.: Smithsonian Miscellaneous Collections, 1937.

———. *Field Notes, Native Pt. Southampton Is. 1954 and 1955.* Ms. on file (no. 1974), Document Collection, Information Management Services, Canadian Museum of Civilization, Hull, Quebec, 1955.

———. The man who buys good-for-nothing things. In *Inua: Spirit World of the Bering Sea Eskimo,* ed. W. W. Fitzhugh and S. A. Kaplan, 29–37. Washington, D.C.: Smithsonian Institution Press, 1982.

———. Untitled. Ms. on file (no. 1973), Document Collection, Information Management Services, Canadian Museum of Civilization, Hull, Quebec, n.d.

Collins, Henry B., Jr., and J. N. Emerson. *Tunirmiut I Site, Native Point.* Ms. on file (no. 1523, Book 1), Document Collection, Information Management Services, Canadian Museum of Civilization, Hull, Quebec, 1954.

Condon, Richard. *Inuit Youth: Growth and Change in the Canadian Arctic.* New Brunswick, N.J.: Rutgers University Press, 1987.

Conkey, Margaret W., and Joan M. Gero. Tensions, pluralities, and engendering archaeology: an introduction to women and prehistory. In *Engendering Archaeology,* ed. J. M. Gero, and M. W. Conkey, 3–30. Cambridge, Mass.: Blackwell, 1991.

———. Programme to practice: gender and feminism in archaeology. *Annual Review of Anthropology* 26:411–437, 1997.

Conkey, Margaret W., and Janet D. Spector. Archaeology and the study of gender. In *Advances in Archaeological Method and Theory, Vol. 7,* ed. M. B. Schiffer, 1–38. New York: Academic, 1984.

Cook, Frederick A. Medical observations among the Esquimaux. *American Gynecological and Obstetrical Journal* 4:282–289, 1894.

Corbeil, Marie-Claude. Analysis of iron and composite artifacts. CCI Analytical Report ARS 3371, Part I. Ottawa: Analytical Research Services, Canadian Conservation Institute, 1995.

———. Determination of nickel in iron and composite artifacts. CCI Analytical Report ARS 3371, Part III. Ottawa: Analytical Research Services, Canadian Conservation Institute, 1996.

Corbeil, Marie-Claude, and Jeremy Powell. Analysis of copper and composite artifacts. CCI Analytical Report ARS 3371, Part II. Ottawa: Analytical Research Services, Canadian Conservation Institute, 1995.

Correll, Thomas Clifton. Ungalaqlingmiut: a study in language and society. Ph.D. diss., University of Minnesota, 1972.

Costin, Cathy Lynne. Exploring the relationship between gender and craft in complex societies: methodological and theoretical issues of gender attribution. In *Gender and Archaeology*, ed. R. P. Wright, 111–140. Philadelphia: University of Pennsylvania Press, 1996.

Crantz, David. *The History of Greenland: Containing a Description of the Country, and Its Inhabitants and Particularly, a Relation of the Mission, Carried on for Above Thefe Thirty Years of the Unitas Fratrum, at New Herrnhuth and Lichtenfels, in That Country.* 2 vols. London: Brethren's Society, 1767.

Crass, Barbara A. Pre-Christian Inuit mortuary practices: a compendium of archaeological and ethnographic sources. Ph.D. diss., University of Wisconsin, Milwaukee, 1998.

———. Material and symbolism associated with gender in Inuit burial practices. In *Interpreting the Body: Insights From Anthropological and Classical Archaeology*, ed. A. E. Rautman. Philadelphia: University of Pennsylvania Press, 2000.

———. Gender and mortuary analysis: what can grave goods really tell us? In *Gender and the Archaeology of Death*, ed. B. Arnold and N. Wicker. Walnut Creek: AltaMira, 2001.

Crowell, Aron L. *Archaeology and the Capitalist World System: A Study From Russian America.* New York: Plenum, 1997.

Cruikshank, Julie, in collaboration with Angela Sidney, Kitty Smith, and Annie Ned. *Life Lived Like a Story: Life Stories of Three Yukon Native Elders.* Lincoln: University of Nebraska Press, 1990.

Czederpiltz, Jessica M.C. Patterns of Aleut exploitation of birds and fish on the Lower Alaska Peninsula. Paper presented at the fifth University of Wisconsin Arctic Archaeology Conference, Madison, Wisconsin, 1997.

Dall, William H. *Alaska and Its Resources.* Boston: Lee and Shepard, 1870.

Davis, D. L., and R. G. Whitten. The cross-cultural study of human sexuality. *Annual Review of Anthropology* 16:69–98. Palo Alto: Annual Reviews, 1987.

Day, Stacey B. *Tuluak and Amaulik: Dialogues on Death and Mourning With the Inuit Eskimo of Point Barrow and Wainwright, Alaska.* Minneapolis: Bell Museum of Pathology, 1973.

Degerbol, M. The former Eskimo habitation in the Kangerdligssuaq District, East Greenland. *Meddelelser om Gronland* 104 (10):1–48. Copenhagen: C. A. Reitzels Forlag, 1936.

Dekin, Albert A., Jr. Sealed in time: ice entombs an Eskimo family for five centuries. *National Geographic* 171 (6):824–836, 1987.

DeLaguna, Frederica. *The Archaeology of Cook Inlet, Alaska.* Philadelphia: University Museum, 1934.

———. The prehistory of northern North America as seen from the Yukon. *American Antiquity,* Memoirs of the Society for American Archaeology 7 (3), Part 2 supplement, 1947.

———. *Chugach Prehistory: The Archaeology of Prince William Sound, Alaska.* Seattle: University of Washington Press, 1956.

———. *The Archaeology of Cook Inlet, Alaska* (originally published Philadelphia: University of Pennsylvania Press, 1934). Anchorage: Alaska Historical Society, 1975.

———. *Tales From the Dena: Indian Stories From the Tanana, Koyukuk, and Yukon Rivers.* Seattle: University of Washington Press, 1995.

DeMarrais, Elizabeth, Luis Jaime Castillo, and Timothy Earle. Ideology, materialization, and power strategies. *Current Anthropology* 37 (1):15–31, 1996.

Desautels, Roger J., Albert J. McCurdy, James D. Flynn, and Robert R. Ellis. *Archaeological Report, Amchitka Island, Alaska, 1969–1970.* California: Archaeological Research, 1970.

Devere Brody, Jennifer. *Impossible Purities: Blackness, Femininity, and Victorian Culture.* Durham, N.C.: Duke University Press, 1998.

Diehl, Michael. Complexity at the root of the socio-evolutionary tree. In *Debating Complexity,* ed. D. Meyer, P. Dawson, and D. Hanna, 274–281. Proceedings of the 26th Annual Chacmool Conference. Calgary: Archaeological Association of the University of Calgary, 1996.

Dietler, Michael, and Brian Hayden. *Feasts: Archaeological and Ethnographic Perspectives on Food, Politics, and Power.* Washington, D.C.: Smithsonian Institution Press, 2001.

di Leonardo, Micaela, ed. *Gender at the Crossroads of Knowledge: Feminist Anthropology in the Postmodern Era.* Berkeley: University of California Press, 1991.

Draper, Patricia. !Kung women: contrasts in sexual egalitarianism in foraging and sedentary contexts. In *Toward an Anthropology of Women,* ed. R. R. Reiter, 77–109. New York: Monthly Review, 1975.

Drucker, Paul, and Robert F. Heizer. *To Make My Name Good.* Berkeley: University of California Press, 1967.

Dumond, Don. *The Eskimos and Aleuts.* London: Thames and Hudson, 1977.

———. Archaeology of the Alaska Peninsula: the Naknek region, 1960–1975. *University of Oregon Anthropological Papers* 21:1–277, 1981.

Dunning, R. W. Differentiation of status in subsistence-level societies. *Transactions of the Royal Society of Canada* 44:25–32, 1960.

Egede, Hans P. *A Description of Greenland by Hans Egede, Who Was a Missionary in That Country for Twenty-five Years.* London: T. and J. Allman, 1818.

Ellanna, Linda J., and George K. Sherrod. *The Role of Kinship Linkages in Subsistence Production: Some Implications for Community Organization.* Technical paper no. 100. Juneau: Division of Subsistence, Alaska Fish and Game, 1984.

———. "Big women": gender and economic management among King Island and Kobuk River Inupiat of northwest Alaska. *Research in Economic Anthropology* 16:15–38, 1995.

Ember, Carol R. Myths about hunter-gatherers. *Ethnology* 17:439–448, 1978.

Emerson, J. N. Field notes, Tunirmiut 1 (T1) Burial 2, Southampton Is., 1954. Ms. on file (no. 1973), Document Collection, Information Management Services, Canadian Museum of Civilization, Hull, Quebec, 1954.

Fall, James A., Ronald T. Stanek, Louis Brown, and Charles Utermohle. *The Harvest and Use of Fish, Wildlife, and Plant Resources in False Pass, Unimak Island, Alaska.* Technical paper no. 183. Juneau: Alaska Department of Fish and Game, Division of Subsistence, 1996.

Fausto-Sterling, Anne. *Sexing the Body: Gender Politics and the Construction of Sexuality.* New York: Basic, 2000.

Felbo, Mette, J. Fog, A. B. Gotfredsen, and H. C. Gullov. *Rapport om det Arkaeologiske Arbejde i Skjoldungen, Ammassalik Kommune, Sydostgronland, Sommerren 1991.* Copenhagen: Dansk Polar Center, 1992.

Felbo, Mette, A. B. Gotfredsen, K. Rosenlund, H. C. Gullov, H. Kapel, and A. Koch. *Illuluarsuk. Rapport om det Arkaeologiske Arbejde i Illuluarsuk Regionen syd for Bernstorffs Isfjord, Ammassalik Kommune, Sydostgronland, Sommeren 1992.* Copenhagen: Dansk Polar Center, 1993.

Fienup-Riordan, Ann. *Nelson Island Eskimo.* Anchorage: Alaska Pacific University Press, 1983.

———. The real people: the concept of personhood among the Yup'ik Eskimos of western Alaska. *Etudes/Inuit/Studies* 10 (1–2):261–270, 1986a.

———. *When Our Bad Season Comes: A Cultural Account of Subsistence Harvesting and Harvest Disruption on the Yukon Delta.* Aurora Monograph Series 1. Anchorage: Alaska Anthropological Association, 1986b.

———. *The Yup'ik Eskimos: As Described in the Travel Journals and Ethnographic Accounts of John and Edith Kilbuck Who Served With the Alaska Mission of the Moravian Church, 1885–1900.* Ontario: Limestone, 1988.

———. *The Real People and the Children of Thunder.* Norman: University of Oklahoma Press, 1991.

———. *Boundaries and Passages: Rule and Ritual in Yup'ik Eskimo Oral Tradition.* Norman: University of Oklahoma Press, 1994.

———. *The Living Tradition of Yup'ik Masks.* Seattle: University of Washington Press, 1996.

Finley, K. J., and W. G. Johnston. *An Investigation of the Distribution of Marine Mammals in the Vicinity of Somerset Island With Emphasis on Bellot Strait,*

August–September 1976. Polar Gas Environmental Program, LGL Ltd. Environmental Research Associates, n.p., 1977.

Finn, Janet L. Ella Cara Deloria and Mourning Dove: writing for cultures, writing against the grain. In *Women Writing Culture,* ed. R. Behar and D. A. Gordon, 131–147. Berkeley: University of California Press, 1995.

Fischer-Moller, K. Skeletal remains of the Central Eskimo. *Report of the Fifth Thule Expedition, 1921–24,* 3 (1). Copenhagen: Gyldendalske Boghandel, Nordisk Forlag, 1937.

Fitzhugh, William W., and Susan A. Kaplan. *Inua: Spirit World of the Bering Sea Eskimo.* Washington, D.C.: Smithsonian Institution Press, 1982.

Flanagan, James G. Hierarchy in simple "egalitarian" societies. *Annual Review of Anthropology* 18:245–266, 1989.

Flanders, Nicholas E. Religious conflict and social change: a case from western Alaska. *Etudes/Inuit/Studies* 1:141–157, 1984.

Flannery, Kent V. Spatial analysis of living floors: an introduction to part VI. In *Guila Naquitz: Archaic Foraging and Early Agriculture in Oaxaca, Mexico.* New York: Academic, 1986.

Flannery, Kent V., and Marcus C. Winter. Analyzing household activities. In *The Early Mesoamerican Village,* ed. K. V. Flannery, 34–47. New York: Academic, 1976.

Flenniken, Jeffrey J. The experimental replication of Paleo-Indian needles from Washington. *Northwest Anthropological Research Notes* 12 (1):61–71, 1978.

Fortescue, Michael. *Eskimo Orientation Systems.* Copenhagen: Meddelelser om Gronland, Man and Society 11, 1988.

Fortuine, Robert. *Chills and Fever: Health and Disease in the Early History of Alaska.* Fairbanks: University of Alaska Press, 1992.

Franklin, U. M., E. Badone, R. Gotthardt, and B. Yorga. *An Examination of Prehistory Copper Technology and Copper Sources in Western Arctic and Subarctic North America.* National Museum of Man Mercury Series, no. 101. Ottawa: Archaeological Survey of Canada, 1981.

Friedl, Ernestine. *Women and Men: An Anthropological View.* New York: Holt, Rinehart, and Winston, 1975.

Frink, Lisa, Brian W. Hoffman, and Robert D. Shaw. Ulu knife use in western Alaska: A comparative ethnoarchaeological study. *Current Anthropology,* forthcoming (February 2003).

Fulton, Robert, and Steven W. Anderson. The Amerindian "man-woman": gender, liminality, and cultural continuity. *Current Anthropology* 33:603–610, 1992.

Gal, Susan. Between speech and silence: the problematics of research on language and gender. In *Gender at the Crossroads of Knowledge: Feminist Anthropology in the Postmodern Era,* ed. M. di Leonardo, 175–203. Berkeley: University of California Press, 1991.

Gero, Joan M. Assessing social information in material objects: how well do lithics measure up? In *Time, Energy, and Stone Tools*, ed. R. Torrence, 92–105. Cambridge: Cambridge University Press, 1989.

Gero, Joan M., and Margaret W. Conkey, eds. *Engendering Archaeology: Women and Prehistory.* Oxford: Basil Blackwell, 1991.

Giddens, Anthony. *Central Problems in Social Theory: Action, Structure, and Contradiction in Social Analysis.* Cambridge: Cambridge University Press, 1979.

———. *The Constitution of Society: Outline of the Theory of Structuration.* Cambridge: Polity, 1984.

Giddings, J. L. *Kobuk River People.* Studies of Northern Peoples, no. 1. Anchorage: University of Alaska Press, 1961.

———. *The Archeology of Cape Denbigh.* Providence, R.I.: Brown University Press, 1964.

Giddings, J. L., and D. L. Andersen. Beach ridge archaeology of Cape Krusenstern–Eskimo and pre-Eskimo settlements around Kotzebue Sound, Alaska. *Publications in Archaeology* 20. Washington, D.C.: National Park Service, U.S. Department of the Interior, 1986.

Giffen, Naomi M. *The Roles of Men and Women in Eskimo Culture.* Chicago: University of Chicago Press, 1930.

Gifford-Gonzales, Diane. Gaps in zooarchaeological analyses of butchery: is gender an issue? In *From Bones to Behavior*, ed. J. Hudson, 181–199. Carbondale: Southern Illinois University Press, 1993.

Gilmore, David. Above and below: toward a social geometry of gender. *American Anthropologist* 98 (1):54–66, 1993.

Ginsburg, Faye, and Anna Lowenhaupt Tsing, eds. *Uncertain Terms: Negotiating Gender in American Culture.* Boston: Beacon, 1990.

Glob, P. V. Eskimo settlements in Kempe Fjord and King Oscar Fjord. *Meddelelser om Gronland* 102 (2). Copenhagen: C. A. Reitzels Forlag, 1935.

Godelier, Maurice. *The Mental and the Material: Thought, Economy, and Society.* Thetford: Verso, 1986.

Gosling, W. G. *Labrador: Its Discovery, Exploration, and Development.* London: Alston Rivers, 1910.

Graburn, Nelson. Television and the Canadian Inuit. *Etudes/Inuit/Studies* 6 (1): 7–18, Laval University, 1982.

Griffin, Dennis. A culture in transition: a history of acculturation and settlement near the mouth of the Yukon River, Alaska. *Arctic Anthropology* 33 (1):98–115, 1996.

Guemple, Lee. Men and women, husbands and wives: the role of gender in traditional Inuit society. *Etudes/Inuit/Studies* 10 (1–2):9–24, 1986.

———. Gender in Inuit society. In *Women and Power in Native North America*, ed. L. Klein and L. Ackerman, 17–27. Norman: University of Oklahoma Press, 1995.

Habu, Junko, and James M. Savelle. Construction, use, and abandonment of a Thule whale bone house, Somerset Island, Arctic Canada. *Dai Yonki Kenkyu* (Quaternary Research) 33 (1):1–18, 1994.

Hager, Lori D., ed. *Women in Human Evolution.* New York: Routledge, 1997.

Hall, Edwin S., Jr., ed. *The Utqiagvik Excavations* 1–3. Barrow, Alaska: North Slope Borough, Commission on Inupiat History, Language, and Culture, 1990.

Haraway, Donna J. A cyborg manifesto: Science, technology, and socialist-feminism in the late twentieth century. In *Simians, Cyborgs, and Women: The Reinvention of Nature,* ed. D. J. Haraway, 149–183. New York: Routledge, 1991.

Hawkes, Ernest William. The Labrador Eskimo. *Canada Department of Mines, Geological Survey Memoir 91.* Anthropological Series 14. Ottawa: Government Printing Bureau, 1916.

Hayden, Brian. Observing women in prehistory. In *Exploring Gender Through Archaeology,* ed. C. Claassen, 33–48. Madison: Prehistory Press, 1992.

———. Practical and prestige technologies: the evolution of material systems. *Journal of Archaeological Method and Theory* 5 (1):1–55, 1998.

Hays-Gilpin, Kelly Ann, and David S. Whitley. *Reader in Gender Archaeology.* New York: Routledge, 1998.

Heizer, Robert. Archaeology of Uyak Site, Kodiak Island, Ala__a. *Anthropological Records* 17:1. Berkeley: University of California Press, 1956.

Hickey, Clifford. The historic Beringian trade network: its nature and origins. In *Thule Eskimo Culture: An Anthropological Retrospective,* ed. A. P. McCartney, 411–434. National Museum of Man Mercury Series, Archaeological Survey of Canada Paper 88, Ottawa, 1979.

Hjarno, Jan, J. Balslec Jorgensen, and M. Vesely. Archaeological and anthropological investigations of Late Heathen graves in Upernavik District. *Meddelelser om Gronland* 202 (1):1–36. Copenhagen: C. A. Reitzels Forlag, 1974.

Hoffman, Brian W. Agayadan village: household archaeology on Unimak Island, Alaska. *Journal of Field Archaeology* 26 (2):147–161, 1999.

———. Unangan seamstresses: gender, prestige, and labor in the North Pacific, ca. A.D. 1000–1800. Paper presented at the 8th Arctic Archaeology Conference, Lawrence, Kansas, 2000.

———. The organization of complexity: a study of late prehistoric village organization in the eastern Aleutian region, Alaska. Ph.D. diss., University of Wisconsin, Madison, 2002.

Hofman-Wyss, Anna Barbara. *St. Lorenz Insel-Studien. Berner Beitrage zur archaeolgischen und ethnologischen Erforschung des Bering-strassengebietes. Band II. Prahitorische Eskimograber an der Dovelavik Bay und bei Kitnepaluk im Westen der St. Lorenz Insel, Alaska.* Bern: Verlag Paul Haupt, 1987.

Holland, Kathryn M. Chulka bone artifacts, Akun Island, Alaska: analysis and description. Unpublished M.S. thesis, Arizona State University, Tempe, 1982.

———. A 1,000 year Akun-Kodiak interaction sphere. In *The Late Prehistoric Development of Alaska's Native People*, ed. R. D. Shaw, R. K. Harritt, and D. E. Dumond, 307–317. Alaska Anthropological Association Monograph Series 4. Anchorage: Aurora, 1988.

Hollimon, Sandra E. The third gender in Native California: Two-spirit undertakers among the Chumash and their neighbors. In *Women and Prehistory: North America and Mesoamerica*, ed. C. Claassen and R. A. Joyce, 173–188. Philadelphia: University of Pennsylvania Press, 1997.

Holm, Gustav. *Ethnological Sketch of the Angmagsalik Eskimo.* Meddelelser om Gronland 39. Copenhagen: Nordisk Forlag, 1914.

Hunn, Eugene S. *Nch'i-wana "The Big River": Mid-Columbia Indians and Their Land.* Seattle: University of Washington Press, 1990.

Isaac, Barry L. Economy, ecology, and analogy: the !Kung San and the generalized foraging model. *Research in Economic Anthropology*, supplement 5:323–335, 1990.

———. Introduction: hunting and gathering: gender as an economic factor. *Research in Economic Anthropology* 16:1–12, 1995.

Issenman, Betty Kobyashi. *Sinews of Survival: The Living Legacy of Inuit Clothing.* Vancouver: University of British Columbia Press, 1997a.

———. Stitches in time: prehistoric Inuit skin clothing and related tools. In *Braving the Cold: Continuity and Change in Arctic Clothing*, ed. C. Buijs and J. Oosten, 34–59. Leiden: CNWS, 1997b.

Jackson, Louise M. Cloth, clothing, and related paraphernalia: a key to gender visibility in the archaeological record of Russian America. In *Those of Little Note: Gender, Race, and Class in Historical Archaeology*, ed. E. M. Scott, 27–54. Tucson: University of Arizona Press, 1994.

Jacobs, Sue-Ellen. Is the "North American berdache" merely a phantom in the imagination of Western social scientists. In *Two-Spirit People: Native American Gender Identity, Sexuality, and Spirituality*, ed. S. Jacobs, W. Thomas, and S. Lang, 21–44. Urbana: University of Illinois Press, 1997.

Jacobs, Sue-Ellen, Wesley Thomas, and Sabine Lang, eds. *Two-Spirit People: Native American Gender Identity, Sexuality, and Spirituality.* Urbana: University of Illinois Press, 1997.

Jacobson, Steven A., ed., and Linda Badten, Vera Oovi Kaneshiro, and Marie Oovi, comps. *A Dictionary of the St. Lawrence Island/Siberian Yupik Eskimo Language, Second Preliminary Version.* Fairbanks: Alaska Native Language Center, 1987.

Janes, Robert R. *Archaeological Ethnography Among Mackenzie Basin Dene, Canada.* Technical paper no. 28. Calgary: Arctic Institute of North America, 1983.

Jarvenpa, Robert, and Hetty Jo Brumbach. Socio-spatial organization and decision making processes: observations from the Chipewyan. *American Anthropologist* 90 (3):598–618, 1988.

———. Ethnoarchaeology and gender: Chipewyan women as hunters. *Research in Economic Anthropology* 16:39–82, 1995.

———. The gendered nature of living and storage space in the Canadian Subarctic. In *From the Ground Up: Beyond Gender Theory in Archaeology*, ed. B. Arnold and N. Wicker. Oxford: BAR International Series 812, 2001.

Jenness, Diamond. *Life of the Copper Eskimos.* Report of the Canadian Arctic Expedition 1913–1918, vol. 12:2–249. Monograph 12, Ottawa, 1922.

Jochelson, Waldemar. *Archaeological Investigations in the Aleutian Islands.* Washington, D.C.: Carnegie Institution of Washington, 1925.

Jolles, Carol Zane. Changing roles of St. Lawrence Island women: clanswomen in the public. *Arctic Anthropology* 34:86–101, 1997.

———. *Faith, Food, and Family in a Yupik Whaling Community.* Seattle: University of Washington Press, 2002.

Jolles, Carol Zane, and Kaningok. *Qayuutat* and *angyapiget*: gender relations and subsistence activities in Sivuqaq (Gambell, St. Lawrence Island, Alaska). *Etudes/Inuit/Studies* 15:23–53, 1990.

Jorgensen, Joseph G. *Oil Age Eskimos.* Berkeley: University of California Press, 1990.

Kalkreuth, Wolfgang D., Karen M. McCullough, and R.J.H. Richardson. Geological, archaeological, and historical occurrence of coal, east-central Ellesmere Island, Arctic Canada. *Arctic and Alpine Research* 25:277–307, 1993.

Kalkreuth, Wolfgang D., and Patricia D. Sutherland. The archaeology and petrology of coal artifacts from a Thule settlement on Axel Heiberg Island, Arctic Canada. *Arctic* 51:345–349, 1998.

Kan, Sergei. Clan mothers and godmothers: Tlingit women and Russian Orthodox Christianity, 1840–1940. *Ethnohistory* 43 (4):613–641, 1996.

Kehoe, Alice. On the incommensurality of gender categories. In *Two-Spirit People: Native American Gender Identity, Sexuality, and Spirituality*, ed. S. Jacobs, W. Thomas, and S. Lang, 265–271. Urbana: University of Illinois Press, 1997.

Kent, Susan, ed. *Gender in African Prehistory.* Walnut Creek: AltaMira, 1998.

Kjellström, Rolf. *Eskimo Marriage: An Account of Traditional Eskimo Courtship and Marriage.* Lund: Nordiska museets Handlingar 80, 1973.

Klein, Laura F., and Lillian A. Ackerman, eds. *Women and Power in Native North America.* Norman: University of Oklahoma Press, 1995.

Kleivan, Inge. West Greenland before 1950. In *Handbook of North American Indians, Volume 5*, ed. D. Damas, 595–621. Washington, D.C.: Smithsonian Institution Press, 1984.

Klichka, Franz N. A report on the voyage of Potap K. Zaikov to islands in the North Pacific Ocean between Asia and America, aboard the Merchant

Vessel Sv. Vladimir, as described for the Academy of Sciences by Franz Nikolaevich Klichka, governor of Irkutsk, September 22, 1772–September 6, 1779. In *Russian Penetration of the North Pacific Ocean: Three Centuries of Russian Eastward Expansion (Vol. 2, 1700–1797)*, ed. B. Dmytryshyn, E.A.P. Crownhart-Vaughan, and T. Vaughan, 259–267. Eugene: Oregon Historical Society Press, 1988.

Knecht, Heidi. Projectile points of bone, antler, and stone: experimental explorations of manufacture and use. In *Projectile Point Technology*, ed. H. Knecht, 191–212. New York: Plenum, 1997.

Knudson, Kelly, Lisa Frink, Brian W. Hoffman, and T. D. Price. Fish heads, fish heads: soil chemistry characterizations in western Alaskan fish camps, n.d.

Koebberling, Ursel. The application of communication technologies in Canada's Inuit communities. *Musk-Ox* 37:202–208. Saskatoon: University of Saskatchewan, Institute of Northern Studies, 1999.

Koranda, Lorraine D. Three bladder festival songs. *Anthropological Papers of the University of Alaska* 14 (1):27–32, 1968.

Kramer, Carol. Ethnographic households and archaeological interpretation. *American Behavioral Scientist* 25 (6):663–675, 1982.

Krenitsyn, Petr K., and Mikhail D. Levashev. An extract from the journals of Captain Petr Kuzmich Krenitsyn and Captain Lieutenant Mikhail Dmitrievich Levashev describing Russian hunting techniques and narratives encountered in the Aleutian Islands during their voyages commencing in 1764. *Russian Penetration of the North Pacific Ocean: Three Centuries of Russian Eastward Expansion (Vol. 2, 1700–1797)*, ed. B. Dmytryshyn, E.A.P. Crownhart-Vaughan, and T. Vaughan, 259–267. Eugene: Oregon Historical Society Press, 1988.

Kreutz, K., P. Mayewski, L. Meeker, M. Twickler, S. Whitlow, and I. Pittalwala. Bipolar changes in atmospheric circulation during the Little Ice Age. *Science* 277:1294–1296, 1997.

Kroeber, Alfred L. The Eskimos of Smith Sound. *Bulletin of the American Museum of Natural History* 12. New York: American Museum of Natural History, 1900.

Kumlien, Ludwig, ed. *Contributions to the Natural Resources of Arctic America, Made in Connection With the Howgate Polar Expedition, 1877–1878.* U.S. National Museum Bulletin 15. Washington, D.C.: U.S. Government Printing Office, 1879.

LaMotta, Vincent B., and Michael B. Schiffer. Formation processes of house floor assemblages. In *The Archaeology of Household Activities*, ed. P. M. Allison, 19–29. New York: Routledge, 1999.

Lang, Sabine. *Men as Women, Women as Men: Changing Gender in Native American Cultures.* Austin: University of Texas Press, 1998.

Langley, Russell. *Practical Statistics Simply Explained.* New York: Dover, 1971.

Lantis, Margaret. The social culture of the Nunivak Eskimo. *Transactions of the American Philosophical Society* 35 (3):153–323. Philadelphia: America Philos Society, 1946.

———. Aleut. In *Handbook of North American Indians, Volume 5, Arctic,* ed. D. Damas, 161–184. Washington, D.C.: Smithsonian Institution Press, 1984.

Larsen, Helge. Dodemandsbugten, an Eskimo settlement of Clavering Island. *Meddelelser om Gronland* 102 (1). Copenhagen: C. A. Reitzels Forlag, 1934.

———. Archaeological investigations in Knud Rasmussen's land. *Meddelelser om Gronland* 119 (8). Copenhagen: C. A. Reitzels Forlag, 1938.

Larsen, Helge, and Froelich Rainey. *Ipiutak and the Arctic Whale Hunting Culture.* Anthropological papers of the American Museum of Natural History 42. New York: American Museum of Natural History, 1948.

Larson, Mary Ann. Determining the function of a "men's house." In *The Archaeology of Gender: Proceedings of the 22nd Annual Chacmool Conference,* ed. D. Walde and N. D. Willows, 165–175. Calgary: University of Calgary Archaeological Association, 1991.

———. And then there were none: The "disappearance" of the *qargi* in northern Alaska. In *Hunting the Largest Animals: Native Whaling in the Western Arctic and Subarctic,* ed. A. P. McCartney, 207–220. Occasional Publication no. 36. Edmonton: Canadian Circumpolar Institute, 1995.

Lawrence, Susan. Toward a feminist archaeology of households: gender and household structure on the Australian goldfields. In *The Archaeology of Household Activities,* ed. P. M. Allison, 121–141. New York: Routledge, 1999.

Leacock, Eleanor. Women's status in egalitarian society: implications for social evolution. *Current Anthropology* 19 (2):247–275, 1978.

Lee, Molly, and Gregory A. Reinhardt. *Eskimo Architecture: Dwelling and Structure in the Early Historic Period.* Fairbanks: University of Alaska Press, n.d.

Left Handed (recorded by Walter Dyk). *Son of Old Man Hat.* Lincoln: University of Nebraska Press, 1995 [1938].

Lenz, Mary, and James H. Barker. Bethel, the first hundred years. A City of Bethel Centennial History Project, 1985.

Lepowsky, Maria. *Fruit of the Motherland: Gender in an Egalitarian Society.* New York: Columbia University Press, 1993.

Levinson, David, and Martin J. Malone. *Toward Explaining Human Culture: A Critical Review of the Findings of Worldwide Cross-Cultural Research.* New Haven: HRAF, 1980.

Lightfoot, Kent G., A. Martinez, and A. M. Schiff. Daily practice and material culture in pluralistic social settings: an archaeological study of culture and persistence from Fort Ross, California. *American Antiquity* 63 (2):199–222, 1998.

Llorente, Segundo, S.J. *Memoirs of a Yukon Priest.* Washington, D.C.: Georgetown University Press, 1988.

Lutz, Bruce J. An archaeological karigi at the site of UngaLaqLiq, western Alaska. *Arctic Anthropology* 10 (1):111–118, 1973.

Lyon, George Francis. *The Private Journal of Captain G. F. Lyon, of H.M.S. Hecla, During the Recent Voyage of Discovery Under Captain Parry,* 2d ed. London: J. Murray, 1825.

Male concubinage. *Musk-Ox* 40:104–105, 1994.

Marcus, George, and Michael J. Fischer. *Anthropology as Cultural Critique: An Experimental Moment in the Human Sciences.* Chicago: University of Chicago Press, 1986.

Maschner, Herbert D.G., and Brian W. Hoffman. The evolution of the North Pacific household. *Alaska Journal of Anthropology,* n.d.

Maschner, Herbert D.G., and Katherine L. Reedy-Maschner. Raid, retreat, defend (repeat): the archaeology and ethnohistory of warfare on the North Pacific Rim. *Journal of Anthropological Archaeology* 17:19–51, 1998.

Mather, Elsie. With a vision beyond our immediate needs: oral traditions in an age of literacy. In *When Our Words Return: Writing, Hearing, and Remembering Oral Traditions of Alaska and the Yukon,* ed. P. Morrow and W. Schneider, 13–27. Logan: Utah State University Press, 1995.

Mathiassen, Therkel. *Archaeology of the Central Eskimo.* Report of the Fifth Thule Expedition 1921–1924, vol. 4 (1–2). Copenhagen: Gyldendalske Boghandel, 1927.

———. Ancient Eskimo settlements in the Kangamiut area. *Meddelelser om Gronland* 91 (1). Copenhagen: C. A. Reitzels Forlag, 1931.

———. Prehistory of the Angmagssalik Eskimos. *Meddelelser om Gronland* 92 (4). Copenhagen: C. A. Reitzels Forlag, 1933.

———. Contributions to the archaeology of Disko Bay. *Meddelelser om Gronland* 93 (2). Copenhagen: C. A. Reitzels Forlag, 1934.

———. The Eskimo archaeology of Julianehaab District. *Meddelelser om Gronland* 118 (1). Copenhagen: C. A. Reitzels Forlag, 1936a.

———. Eskimo finds from the Kangerlugssuak Region. *Meddelelser om Gronland* 104 (9). Copenhagen: C. A. Reitzels Forlag, 1936b.

———. The former Eskimo settlements on Frederik VI's coast. *Meddelelser om Gronland* 109 (2). Copenhagen: C. A. Reitzels Forlag, 1936c.

Matthiasson, John S. Northern Baffin Island women in three cultural periods. In *Sex Roles in Changing Cultures,* ed. A. McElroy and C. Matthiasson, 61–71. Occasional Papers in Anthropology, no. 1. Buffalo: State University of New York at Buffalo, 1979.

Maxwell, Moreau S. *Prehistory of the Eastern Arctic.* Orlando: Academic, 1985.

Maynard, Eileen. Changing sex roles and family structure among the Oglala Sioux. In *Sex Roles in Changing Cultures,* ed. A. McElroy and C. Matthiasson,

11–19. Occasional Papers in Anthropology, no. 1. Buffalo: State University of New York at Buffalo, 1979.

Maynes, Mary Jo, Ann Waltner, Birgitte Soland, and Ulrike Strasser, eds. *Gender Kinship Power: A Comparative and Interdisciplinary History.* New York: Routledge, 1996.

McCartney, Allen P. An analysis of the bone industry from Amaknak Island, Alaska. M.S. thesis, University of Wisconsin, Madison, 1967.

———. Thule Eskimo prehistory along northwestern Hudson Bay. Ph.D. diss., University of Wisconsin, Madison, 1971.

———. *Thule Eskimo Prehistory Along Northwest Hudson Bay.* National Museum of Man Mercury Series, no. 70. Ottawa: Archaeological Survey of Canada, 1977.

———. Prehistory of the Aleutian region. In *Handbook of North American Indians, Volume 5, Arctic,* ed. D. Damas, 119–135. Washington, D.C.: Smithsonian Institution Press, 1984.

———. Late prehistoric metal use in the New World Arctic. In *The Late Prehistoric Development of Alaska's Native People,* ed. R. Shaw, R. Harritt, and D. Dumond, 57–79. Alaska Anthropological Association Monograph Series no. 4. Fairbanks: Aurora, 1988.

———. Canadian Arctic trade metal: reflections of prehistoric to historic social networks. In *Metals in Society: Theory Beyond Analysis,* ed. R. M. Ehrenreich, 26–43. MASCA Research Papers in Science and Archaeology 8, part 2. Philadelphia: University of Pennsylvania Museum, 1991.

McCartney, Allen P., and D. J. Mack. Iron utilization by Thule Eskimos of central Canada. *American Antiquity* 38:328–339, 1973.

McCullough, Karen M. *The Ruin Islanders: Early Thule Culture Pioneers in the Eastern High Arctic,* Archaeological Survey of Canada Mercury Series, no. 141. Ottawa: Canadian Museum of Civilization, 1989.

McElroy, Ann. The negotiation of sex-role identity in eastern Arctic culture change. In *Sex Roles in Changing Cultures,* ed. A. McElroy and C. Matthiasson, 49–60. Occasional Papers in Anthropology, no. 1. Buffalo: State University of New York at Buffalo, 1979.

McFadyen Clark, Annette. *Who Lived in This House? A Study of Koyukuk River Semi-subterranean Houses.* Mercury Series Archaeological Survey of Canada Paper 153. Hull, Quebec: Canadian Museum of Civilization, 1996.

McGhee, Robert. *Copper Eskimo Prehistory.* National Museum of Man Publications in Archaeology, no. 2. Ottawa: National Museum of Canada, 1972.

———. Ivory for the sea woman: the symbolic attributes of a prehistoric technology. *Canadian Journal of Archaeology* 1:141–149, 1977.

———. Contact between Native North Americans and the Medieval Norse: a review of the evidence. *American Antiquity* 49:4–26, 1984a.

———. Thule prehistory of Canada. In *Handbook of North American Indians, Arctic, Vol. 5,* ed. D. Damas, 369–376. Washington, D.C.: Smithsonian Institution Press, 1984b.

———. *The Thule Village at Brooman Point, High Arctic Canada.* National Museum of Man Mercury Series, no. 125. Ottawa: Archaeological Survey of Canada, 1984c.

———. *Ancient People of the Arctic.* Vancouver: University of British Columbia Press, 1996.

Menager, Francis M. *The Kingdom of the Seal.* Chicago: Loyola University Press, 1962.

Merbs, Charles F. Human burials of Silumiut, a Thule culture site north of Chesterfield Inlet, Northwest Territories, preliminary report. Ms. on file (no. 605), Document Collection, Information Management Services, Canadian Museum of Civilization, Hull, Quebec, 1967.

———Eskimo burial studies: the Kamarvik and Silumiut Sites, preliminary report. Ms. on file (no. 607), Document Collection, Information Management Services, Canadian Museum of Civilization, Hull, Quebec, 1968a.

———. Report of field operations. Ms. on file (no. 606), Document Collection, Information Management Services, Canadian Museum of Civilization, Hull, Quebec, 1968b.

Merck, Carl H. Siberia and Northwestern America, 1788–1792: the journal of Carl Heinrich Merck, naturalist with the Russian Scientific Expedition led by Captains Joseph Billings and Gavriil Sarychev. *Alaska History* 17. Ontario: Limestone, 1980.

Meskell, Lynn M. Dying young: the experience of death at Deir el Medina. *Archaeological Review From Cambridge* 13:35–45, 1994.

———. The somatization of archaeology: institutions, discourses, corporeality. *Norwegian Archaeological Review* 29:1–16, 1996.

Michael, Henry N., ed. *Lieutenant Zagoskin's Travels in Russian America, 1842–1844: The First Ethnographic and Geographic Investigations in the Yukon and Kuskokwim Valleys of Alaska.* Toronto: University of Toronto Press, 1967.

Mitchell, Donald Craig. *Sold American: The Story of Alaska Natives and Their Land, 1867–1959: The Army to Statehood.* Hanover: University Press of New England, Dartmouth College, 1997.

Moller Okin, Susan. *Is Multiculturalism Bad for Women?* Princeton: Princeton University Press, 1999.

Moore, Henrietta. *A Passion for Difference: Essays in Anthropology and Gender.* Bloomington: Indiana University Press, 1994a.

———. Understanding sex and gender. In *Companion Encyclopaedia of Anthropology,* ed. T. Ingold, 813–830. London: Routledge, 1994b.

Moore, Jenny, and Eleanor Scott, eds. *Invisible People and Processes: Writing Gender and Childhood Into European Archaeology.* London: Leicester University Press, 1997.

Morris, Rosalind. All made up: performance theory and the new anthropology of sex and gender. *Annual Review of Anthropology* 24:567–592, 1995.

Morrison, David A. *Thule Culture in Western Coronation Gulf.* National Museum of Man Mercury Series, no. 116. Ottawa: Archaeological Survey of Canada, 1983.

———. Thule and historic copper use in the Copper Inuit area. *American Antiquity* 52 (1):3–12, 1987.

———. The Copper Inuit soapstone trade. *Arctic* 44 (33):239–246, 1991.

Morrow, Phyllis, and William Schneider, eds. *When Our Words Return: Writing, Hearing, and Remembering Oral Traditions of Alaska and the Yukon.* Logan: Utah State University Press, 1995.

Moss, Madonna L. Shellfish, gender, and status on the northwest coast: Reconciling archaeological, ethnographic, and ethnohistorical records of the Tlingit. *American Anthropologist* 95 (3):631–652, 1993.

Mukopudhyay, Carol C., and Patricia J. Higgins. Anthropological studies of women's status revisited: 1977–1987. *Annual Review of Anthropology* 17:461–495, 1988.

Murdoch, John. Ethnological results of the Point Barrow expedition. *Smithsonian Institution, Bureau of Ethnology, Ninth Annual Report,* 3–441. Washington, D.C.: U.S. Government Printing Office, 1988 [1892].

Murray, S. On subordinating Native American cosmologies to the empire of gender. *Current Anthropology* 35 (1):59–62, 1994.

Nelson, Edward W. A sledge journey in the Delta of the Yukon, northern Alaska. *Proceedings of the Royal Geographical Society and Monthly Record of Geography* 4 (11):660–670, 712, 1882.

———. *The Eskimo About Bering Strait.* Smithsonian Institution, Bureau of American Ethnology, 18th Annual Report 1:3–518, 1983 [1899].

Nelson, Sara Milledge. *Gender in Archaeology: Analyzing Power and Prestige.* Walnut Creek: AltaMira, 1997.

Newell, Raymond, R. The archaeological, human biological, and comparative contexts of a catastrophically terminated Kataligaaq house at Utqiagvik, Alaska (BAR-2). *Arctic Anthropology* 21 (1):5–51, 1984.

Noss, Andrew J., and Barry S. Hewlett. The contexts of female hunting in central Africa. *American Anthropologist* 103 (4):1024–1040, 2001.

Nuttall, Mark. *Arctic Homeland: Kinship, Community, and Development in Northwest Greenland.* Toronto: University of Toronto Press, 1992.

Oakes, Jillian E. Copper and Inuit skin clothing production. *Canadian Ethnology Service, Mercury Series Paper no. 118.* Hull, Quebec: Canadian Museum of Civilization, 1991.

Oakes, Jillian, and Rick Riewe. *Our Boots: An Inuit Women's Art.* Vancouver: Douglas and McIntyre, 1995.

O'Connor, Paul, S.J. *Eskimo Parish.* Milwaukee: Bruce, 1947.

Okada, Hiro, Atsuko Okada, Kunio Yajima, Osahito Miyaoka, and Chikuma Oka. *The Qaluyaarmiut: An Anthropological Survey of the Southwestern Alaska Eskimos.* Faculty Letters. Japan: Hokkaido University, 1982.

O'Leary, Beth L. Salmon and storage: southern Tutchone use of an "abundant" resource. *Occasional Papers in Archaeology,* no. 3. Yukon Tourism Heritage Branch, n.p., 1992.

Ong, Aihwa. Women out of China: traveling tales and traveling theories in postcolonial feminism. In *Women Writing Culture,* ed. R. Behar and D. A. Gordon, 350–372. Berkeley: University of California Press, 1995.

Ortner, Sherry B. Is female to male as nature is to culture? In *Woman, Culture, and Society,* ed. M. Zimbalist Rosaldo and L. Lamphere, 67–87. Stanford: Stanford University Press, 1974.

Osgood, Cornelius. *Ingalik Material Culture.* Yale University Publications in Anthropology 22. New Haven: Yale University Press, 1940.

———. *Ingalik Social Culture.* Yale University Publications in Anthropology 53. New Haven: Yale University Press, 1958.

———. *Ingalik Mental Cutlure.* Yale Publications in Anthropology 56. New Haven: Yale University Press, 1959.

Ostermann, Hother. Knud Rasmussen posthumous notes on the life and doings of the east Greenlanders in olden times. *Meddelelser om Gronland* 109 (1). Copenhagen: Nordisk Forlang, 1938.

Oswalt, Wendell H. The archaeology of Hooper Bay village, Alaska. *Anthropological Papers of the University of Alaska* 1 (1):46–91, 1952.

———. *Mission of Change in Alaska: Eskimos and Moravians on the Kuskokwim.* San Marino, Calif.: Huntington Library, 1963a.

———. *Napaskiak.* Tucson: University of Arizona Press, 1963b.

———. *Alaskan Eskimos.* San Francisco: Chandler, 1967.

———. *Eskimos and Explorers.* Novato: Chandler and Sharp, 1979.

———. Kolmakovskiy Redoubt: the ethnoarchaeology of a Russian fort in Alaska. *Institute of Archaeology Monumenta Archaeologica, Vol. 8.* Los Angeles: Regents of the University of California, 1980.

———. *Bashful No Longer: An Alaskan Eskimo Ethnohistory, 1778–1988.* Norman: University of Oklahoma Press, 1990.

Oswalt, Wendell H., and James W. VanStone. *The Ethnoarchaeology of Crow Village, Alaska.* Smithsonian Institution Bureau of American Ethnology Bulletin 199. Washington, D.C.: U.S. Government Printing Office, 1967.

Owen, Linda R. Questioning stereotypical notions of prehistoric tool functions: ethnoanalogy, experimentation, and functional analysis. In *Ethno-Analogy and the Reconstruction of Prehistoric Artefact Use and Production,* ed. L. R. Owen and M. Porr, 17–30. Tubingen: Mo Vince Verlag, 1999.

Oyama, Susan. *Evolution's Eye: A Systems View of the Biology-Culture Divide.* Durham, N.C.: Duke University Press, 2000.

Pader, Ellen J. Inside spatial relations. *Architecture and Comportment/Architecture and Behavior* 4 (3):251–267, 1988.

Peary, Robert E. *Northward Over the "Great Ice": A Narrative of Life and Work Along the Shores and Upon the Interior Ice-cap of Northern Greenland in the Years 1886 and 1891–1897,* 2 vols. New York: Frederick A. Stokes, 1898.

Pete, Mary C. *Subsistence Herring Fishing in the Nelson Island and Nunivak Island Districts, 1990.* Technical Paper no. 196. Fairbanks: Alaska Department of Fish and Game, Division of Subsistence, 1991.

Pollock, Susan. *Ancient Mesopotamia: The Eden That Never Was.* New York: Cambridge University Press, 1999.

Porter, Robert P. *Report on Population, Industries, and Resources of Alaska.* Department of Interior, Census Office. Washington, D.C.: U.S. Government Printing Office, 1893.

Pratt, Mary Louise. Fieldwork in common places. In *Writing Culture: The Poetics and Politics of Ethnography,* ed. J. Clifford and G. E. Marcus, 27–50. Berkeley: University of California Press, 1986.

Rainey, Froelich G. The whale hunters of Tigara. *Anthropological Papers of the American Museum of Natural History* 41 (2):231–283. New York, n.pub., 1947.

———. Grave sketches. Box 2, Folder 38. Archives, Alaska and Polar Regions Department, Rasmuson Library, University of Alaska Fairbanks, n.d.

Rasmussen, Knud. *People of the Polar North: A Record.* Compiled from the Danish originals: I. The New People: Polar Eskimo; II. The West Greenlanders; III. The East Greenlanders, ed. G. Herring. London: Kegan Paul, Trench, Trubner, 1908.

———. Intellectual culture of the Iglulik Eskimos. *Report of the Fifth Thule Expedition 1921–24* 7 (1). Copenhagen: Gyldendalske Boghandel, Nordisk Forlang, 1929.

———. Observations on the intellectual culture of the Caribou Eskimos. *Report of the Fifth Thule Expedition 1921–24* 7 (2). Copenhagen: Gyldendalske Boghandel, Nordisk Forlag, 1930.

———. The Netsilik Eskimos: social life and spiritual culture. *Report of the Fifth Thule Expedition 1921–24* 8. Copenhagen: Gyldendalske Boghandel, Nordisk Forlag, 1931.

Ray, Dorothy J. The Eskimo of St. Michael and vicinity as related by H. M. Edmonds, ed. D. J. Ray. *Anthropological Papers of the University of Alaska* 13 (2):1–143, 1966.

———. *The Eskimos of Bering Strait, 1650–1898.* Seattle: University of Washington Press, 1975.

Reimer, Gwen D. Female consciousness: an interpretation of interviews with Inuit women. *Etudes/Inuit/Studies* 20:77–100, 1996.

Reinhardt, Gregory A. The dwelling as artifact: analysis of ethnographic Eskimo dwellings, with archaeological implications. Ph.D. diss., University of California, Los Angeles, 1986.

———. A head-count of six people from Mound 44 at the Utqiagvik Site, Barrow, Alaska. Paper presented at the Annual Meeting of the Alaska Anthropological Association, Fairbanks, Alaska, 1990.

———. Frozen bodies, frenzied digging, fractured data: human remains and the weighing of archaeological desires against community wishes. n.d.a.

———. Mound 44, general notes, 20 August 1982, n.d.b.

Reinhardt, Gregory A., and Albert A. Dekin Jr. House structure and interior features. In *Excavation of a Prehistoric Catastrophe: A Preserved Household From the Utqiagvik Village, Barrow, Alaska, the Utqiagvik Excavations—Vol. 3*, ed. E. S. Hall Jr., 38-112. Barrow, Alaska: North Slope Borough, Commission on Inupiat History, Language, and Culture, 1990.

Reiter, Rayna R., ed. *Toward an Anthropology of Women*. New York: Monthly Review, 1975.

Remie, Cornelius. Towards a new perspective on Netsilik Inuit female infanticide. *Etudes/Inuit/Studies* 9 (1):67-76, 1985.

Reynolds, Georgeanne Lewis. Expanded definitions of a "tool kit" and "assemblage": evidence from the Utqiagvik Village Site, Barrow, Alaska. Ms., n.d.

Robert-Lamblin, Joelle. Changement desexe de certains enfants d'Ammassalik. *Etudes/Inuit/Studies* 5 (1):117-126, 1981.

Romanoff, Steven. Frasier Lillooet salmon fishing. In *A Complex Culture of the British Columbia Plateau: Stl'atl'imx Resource Use*, ed. B. Hayden, 222-265. Vancouver: University of British Columbia Press, 1992.

Sahlins, Marshall. *Stone Age Economics*. New York: Aldine de Gruyter, 1972.

Rosaldo, Michelle Zimbalist, and Louise Lamphere, eds. *Woman Culture and Society*. Stanford: Stanford University Press, 1974.

Saladin d'Anglure, Bernard. Iqallijuq ou les reminiscences d'une ame-nom Inuit. *Etudes/Inuit/Studies* 1 (1):33-63, 1977.

———. Nanoo, super male: the polar bear in the imaginary space and social time of the Inuit of the Canadian Arctic. In *Signifying Animals: Human Meaning in the Natural World*, ed. R. Willis, 178-195. New York: Routledge, 1990.

———. The shaman's share, or Inuit sexual communism in the Canadian central Arctic. *Anthropologica* 35 (1):59-103, 1993.

———. Brother moon, sister sun, and the direction of the world: from Arctic cosmography to Inuit cosmology. In *Circumpolar Religion and Ecology: An Anthropology of the North*, ed. T. Irimoto and T. Yamada, 187-212. Tokyo: University of Tokyo Press, 1994a.

———. From foetus to shaman: the construction of an Inuit third sex. In *Amerindian Rebirth: Reincarnation Belief Among North American Indians and Inuit*, ed. A. Mills and R. Slobodin, 82-106. Toronto: University of Toronto Press, 1994b (translation of Du foetus au shaman: la construction d'un < troisieme sexe > Inuit. *Etudes/Inuit/Studies* 10 (1-2):25-114, 1987).

Salter, Elizabeth Mary. Skeletal biology of Cumberland Sound, Baffin Island, N.W.T. Ph.D. diss., University of Toronto, 1984.

Sanday, Peggy R. Female status in the public domain. In *Woman, Culture, and Society,* ed. M. Zimbalist Rosaldo and L. Lamphere, 189–206. Stanford: Stanford University Press, 1974.

Sarychev, Gavriil. *Account of a Voyage of Discovery to the North-East of Siberia, the Frozen Ocean, and the North-East Sea* (Originally published London: Richard Phillips, 1806–1807). New York: DaCapo, 1969.

Sassaman, Kenneth. Gender and technology at the Archaic-Woodland transition. In *Exploring Gender Through Archaeology: Selected Papers From the 1991 Boone Conference,* ed. C. Claassen, 71–79. Madison: Prehistory, 1992.

Saunders, Thomas. The feudal construction of space: power and domination in the nucleated village. In *The Social Archaeology of Houses,* ed. R. Samson, pp. 181–196. Edinburgh: Edinburgh University Press, 1990.

Savelle, James M. The nature of nineteenth century Inuit occupations of the High Arctic islands of Canada. *Etudes/Inuit/Studies* 5:109–123, 1981.

———. Effects of nineteenth century European exploration on the development of the Netsilik Inuit culture. In *The Franklin Era in Canadian Arctic History 1845–1859,* ed. P. Sutherland, 192–214. National Museum of Man Mercury Series, no. 131. Ottawa: Archaeological Survey of Canada, 1985.

———. Thule Eskimo whaling systems in the Canadian Arctic islands. *Proceedings of the International Abashiri Symposium* 10:41–56, 1996.

Savelle, James M., and Allen P. McCartney. Geographical and temporal variation in Thule Eskimo subsistence economies: a model. *Research in Economic Anthropology* 10:21–72, 1988.

———. Thule Inuit bowhead whaling: a biometrical analysis. In *Threads of Arctic Prehistory: Papers in Honour of William E. Taylor Jr.,* ed. D. Morrison, and J. L. Pilon, 281–310. Archaeological Survey of Canada Mercury Series, no. 149. Hull, Quebec: Canadian Museum of Civilization, 1994.

———. Thule Eskimo bowhead whale interception strategies. *World Archaeology* 30 (3):437–451, 1999.

Schalk, Robert F. The structure of an anadromous fish resource. In *For Theory Building in Archaeology,* ed. L. R. Binford, 207–250. New York: Academic, 1977.

Scheinsohn, Vivian, and Jose L. Ferretti. The mechanical properties of bone materials in relation to the design and function of prehistoric tools from Tierra-Del-Fuego, Argentina. *Journal of Archeological Science* 22 (6):711–717, 1995.

Schiffer, Michael B. Is there a "Pompeii premis" in archaeology? *Journal of Anthropological Research* 41:18–41, 1983.

Schlegel, Alice. Toward a theory of sexual stratification. In *Sexual Stratification: A Cross-Cultural View,* ed. A. Schlegel, 1–40. New York: Columbia University Press, 1977.

Schmidt, Robert A., and Barbara L. Voss, eds. *Archaeologies of Sexuality.* New York: Routledge, 2000.

Schneider, Lucien. *Ulirnaisigutit: An Inuktitut-English Dictionary of Northern Quebec, Labrador, and Eastern Arctic Dialects.* Quebec: La Oresse de l'Universite Laval, 1987.

Schultz-Lorentsen, C. W. Intellectual culture of the Greenlanders. In *Greenland: The Present and Past Population,* ed. M. Vahl, G. C. Amdrup, L. Bobe, and A. S. Jensen. Copenhagen and London: C. A. Reitzel and Oxford University Press, 1927.

Schwalbe, Anna Buxbaum. *Dayspring on the Kuskokwim: The Story of the Moravian Missions in Alaska.* Bethlehem: Moravian, 1951.

Scott, Elizabeth M. *Those of Little Note: Gender, Race, and Class in Historical Archaeology.* Tucson: University of Arizona Press, 1994.

Seitz, Jody. Subsistence salmon fishing in Nushagak Bay, southwest Alaska. Technical paper no. 195. Juneau: Division of Subsistence, Alaska Department of Fish and Game, 1996.

Selkregg, Lidia L. *Alaska Regional Profiles: Yukon Region.* Anchorage: University of Alaska Arctic Environmental Information and Data Center, 1976.

Shaw, Robert D. The expansion and survival of the Norton tradition on the Yukon-Kuskokwim Delta. *Arctic Anthropology* 19:59–73, 1982.

———. The archaeology of the Manokinak Site: a study of the cultural transition between Late Norton tradition and historic Eskimo. Ph.D. diss., Washington State University, 1983.

———. An archaeology of the central Yupik: a regional overview for the Y-K Delta, northern Bristol Bay, and Nunivak Island. *Arctic Anthropology* 35 (1):234–246, 1998.

Sheehan, Glenn W. Whaling as an organizing focus in northwestern Alaska Eskimo society. In *Prehistoric Hunter-Gatherers: The Emergence of Cultural Complexity,* ed. T. D. Price and J. Brown, 133–154. Orlando: Academic, 1985.

———. *In the Belly of the Whale: Trade and War in Eskimo Society.* Alaska Anthropological Association Monograph Series, no. 6. Anchorage: Aurora, 1997.

Shepard, Rita Stuart. Rivers of change: Eskimo and Athapaskan domestic culture in contact era western Alaska. Ph.D. diss., University of California, Los Angeles, 1997.

Shnirleman, Victor A. Cherchez le Chien: perspectives on the economy of the traditional fishing-oriented people of Kamchatka. In *Key Issues in Hunter-Gatherer Research,* ed. E. S. Burch Jr. and L. J. Ellanna, 169–188. Washington, D.C.: Berg, 1994.

Shostak, Marjorie. *Nisa: The Life and Words of a !Kung Woman.* Cambridge: Harvard University Press, 1981.

Simeone, William E. A history of Alaskan Athapaskans: a history of Alaskan Athapaskans including a description of Athapaskan culture and a historical narrative, 1785–1971. Anchorage: Alaska Historical Commission, 1982.

Siemoneit, Beate. *Das Kind in der Linienbandkeramik Befunde aus Graberfelden und Siedlungen in Mitteleuropa.* Rahden/Westf: Verlag Marie Leidorf GmbH, 1997.

Snow, Jeanne H. Ingalik. In *Handbook of North American Indians, Subarctic, Vol. 6*, ed. J. Helm, 602–617. Washington, D.C.: Smithsonian Institution Press, 1981.

Sofaer Derevenski, J. Where are the children? accessing children in the past. *Archaeological Review From Cambridge* 13:7–20, 1994.

———. Engendering children, engendering archaeology. In *Invisible People and Processes: Writing Gender and Childhood Into European Archaeology*, ed. J. Moore and E. Scott, 192–202. Leicester: Leicester University Press, 1997.

Soja, Edward. *Postmodern Geographics.* New York: Verso, 1989.

Sorenson, Laila. The Inuit Broadcasting Corporation and Nunavut. In *Nunavut: Inuit Regain Control of Their Lands and Their Lives*, eds. J. Dahl, J. Hicks, and P. Jull, 170–179. Copenhagen: International Work Group for Indigenous Affairs, 2000.

Spencer, Robert F. *The North Alaskan Eskimo: A Study in Ecology and Society.* Bulletin 171. Washington, D.C.: Bureau of American Ethnology, 1959.

———. The social composition of the North Alaskan whaling crew. In *Alliance in Eskimo Society*, ed. L. Guemple, 110–120. Proceedings of the American Ethnological Society, 1971, Supplement. Seattle: University of Washington Press, 1972.

Spencer-Wood, Suzanne M. The world their household: changing meanings of the domestic sphere in the nineteenth century. In *The Archaeology of Household Activities*, ed. P. M. Allison, 162–189. New York: Routledge, 1999.

Sperling, Susan. Baboons with briefcases vs. langurs in lipstick: feminism and functionalism in primate studies. In *Gender at the Crossroads of Knowledge: Feminist Anthropology in the Postmodern Era*, ed. M. di Leonardo, 204–235. Berkeley: University of California Press, 1991.

Speth, John D. Seasonality, resource stress, and food sharing in so-called "egalitarian" foraging societies. *Journal of Anthropological Archaeology* 9:148–188, 1990.

Stahl, Ann. Concepts of time and approaches to analogical reasoning in historical perspective. *American Antiquity* 58 (2):235–260, 1993.

Staley, David P. A view of the early contact period in southwestern Alaska: the archaeological analysis of House 15, Chagvan Bay Beach Site. *Anthropological Papers of the University of Alaska* 24 (1–2):15–31, 1992.

Steensby, Hans Peder. Contributions to the ethnology and anthropogeography of the Polar Eskimos. *Meddelelser om Gronland* 34 (7). Copenhagen: C. A. Reitzels Forlag, 1910.

Stefansson, Vilhjamlmur. *Prehistoric and Present Commerce Among the Arctic Coast Eskimo.* Museum Bulletin no. 6. Ottawa: Geological Survey of Canada, 1914.

———. *My Life Among the Eskimos.* New York: Collier, 1962 (reprint).

Stenbaek, Marianne. Sustainable development and mass media in the Arctic: the case of the Inuit Circumpolar Communications Commission. In *Dependency, Autonomy, Sustainability in the Arctic,* ed. H. Petersen and B. Poppel, 277–288. Aldershot: Ashgate, 1999.

Sweely, Tracy L. *Manifesting Power: Gender and the Interpretation of Power in Archaeology.* New York: Routledge, 1999.

Sun Chief (Don Talayesva). *Sun Chief: The Autobiography of a Hopi Indian,* ed. L. W. Simmons. New Haven: Yale University Press, 1970 [1942].

Taylor, William E., Jr. *Deblicquy, a Thule Culture Site on Bathurst Island, N.W.T., Canada.* Archaeological Survey of Canada Mercury Series, no. 102. Ottawa: National Museum of Man, 1981.

Testart, Alain. The significance of food storage among hunter-gatherers: residence patterns, population densities, and social inequalities. *Current Anthropology* 23 (5):523–537, 1982.

———. Appropriations of the social product and production relations in hunter-gatherer societies. *Dialectical Anthropology* 12:147–164, 1988a.

———. Food storage among hunter-gatherers: more or less security in the way of life? In *Coping With Uncertainty in the Food Supply,* ed. I. Degarne, and G. A. Harrison, 170–174. Oxford: Clarendon, 1988b.

———. Some major problems in the social anthropology of hunter-gatherers. *Current Anthropology* 29 (1):1–10, 1988c.

Thalbitzer, William. Ethnographical collections from east Greenland (Angmagsalik and Nualik), made by G. Holm, G. Amdrup, and J. Petersen and described by W. Thalbitzer. The Ammassilik Eskimo 1 (7). *Meddelelser om Gronland* 39:319–755. Copenhagen: C. A. Reitzels Forlag, 1912.

———. Language and folklore: the Ammassilik Eskimo, part 2 (3). *Meddelelser om Gronland* 40 (2):113–564. Copenhagen: C. A. Reitzels Forlag, 1923.

———. The Ammassilik Eskimo: ethnology of east Greenland Natives. *Meddelelser om Gronland* 40 (2):1–739. Copenhagen: C. A. Reitzels Forlag, 1941.

Therrien, Michele. La maison de neige (illuvigaq), une metaphore du corps humain. *Inter-Nord* 16:121–126, 1982.

Tilley, Christopher. *A Phenomenology of Landscape: Paths, Places, and Monuments.* Oxford: Berg, 1994.

Tobey, Jennifer A. House and spatial organization of gender differentiated activities: a basis for household archaeology in southwest Alaska. Master's thesis, Binghamton University, Binghamton, 1998.

Tonkin, Elizabeth. *Narrating Our Pasts: The Social Construction of Oral History.* Cambridge: Cambridge University Press, 1992.

Tringham, Ruth. Households with faces: the challenge of gender in prehistoric architectural remains. In *Engendering Archaeology: Women and Prehistory,* ed. J. M. Gero, and M. W. Conkey, 93–131. Oxford: Basil Blackwell, 1991.

Turner, Lucien M. Ethnology of the Ungava District, Hudson Bay Territory. In *Eleventh Annual Report of the Bureau of American Ethnology for the Years 1889–1890.* Washington, D.C.: U.S. Government Printing Office, 2001 [1894].

Vansina, Jan. *Oral Tradition as History.* Madison: The University of Wisconsin Press, 1985.

———. Deep-down time: political tradition in central Africa. *History in Africa* 16:341–362, 1989.

VanStone, James. Archaeological excavations at Kotzebue, Alaska. In *Anthropological Papers of the University of Alaska* 3 (2):75–155. Fairbanks: University of Alaska Press, 1955.

———. Russian exploration in interior Alaska: an extract from the journal of Andrei Glazunov. In *Pacific Northwest Quarterly* 50 (2):37–47, 1959.

———. *Eskimos of the Nushagak River: An Ethnographic History.* Seattle: University of Washington Press, 1967.

———. Tikchik village. In *Fieldiana: Anthropology* 56 (3). Chicago: Field Museum of Natural History, 1968.

———. Historic settlement patterns in the Nushagak River region, Alaska. *Fieldiana: Anthropology* 61. Chicago: Field Museum of Natural History, 1971.

———. *Athapaskan Adaptations: Hunters and Fisherman of the Subarctic Forests.* Chicago: Aldine, 1974.

———. Historic Ingalik settlements along the Yukon, Innoko, and Anvik Rivers, Alaska. *Fieldiana: Anthropology* 72. Chicago: Field Museum of Natural History, 1979a.

———. Ingalik contact ecology: an ethnohistory of the lower-middle Yukon, 1790–1935. *Fieldiana: Anthropology* 71. Chicago: Field Museum of Natural History, 1979b.

———. Mainland southwest Alaska Eskimo. In *Handbook of North American Indians, Arctic* 5, 224–242. Washington, D.C.: Smithsonian Institution Press, 1984a.

———. Southwest Alaska Eskimo: introduction. In *Handbook of North American Indians, Arctic* 5, 205–208. Washington, D.C.: Smithsonian Institution Press, 1984b.

Veniaminov, Ivan. Notes on the islands of the Unalaska District, ed. L. T. Black and R. H. Geoghegan. *Alaska History* 27. Ontario: Limestone, 1984.

Walde, Dale, and Noreen D. Willows, eds. *The Archaeology of Gender: Proceedings of the 22nd Annual Chacmool Conference.* Calgary: University of Calgary Archaeological Association, 1991.

Washburn, Sherwood L., and C. S. Lancaster. The evolution of hunting. In *Man the Hunter,* ed. R. B. Lee and I. DeVore, 293–303. Chicago: Aldine, 1968.

Watson, Linvill. Television and early social effects among Rankin Inlet Inuit. *Musk-Ox* 27:60–66. Saskatoon: University of Saskatchewan Institute for Northern Studies, 1980.

Way, Jacob Edson, III. An osteological analysis of a late Thule/early historic Labrador Eskimo population. Ph.D. diss., University of Toronto, 1978.

Whitridge, Peter. Gender, labour, and the divisions of space in Thule society. Paper presented at the 30th Annual Meeting of the Canadian Archaeological Association, Saskatoon, 1997.

———. The construction of social difference in a prehistoric Inuit whaling community. Ph.D. diss., Arizona State University, Tempe, 1999a.

———. The prehistory of Inuit and Yupik whale use. *Revista de Arqueologia Americana* 16:99–154, 1999b.

———. Zen fish: a consideration of the discordance between artifactual and zooarchaeological indicators of Thule Inuit fish use. *Journal of Anthropological Archaeology* 20:3–72, 2001.

———. Social and ritual determinants of whale bone transport at a Classic Thule winter site in the Canadian Arctic. *International Journal of Osteoarchaeology* 12 (1):65–75, 2002.

Whymper, Frederick. Russian America, or "Alaska": the Natives of the Youkon River and adjacent country. *Journal of the Ethnological Society of London*, 167–184. London: Trübner, 1868.

Wolf, Eric. *Europe and the People Without History.* Berkeley: University of California Press, 1982.

Wolfe, Robert J. Commercial fishing in the hunting-gathering economy of a Yukon River Yup'ik society. *Inuit/ Studies/Etudes* 8:159–184, 1984.

———. Myths: what have you heard? *Alaska Fish and Game* 21 (6):16–19, 1989a.

———. Tools: a crucial difference. *Alaska Fish and Game* 21 (6):20–23, 1989b.

Wolfe, Robert J., Joseph J. Gross, Steven J. Langdon, John M. Wright, George K. Sherrod, Linda J. Ellana, and Valerie Sumida. *Subsistence-Based Economies in Coastal Communities of Southwest Alaska.* Technical paper no. 89. Juneau: Alaska Department of Fish and Game, Division of Subsistence, 1984.

Woodbury, Anthony C. *Cev'armiut Qanemciit Qulirait—Ilu Eskimo Narratives and Tales From Chevak, Alaska.* Alaska Native Language Center. Anchorage: University of Alaska Press, 1992.

Woodhouse-Beyer, Katharine. Artels and identities: gender, power, and Russian America. In *Manifesting Power: Gender and the Interpretation of Power in Archaeology,* ed. T. L. Sweely, 129–154. New York: Routledge, 1999.

Wright, Rita P., ed. *Gender and Archaeology.* Philadelphia: University of Pennsylvania Press, 1996.

Wylie, Alison. Gender theory and the archaeological record: why is there no archaeology of gender? In *Engendering Archaeology: Women and Prehistory,* ed. J. M. Gero and M. W. Conkey, 31–54. Oxford: Basil Blackwell, 1991.

Yanagisko, Sylvia Junko. Family and household: the analysis of domestic groups. *Annual Review of Anthropology* 8:161–205, 1979.

Yava, Albert. *Big Falling Snow: A Tewa Indian's Life and Times and the History and Traditions of His People,* ed. H. Courlander. Albuquerque: University of New Mexico Press, 1996 [1978].

Yow, Valerie Raleigh. *Recording Oral History: A Practical Guide for Social Scientists.* Thousand Oaks: Sage, 1994.

The Yukon-Kuskokwim Delta. *Alaska Geographic* 6 (1):3–13, 1979.

Ziff, Alan, Kenneth Pratt, and Robert Drozda. Historical overview of new Chevak. Ms. in possession of authors, 1982.

Zimmerman, Michael R., and Arthur C. Aufderheide. The frozen family of Utqiagvik: the autopsy findings. *Arctic Anthropology* 21 (1):53–64, 1984.

LIST OF CONTRIBUTORS

Lillian A. Ackerman
Washington State University

Hetty Jo Brumbach
University at Albany, State University of New York

Barbara A. Crass
University of Wisconsin, Milwaukee

Lisa Frink
University of Wisconsin, Madison

Brian W. Hoffman
Hamline University

Robert Jarvenpa
University at Albany, State University of New York

Carol Zane Jolles
University of Washington, Seattle

Gregory Reinhardt
University of Indianapolis

Rita S. Shepard
University of California, Los Angeles

Henry Stewart
Showa Women's University, Tokyo

Jennifer Ann Tobey
Lake Clark–Katmai National Park and Reserve, Anchorage

Peter Whitridge
University of North Carolina at Chapel Hill

INDEX

Abandonment, of houses, 121-22
Ackerman, Robert, 73-74, 148
Adams, George, 66
Afterlife, Inuit, 118, 119
Agayadan Village, 9, 152, 161-62
Alaska, 85, 113, 153; missionization in, 198-99. *See also various places by name*
Alaska Native Language Center, 54
Aleutian Islands, 85; bone needles from, 151-52, 153, 161-63
Aleuts, 9, 18, 198, 206
Amchitka Island, 2, 161-62
American Commercial Company, 85
Ammassalik (Angmagsalik), 2, 19, 15-16, 22, 212(n4)
Anasik, 18
Animal Ceremony, Deg Hit'an, 86
Animals, 209; in Inupiaq hunting, 34-35; in Koyukon Athapaskan houses, 74-75; and Netsilik *kipijuituq*, 14, 15-16, 20

Anthropology, interdisciplinary approach to, 5-6
Anvik, 2, 82, 88-89
Aranu'tiq, 18
Archaeology, 2, 3, 4-6, 9, 107, 111, 198, 200; at Chevak, 98-99; culture change and, 77-79; experimental, 154, 157-61; formation processes in, 122-23; gender identification in, 73-74, 87, 130-48, 168, 206-7; household in, 64-65, 82-83; ideological systems and, 63-64; needle manufacture and, 156-57; semisubterranean house, 121-22; sex and gender in, 167-68; slot width analysis in, 177-82; social change, 61-62; social differentiation in, 165-66; on Unalakleet River, 69-73; Yukon-Kuskokwim delta, 96-97
Artifacts: chert flakes, 142-44; distributional analysis of, 123-25;

fishing-related, 69; gender identification and, 87, 125–47; metal, 176–77; 187–89, 190; Mound 44 floor-related, 132–137; in needle manufacture, 156–57; sewing scraps, 142–43; slot width analysis of, 177–82
Artists, St. Lawrence Island, 42
Arvillingjuarmiut. *See* Netsilik
Athapaskans, 8, 39, 197; household patterns, 74–75, 81–82; premissionary life of, 85–86

Badten, Linda Womkon (Adelinde Aghanaghaughpik Womkon), 40, 41–43, 200, 209–10; life history of, 44, 47–54
Barrow, 2, 197; house mound excavation in, 121–25, 203, 206–7, 210
Bears, in Koyukon houses, 74, 75, 209. *See also* Polar bears
Berdache, 18, 212(n7)
Bering Sea, 97
Bethel, 2, 68
Big Man systems, North Alaskan, 170–72
Billings, Joseph, 154
Billings-Sarychev Expedition, 154
Blackman, Margaret, 38–39
Boarding schools, 88, 98, 213–14(n4)
Boat owners, status of, 170–72
Bodenhorn, Barbara, 34–35
Boys, 46, 144, 145. *See also* Children
Bronze, 175
Burial goods, with children and infants, 115–18, 119
Burials, 201; Eskimo and Inuit, 8, 111–19
Butler, Stephanie, 159, 161

Cairns, 113–14, 115; burial goods in, 116–17
Canadian Arctic, 113, 170, 197

Canoe villages, Deg Hit'an, 85, 86
Cape Newenham, 2, 73–74
Cape York, meteorite from, 175
Caribou, 170
Catamites, 18, 212(n7)
Caves, burials in, 113
Ceremonial life, 67, 86, 89; men's houses and, 97, 171, 172, 189–90, 203
Chagvan beach, 73
Cherchez le Chien, 96
Chevak, 2, 36, 94, 197, 214(n3); food management at, 103–5; research at, 98–99
Child care, 201–2
Children, childhood, 67, 98, 111, 144; custody of, 31, 32; household economy and, 88, 91; household organization and, 76, 97, 145; mortuary practices and, 2, 8, 113–19, 201; Yupik, 50–51
Chipewyan, 2, 204, 208
Christianity, 62, 68, 69, 78, 85
Chugach, 18
Chukchi, 18
Clan system, Yupik, 42
Clark, A. McFadyen, 74–75, 123
Classic Thule, 166, 204; metal use, 175–76; social differentiation among, 170–73, 204–5; tool slots and, 177–82; trade networks, 174–75
Climate change, 170
Clothing, Unangan manufacture of, 162–63
College of Emporia, 52
Colville Indians, 7
Colville Indian Reservation, 2, 27–28; economic equality on, 29–30, 208; gender equality on, 32–34, 36, 200–201; family economy on, 31–32
Communities, 5, 9. *See also* Villages
Complementarity, in social status and power, 34–35

Index

Compounds, multi-dwelling, 172
Convert, Jules, 98
Copper, 175; as female-associated, 187–89
Copper Inuit, 165–66
Cosmology, Inuit, 23–24
Cruikshank, Julie, 39, 40
Culture, 197; and gender, 84, 166–67; material culture, 168–69
Culture change, 197, 199–200; archaeological evidence of, 77–78; and gender roles, 75–76
Cumberland Sound, 19
Cup'ik, Cupiit, 94, 214(n5), 214(n6); Chevak and, 98–99; fish processing by, 100–103, 197, 199, 200, 209; hunting and gathering by, 95–96

Davidson, Florence Edenshaw, 39
Deaths, 114, 202; in house collapse, 121, 22; violent, 118–19
Debt, gift-incurred, 170–72
Deg Hit'an Athapaskan, 2, 8, 85, 197, 199, 213(nn1, 2, 3); households, 81–82; missionaries and, 88–90, 91, 203–4; premissionary life of, 85–86
Deposition, primary and secondary, 122–23
Disease, 49, 98
Division of labor, 203; Deg Hit'an, 86–87; in fish processing, 100–103; Cup'ik, 99, 214(n6)
Divorce, and child custody, 31, 32
Dogs, in burials, 114–15
Dog teams, 104
Domestic system, 62; Kuskokwim Eskimo, 65–67
Dualism, sexual, 22, 24

Eastern Thule, 166
Economy, 208; on Colville Reservation, 7, 28, 29–30; equality in, 35–36; household, 31–32, 88, 91; women's role in, 7, 108, 197

Education: Linda Badten's, 51–52; Yupik, 49–51
Effigies, animal, 16
Egalitarianism, and social differentiation, 165–66
Ekwen, 2 (map), 113
Elections, on Colville Reservation, 32
Ena, 97
Episcopalians, 89
Equality, 5, 208; on Colville Reservation, 28–34, 36, 200–201; gender, 8, 27, 200–201, 202
Eskimos, 94, 95, 99, 198, 213(n3), 214–15(n1); burial practices of, 8, 111–13; gender complementarity in, 34–35. *See also* Inuit; Yupik, Yup'ik
Ethnoarchaeology, 98–99, 198–99, 208
Ethnography, 8, 64–65, 200
Ethnohistory, 8
European contact, 6, 197
Evil spirits, warding off, 18, 19

Fairbanks, 2, 41, 52
False Pass, 2, 154; needle replicating project at, 157–61
Families, 1, 35, 87, 214(n3); Linda Badten's, 41, 43, 45, 48–49; on Colville Reservation, 31–32; St. Lawrence Islander, 46–47
Faunal analysis, 71
Faunal material, 74–75
Female, 3, 20; *kipijuituq* and, 14–15. *See also* Women
Feminist theory, 38
Fetuses, sex of, 21–22
Fish, 96; processing of, 100–103, *106*, 108, 200, 214(n3); women's management of, 103–5, 197, 199, 209
Fish camps, 8, 100; women's roles at, 93–94, 100, 209
Fissures, child and infant burials in, 113, 115, 119

Food, 36; management and ownership of, 103–5, *105;* processing and production of, 93–94, 100–103, *106,* 108; on Yukon-Kuskokwim delta, 94–96
Food production, shared, 36. *See also* Fish
Formation processes, 122–23, 198
Fort Yukon, 52
Fur trade, Aleutian Islands, 85

Gambell (St. Lawrence Island), 2, 41, 42; life in, 44–46
Geist, Otto, 47
Gender, 3, 7, 13, 64, 99, 204, 212(n8); in archaeology, 4–5, 9, 74–75, 123, 125–30, 147–49, 206–7, 210; assignment of, 17–18; as cultural construct, 166–67; as social category, 83–84; and floor assemblages, 130–47; and floor space, 124–25; household activities and, 73–75; inequality of, 172–73; material culture and, 168–69, 189–91; and metal consumption, 185–89, 191–92; needles and, 152–53; reproduction and child care and, 201–2; research on, 195–96; and sex, 21–22, 167–68; social organization and, 86–88, 207–8
Gender change, 13, 18–20, 22–23; Netsilik *kipijuituq* and, 14–15
Gender equality, 27, 202, 208; on Colville Reservation, 28–34, 200–201; Yup'ik, 35–36
Gender mixing, 73
Gender relations, Inuit, 172–73
Gender roles, 4, 19, 34, 208–9; culture change and, 75–76; in fish processing, 100–103; Inupiaq, 34–35; Netsilik, 14–15, 17–18, 207
Gender studies, 13
Genealogy, Plateau Culture, 33
Ger, 75–76

Girls: St. Lawrence Island, 46–47; in Yupik stories, 54–55
Glazunov, Andrey, 97
Goodnews Bay, 2, 35, 73
Grand Coulee Dam, 28
Grandparents, *kipijuituq* and, 14, 16, 209
Graves, 113; burial goods in, 116–17, 119; skeletal elements in, 117–18
Greenland, 22, 175; child and infant burials in, 113, 114–15. *See also* Classic Thule; Thule

Haida, 39
Hair trimming, 15–16, 212(n4)
Herring (*Culpe harengus*), 100; processing, 102–3
Hill, Chance, *99*
Holy Cross, 2, 88–89
Homosexuality, 13
House-floor assemblages, 4–5; gender identification and, 130–47
Households, 1, 62–63; archaeological reconstruction of, 82–83; on Colville Reservation, 31–32; Deg Hit'an, 81–82, 90–91; economy of, 31–32; fish distribution and, 104–5; hunter-gatherer society and, 202–3; identifying gender in, 73–74, 75–76; Koyukon Athapaskan, 8, 74–75; missionary impact on, 67–69, 90–91, 203–4; organizational changes of, 64–65; Qariaraqyuk, 182–85; social organization and, 84–85, 87–88, 206; Thule, 9, 172
Houses, 97, 172; burials in, 113, 115; culture change and, 78–79; Deg Hit'an Athapaskan, 86, 87–88; floor space in, 124–25; gender identification in, 130–47; Koyukon Athapaskans, 74–75, 198; mission influence on, 89, 198–99; semisubterranean, 67,

INDEX

86, 121–22, 206–7; at Tagilgayak site, 69–73; technological change in, 7–8, 65–68, 77–78, 200; Unangan, 151, 163; Yupik, 47–48. *See also* Men's houses
Hudson Bay, 19, 118
Hunter-gatherers, 28, 99; gender equality and, 29, 34; households and, 202–3; social differentiation among, 165–66; on Yukon-Kuskokwim delta, 94–96
Hunting, hunters, 208; Cup'ik, 95, 99; men as, 34–35, 46

Ideology, archaeological identification of, 63–64
Iglulik Inuit, 21–22
Industrialization, 27
Inequality, 7; gender, 172–73
Infants, 111; *kipijuituq* and, 14–15, 209; mortuary practices and, 2, 8, 113–19, 201; sex and gender of, 21–22, 23–24
Influenza, 98
Ingalik, 198, 213(n1). *See also* Deg Hit'an, 199
Interdisciplinary approach, 5–6
Intermarriage, on Colville Reservation, 27–28
Inuit, 13, 34, 212(n1), 214–15(n1); cosmology, 23–24; gender assignment in, 17–18; gender relations among, 172–73; mythology, 20–21; pre-Christian burials, 8, 111–19, 201; sex and gender among, 21–22; social differentiation, 165–66. *See also* Yupik, Yup'ik
Inuk, 24
Inupiaq, 34–35, 36, 39
Inupiat, 123, 170, 197, 208, 209; houses and gender in, 141–42, 143–44; winter houses, 121–22
Iron, 175; as male-associated, 187–89

Kamchatka Peninsula, 96
Karlsen, Axel, 68–69
Kashim, 66, 86, 88, 89–90. *See also* Men's houses
King Island, 35
Kinship, 14–15, 21, 46
Kipijuituq, 5, 7, 207, 212(nn2, 3, 5, 7); becoming, 14–15, 209; hair trimming and, 15–16; polar bear and, 21, 23; release from, 16–17
Kodiak Archipelago, 153
Kotzebue Sound, 18, 22
Koyukon Athapaskans, 8, 74–75, 123, 198, 209
Koyukuk River, 2, 74
Krauss, Michael, 52, 54
Kuskokwim Eskimos: domestic life of, 65–67, 203; missionaries and, 67–69
Kuskokwim River, 68, 85, 94, 197

Lamp. *See* Oil lamp
Land, mission, 88–89
Late Aleutian Tradition, 151–52
Leadership, 34; female, 32, 33, 201
Life histories, 209–10; narrative, 37–38; Yupik, 44–54
Little Ice Age, 170
Longhouses, Unangan, 151, 163
Lucchessi, Father, 89
Lynx, 75

McKenzie Basin Slavey, 198
Mahlemut (Malimiut), 18
Males: as *kipijuituq*, 14–17, 18, 23; and polar bear, 20–21
Man-woman, 18, 212(n7)
Marriage, 34, 46, 68, 173; and family economy, 31–32, 87
Mask Dance, Deg Hit'an, 86
Material culture: and culture change, 77–78; and gender, 168–69, 189–91. *See also* Artifacts
Materialization, of ideological system, 63–64

Men, 6, 67, 75, 143, 208; and children, 201-2; Deg Hit'an, 86, 88; as hunters, 34-35, 46; metal use by, 185-86, 187-89; status and power of, 172, 203; whaling and, 204-5

Men's houses, 35, 97, 143, 145, 189-90, 191-92, 203, 204, 205, 213(n2); archaeological identification of, 69-71; artifact distribution in, 146, 147; Deg Hit'an, 86, 88, 89-90; Kuskokwim Eskimo, 65-66, 67-69; mission and, 89-90; North Alaskan, 171-72. See also Kashim; Qargi; Qariyit; Qasgis; Qaygiq

Merck, Carl, 154

Metals: Qariaraqyuk consumption of, 182-89, 191-92, 210; and social differentiation, 166, 169; Thule use, 175-76; tool slots and, 177-82

Meteorites, as iron source, 175

Middens, child and infant burials in, 113, 115, 119

Missionization, 85, 98; Deg Hit'an Athapaskans and, 88-90, 91; disease and, 98; household and, 62, 203-4; impacts of, 67-69, 198-99, 200; and Plateau Cultures, 33, 201

Mongolians, households, 75-76

Moravians, 67-68, 98

Mortuary behavior, in child and infant burials, 2, 8, 113-19

Mound 44, 121-22, 210; archaeological characteristics of, 122-23; artifact distributions in, 123-25; gender identification in, 130-49

Mythology, Inuit, 20-21, 23-24

Naming, and gender roles, 14-15

Narratives, life-history, 37-38

Narssarssuaq, 2 (map), 113

Neakok, Sadie Brower, 39

Ned, Mrs., 39

Needlefish, storage of, 103

Needles, 9, 206; as gendered items, 152-53; manufacture and use of, 154-57; replicating manufacture of, 157-61, 198; technological change in, 151-52, 153-54, 161-63, 199

Nelson, Edward W., 66, 97-98

Nelson Island, 36, 102

Netsilik, 22, 197, 212(n2); gender assignment, 17-18; kipijuituq, 5, 7, 14-17, 207, 209, 212(n5); social differentiation among, 165-66

New Chevak, 99, 197

Norse, metals traded from, 169, 175, 189

North Alaska, wealth and status in, 170-72

Norton Sound, 197

Nunamiut, 198

Nunaraluq, 98, 99, 100

Nunavut Territory, 14

Nunivak Islanders, 36

Nushagak River Eskimo, 198

Oil lamps, 142, 144, 146-47

Old Chevak, 99, 100

Osgood, Cornelius, 82, 86, 199

Ownership: boat, 170-72; of fish, 101-2, 197; of food, 103-5

Ownership marks, on fish, 104-5, *105*

Pader, Ellen, 75-76

Pelly Bay, 2, 14, 15, 21

Piaarqusiaq (piaaqqusitat), 19

Plants, wild, 28

Plateau Cultures, 27-28; equality in, 33, 200-201

Point Barrow, 35

Point Hope, 2

Polar bear: and *kipijuituq*, 15, 16, 20-21, 23

Politics, Colville Reservation, 32

Postmodernism, 38, 40

Index

Processing activities, women's role in, 93–94
Processual stages, in archaeology, 122–23, 198
Property ownership, 31–32, 86. *See also* Ownership
Ptarmigan (*Lagopus* sp.), used in needle manufacture, 157–58, 159

Qariaraqyuk, 2, 9, 141, 146–47, *167*, 173, 208; gender and material culture at, 189–91; household metal consumption at, 182–89, 191–92, 210; slot width analysis at, 177–82; social differentiation, 166, 169, 204–5; trade and, 174–75
Qargi, 143, 146–47, 171–72, 205; at Qariaraqyuk, 174, 190–91, 204. *See also* Men's houses
Qariyit, 172. *See also* Men's houses
Qasgis, 65–66, 67–68, 213(n2); archaeological identification of, 69–71; culture change and, 77, 78, 203. *See also* Men's houses
Qavinaq, 98
Qaygiq, 97. *See also* Men's houses
Quebec, gender change in, 22–23

Rasmussen, Kund, 21–22
Reproduction, gender and, 201–2
Roman Catholic Church, 89, 98
Russian American Company, 85
Russian Orthodox church, 85, 98
Russian Revolution, 76
Russians, 85, 97

St. Lawrence Island, 18, 22, 41, 197, 200, 213(n1); Yupik life histories from, 40, 44–54
St. Michael (Alaska), 66
Salmon, 28, 103, *105*, *106*
Sauyaq, 67
Scavenging, from houses, 123
Seals, 174, 212(n4)

Self, 48; perception of, 7, 40
Sewing, 162–63, 206. *See also* Needles
Sex, 212(n8); and gender, 21–22, 83–84, 167–68; Inuit cosmology and, 23–24
Sex ratios, and gender change, 19, 22
Sexuality, 3, 22, 212(n8)
Sexual partners, male, 18
Shageluk, 88, 213–14(n4)
Shamans, 16, 18, 89; female, 173, 209; Koyukon Athapaskan, 75, 209
Sharing, food, 36, 104–5
Sheldon Jackson High School, 52
Shostak, Marjorie, 37–38
Shupan, 18
Siberia, 85, 113, 213(n1)
Sidney, Mrs., 39
Silook, Paul, 51
Sitka, 2, 52
Slots, for metal tools, 176, 177–82
Smallpox, 98
Smith, Mrs., 39
Smithsonian Institution, 66, 98
Social differentiation, 169; among Classic Thule, 170–73, 204–5; metal and, 191–92; in small-scale societies, 165–66
Social order, Yupik stories and, 54–55
Social organization, 151, 170; archaeological evidence of, 61–62; gender and, 83–84, 207–8; household and, 84–85, 86–88, 202–3, 204
Social spheres, complementary access to, 34–35
Social transformation, markers of, 61
Somerset Island, 166, *167*, 173–74
Southern Tutchone, 96
Space: house floor, 124–25; social organization of, 84–85, 86–87, 204

Spirits, avoiding malevolent, 18, 19
Status, 206; Classic Thule, 170–72, 204–5; of Colville women, 33–34, 201; in hunter-gatherer societies, 165–66; of polar bears, 20–21
Storage, fish, 103, 214(n2)
Storytelling, stories: Deg Hit'an, 86; Yupik, 54–56
Strangling, of children, 114, 118
Subsistence, 93–94, 202
Surface burials, 113, 115
Summer villages, Deg Hit'an, 85, 86
Swedish Covenant Mission Church, 68–69

Taboos, 21, 212(n6); food, 74, 75; hair trimming, 15–16; on women's behavior, 173, 209
Tagilgayak, 2; house structures at, 71–73; *qasgi* at, 69–71
Technology, 61; changes in, 9, 151–52, 153–54
Television, 17
Tents, Mongolian, 75–76
Thompson, Mr., 51
Thule, 2, 9, 96, 169; gender change among, 18–19; metal use by, 166, 175–76. See also Classic Thule
Tlingit, 39
Trade, 85, 206; Classic Thule, 174–75, *176*, 208
Transvestism, 13
Traveler-Gypsies, 75
Tuberculosis, among Yupik, 4, 50
Tuluaqmiut, 198
Tzahavagamute, 73

Ulroan, Mrs. Angela, *102*
Ulroan, Ulrich, *101*
Ulukuk, 66
Umialit, umialik, 185; role of, 170–72
Unalakleet, 2, 66, 68–69
Unalakleet River, 66; archaeology on, 69–73

Unangan, 9, 199, 206; clothing manufacture, 162–63; needle manufacture and use, 151–57
Unemployment, on Colville Reservation, 28
Unimak Island, 9, 152, 157, 198
United States, 85
University of Alaska, 54
Upsiksui, 172
Utqiagvik Archaeology Project, 121, 122; data reanalysis in, 125–30; gender identification in, 130–47; house floor excavated in, 124–25

Victoria Island, native copper on, 175
Villages: Deg Hit'an, 85–86, 213(n3); winter, 85, 86, 97, 121–22, 143, 166

Walrus, 170
Wamkun, Patrick, 47
Warfare, Unangan, 151
Waterfowl, 95, 214(n1)
Wealth: Classic Thule, 170–72; in hunter-gatherer societies, 165–66
Western Union Telegraph Expedition, 66
Whale bone, 174
Whales, 35, 174
Whaling, 170, 172, 185, 189
Whaling villages, 2, 166, 204–5. See also Qariaraqyuk
Whitefish (*Coregonus* spp.), 100, 103
Winter houses, Birnik, 172
Winter villages, 85, 86, 97, 121–22, 143, 166
Witchcraft, 16
Woman-man, 18, 218(n9)
Woman's house, 97. See also Ena
Women, 6, 18, 76; as animal attractors, 34–35; Athapaskan, 8, 86; and children, 201–2; on Colville Reservation, 29–30, 32, 33–34; in creation myths, 21–22; economic roles of, 5, 7, 197; fish

processing by, 96, 100–103, 108; food management by, 103–5, 199; house use and, 71–73, 87, 88, 143–45, 189, 204; Kuskokwim Eskimo, 67, 71–72; metal use, 185–86, 187–89; narrative life histories of, 37–38; needle design and use by, 152–54; productive role of, 93–94; status and power of, 172, 205; Unangan, 152–53; Yupik, 7–8, 44–56

Work areas, in houses, 142, 144, 146–47

Work habits, on Colville Reservation, 29–30

Yukon, 39

Yukon-Kuskokwim delta, 197, 200; culture history of, 96–97; food resources on, 94–96; population of, 97–98

Yukon River, 85, 94, 197

Yupik, Yup'ik, 2, 7–8, 34, 196–97, 205, 212(n1), 213(n1), 214–15(n1); gender assignment in, 17–18; gender status in, 35–36, 203; life histories of, 40, 44–54; stories, 54–56. *See also* Inuit

Yupik language, 52, 54

Zagoskin, Lavrentiy, 65